MW01058247

Secrets Behind the Door

By

Marti Wibbels

PRESS

Xulon Press
www.XulonPress.com

Xulon Press books are available in bookstores everywhere, and on the Web at www.XulonPress.com.

The Spirit of the Sovereign LORD is on me, because the LORD has anointed me to preach good news to the poor. He has sent me to bind up the brokenhearted, to proclaim freedom for the captives and release from darkness for the prisoners, to proclaim the year of the LORD's favor and the day of vengeance of our God, to comfort all who mourn, and provide for those who grieve in Zion—to bestow on them a crown of beauty instead of ashes, the oil of gladness instead of mourning, and a garment of praise instead of a spirit of despair.

Isaiah 61:1-3

Acknowledgments

➤⟡

This book would never have been completed without the continual encouragement of my beloved husband, Alan. Thank you for urging me to keep writing on behalf of those who live *behind the door.*

Warm thanks to Leah Eckberg Feldman, who superbly edited *Secrets Behind the Door.* When friends told me of a New York writer who might look at my manuscript, I couldn't imagine her being willing to review the work of an unfamiliar novelist. We met after Leah and her family moved to Southern California—and instantly enjoyed working together. While her professional skills transformed this book, our friendship quickly became one of my life's great treasures. I am grateful to our husbands for giving us time to work together—especially since we both hope this is the first of many collaborative works!

To our daughters and sons-in-law: Kristen and Steve McHargue, Amy and Aaron Weeks and Carrie and Jeff VanTuyl, and to our grandchildren: thank you for your excellent ideas (and patience) during the writing process.

The novel benefited from the professional input of Diane Larson, a biblical counselor in Colorado Springs.

Thank you to Jessica Knapp, Franziska Nabb, Jerrid Washburn, and Wendy Widger for their thoughts concerning music; Will Sarris for help with car scenes; and David Rozema, Ph.D., whose skill as a philosophy professor is reflected in Molly's college classrooms; and Joleen Hicken for financial expertise. I am also grateful for the excellent recommendations of Audrey and Chris Conrad, Mark Hadenfeldt, Joleen Hicken, Krystal Kroeker, Jeremy Smith, Sandra and Bentley Tate, M.D., Cheri L. Jensen, M.D., and Kimberly Bush, D.D.S.

Many thanks to the friends and relatives who generously offered advice after reading various editions of the manuscript! To everyone who helped me find answers during every phase of this project: I appreciate you! Special thanks go to all who faithfully prayed for this undertaking—especially to dear friends Suzan and George Sarris.

Above all, my gratitude is to God, who cares about everyone trapped behind all sorts of doors.

Chapter One

S he huddled next to the tree, trying to shield herself from the steady drips of rain. *I'm glad it's not raining hard*, Molly thought. "And Cotton is here." She hugged the once-white bear who faithfully accompanied her on all her trips to the forest. Then she pulled a soggy cracker from her lunch box. "It's a good day, Cotton, I even remembered to wear my raincoat!" she murmured.

Hours later, Molly was still there, crouching under the same tree—drenched, blue and shivering. She studied her watch. "Mom comes home when it says five—four—five," she said aloud, sounding old and tired for just five years old. "OK, Cotton, we better go."

As she neared the big house that bordered the forest, Molly checked her watch once more. "Nana said it's water-proof," she said to no one in particular. She looked up and saw her mother's car pulling into the driveway. "Oh, no, I have to hurry! She's here!"

It was too late. Before Molly could reach the house, her mother was already in the kitchen screaming at Jennifer. "Where is your sister? What is that little brat thinking? Is she thinking? I can't come home to this every day."

Her face softened when Jeremy, her only son, entered the room. "I know you've had a tough day," he said, giving her an understanding hug. "I'm trying to do a good job with Molly, but she won't listen to me."

"Well, honey, you'd better find a way. This is your summer job."

"I know, but Molly's always sneaking off somewhere."

Molly tried to slip upstairs quietly, but her sneeze gave her away. Her mother caught her in the hallway, grabbing her arm and pulling her so close that Molly smelled her smoky breath.

"Don't you have anything to say for yourself, young lady?"

She didn't.

"You can forget about dinner! Look at this mess—you got mud on my clean carpet! I expect you to stay in this house from now on—and do what your brother tells you!"

Without a word, Molly went to her room. As she peeled off her wet clothes, the bedroom door quietly opened and closed. She stood frozen, trying to shield her body with her slender arms. When Jeremy touched the back of her neck, she shivered more than she had all day.

"Why didn't you stay and play with me today, little friend? I had a party planned." He didn't wait for an answer. "It's OK, we can play my games tomorrow. Sweet dreams, sweetie," he sneered.

He turned away and Molly scrambled to pull her nightgown over her head. She didn't see him pick up her bear.

He waited, staring at his sister, his pocketknife poised over the bear. "Looks like your little friend here needs surgery," he said.

Molly cringed, watching him slit open Cotton's neck. "Please, Jeremy," she cried, as stuffing fell across the floor.

He choked her with his eyes. "You'd better be here tomorrow."

Tears trickled down Molly's cheeks as the door shut behind him. She crawled around the room, gathering bits of stuffing and pushing them back into Cotton's scruffy face. Clutching her best friend, Molly fell asleep on the floor.

No one checked to see that she was covered or warm.

Downstairs, Jameson Montgomery arrived home from work to his customary greeting, "Why are you late again?" Without waiting for a response, his wife persisted, "I could use some help around here."

"I pay Jeremy to help," he said, studying his cell phone.

"Stop checking your stock quotes long enough to do one thing," she whined. "Molly totally disregards Jeremy's authority. You pay him to baby-sit, so you can handle this."

With a sigh, Jameson took off his cashmere topcoat and carefully hung it on a polished wooden hanger. "I've been dealing with bank examiners all day. You handle this one," he said.

The Montgomery parents and two of their children ate pizza with the evening news. Afterwards, Jeremy played computer games; Jennifer watched her favorite TV show. Both parents had important projects to do. Babs was on the phone. Jameson was at his computer. Molly was forgotten.

* * *

She woke up the next day, coughing, with a temperature of 103 degrees, so her mother stayed home from work to take her to the doctor.

"Hurry up and shower, Molly. What did you do up here all evening? You didn't even say good night to us."

Molly stood on tiptoes to hang her robe on the gilded hook on her bathroom door, rushing to keep up with the click, click of her mother's heels against the ceramic tile floor.

Her mother's angry voice carried above the sound of the shower. "So why were you out in the rain all day? You are making me miss some very important appointments." She continued talking as she found an outfit and matching hair bow for her daughter to wear. "Hurry up, Molly, we have an 8:30 appointment. I can't be gone from work all day," she yelled into the bathroom. "Get dressed and get downstairs. I'll set the cereal out."

Molly stood to eat at the breakfast bar while her mother brushed her long blonde hair.

"Hurry up, Molly. We've got to be there in thirty minutes."

It hurt to swallow.

"OK, brush your teeth and get into the car."

Her mother was backing out of the garage when Molly ran back downstairs. The automatic garage door rolled quietly down as she jumped in. Her head hurt; she closed her eyes and fell asleep as the car backed out of the long, curving driveway.

Mrs. Montgomery tapped the steering wheel impatiently with her perfectly manicured nails. "Molly, wake up. We're here." Turning to Molly, she added, "Don't tell Dr. Carlson that you were out in the rain."

Molly didn't ask why.

"Mrs. Montgomery, Molly has bronchitis. We can give her some antibiotics. Be sure to give her lots of fluids and keep her in bed—if you can." Dr. Carlson smiled at Molly, sure she was like most kids, in a hurry to get up and play. He didn't really know her; in fact, he had only seen Molly a time or two since her routine baby visits were completed. He didn't notice anything out of the ordinary.

No one noticed anything out of the ordinary in the Montgomery household. Jameson Wythe (J. W.) Montgomery was a successful banker who was at the office six days a week. The seventh day was devoted to golf. Barbara—Babs to her friends—Montgomery owned her own real estate company in their affluent Chicago suburb–and was proud of it. Fortunately, her three kids were old enough, in her opinion, to be left alone all summer. Jeremy was a remarkably responsible thirteen-year old. When he wasn't busy with boys' club events, he was babysitting ten-year-old Jennifer and five-year-old Molly. He never complained or was any cause for complaint. In fact, Babs bragged to her friends that no one could find such a reliable teenager. She was the envy of her bridge club.

Molly had a different opinion of summer. She didn't want to be left at home. She had begged to go back the KidzVille Nursery School, but her mother had said she was big enough to stay home and be useful for a change. Molly didn't dare tell her what happened the summer before—the real reason she didn't want to stay at home.

* * *

It all started the night Jeremy came come home from a boys' club meeting in a bad mood. "Read me a story, Jer, read me a story," then four-year-old Molly begged.

"No way," he snapped, stomping off.

Molly knew when to leave him alone. She heard his computer start up and went to her own room to play dolls. She heard Jennifer leave for her friend's house but was having too much fun to stop playing to say goodbye.

Soon after Jennifer left, Molly was startled when she looked up and saw that Jeremy had silently slipped into her room. He was staring at her. "Hey, sis," he said as he turned to close the door. "I didn't mean to be such a grouch."

At twelve, Jeremy was Molly's hero. "It's OK," she said, giving him a big hug, her blue eyes focused on him with absolute trust. "Will you read to me now?"

"Um, well, I'll do something even better … I want to play a special new game with you."

Molly loved games, and her big brother was usually too busy to play with her. Her eyes sparkled.

"Come, sit with me," he said, patting her bed as he sat down.

Soon the look in her eyes was replaced by confusion, then fear. Her long, dark lashes were moist with tears; the tears her brother ignored when she begged him to stop making her play his game.

"Please, please can we play another game, can we play dominoes, or ..." she whispered, desperate to think of something, "Please can we play computer games, Jeremy?"

"Shut up."

Her brother had never told her to shut up before. Who was this monster, why was he doing these things, making her do them to him? He told Molly his game was fun and good, but it didn't feel that way. It made her sad. He seemed mean, not happy. Jeremy made her promise to keep the new game a secret. He wanted to play his game often, but Molly never wanted to play. Soon she didn't even want to see her brother.

* * *

Every Monday through Friday of her fifth summer, Jeremy was Molly's babysitter. He didn't let her go play with her toys until they played his games. She was terrified. Finally, she realized she could hide from him in the woods behind their house. She even taught herself to awaken early so she could slip out of the house right after her parents' cars backed out of the driveway—an hour before Jeremy got up. Cotton was the only one who knew the secret, and he would never tell.

Chapter Two
➔←

Molly awoke thinking *the sunshine is tickling my eyes.* She felt so happy that she laughed aloud. She wiggled her toes and felt the silky softness of Nana Montgomery's sheets. "I like barn kiteus," she said to herself, coughing a deep, raspy bark.

Jameson Wythe Montgomery's parents, Abby and J.W., Senior, lived an hour from their son and his family. Abby had called him the day Molly was diagnosed.

"Jamie," she said.

"Mom, no one calls me that any more."

"I do. Jamie, you let Dad and me help out for awhile. You and Babs both have demanding jobs, and Dad and I are retired. We can come and get Molly tomorrow morning."

Her offer was accepted without hesitation.

* * *

Hearing Molly's cough, Nana headed upstairs from her kitchen, medicine in hand. "Good morning, Molly Dolly! How are you feeling, sweetheart? Bronchitis is no fun."

"I'm OK, Nana," croaked the little patient.

"I love you, sweetie," Nana said, bending down to kiss her granddaughter and give her a spoonful of cough medicine.

To be able to lie in bed—and know that no one would bother her—brought Molly more happiness than she could bear. She smiled, thinking, *Today I get to be with my favorite person in the whole world, my Nana.*

Abby Montgomery was a woman of action. She smoothed Molly's sheets, popped a thermometer under her tongue and opened the curtains. Then she went out the door, promising Molly she'd be back in three minutes to check her temperature.

The phone rang, and three minutes became ten. Nana breezed into her patient's room, apologizing profusely. "Here you are, waiting so patiently, with that silly thermometer still in your mouth. I am so sorry I let time get away from me, Sweet Pea."

Molly didn't complain. The thermometer hadn't bothered her.

"101 degrees. Not good, but not terrible," murmured Nana, tidying up the already- clean room. "How about some breakfast?" Nana was already heading for the stairway, and it seemed like only seconds before she was back.

The silver tray in her hands was covered with a lace napkin. A hard-boiled egg, in its own special cup sprinkled with blue flowers, orange juice, cinnamon toast and a steaming little pot of tea sat on top. "Oh, Nana," whispered the contented child. "The tea cup is my size!"

Molly could only force a few bites down her raw throat. She fared somewhat better with the tea, especially after her grandmother liberally dosed it with sugar and ice chips.

Breakfast done, Molly ventured a question. "Could we play dominoes, Nana?" Always their favorite, dominoes were spread on Molly's lap table and the two sailed through happy hours.

"I'm so sorry you don't feel well, honey," Nana said, stroking Molly's long, blonde hair.

Molly's eyes overflowed with gratitude. Her little mouth was earnest as she replied, "Oh, I like being sick, Nana, as long as I can be here with you."

Abby laughed lightly. "It's high time I get these breakfast dishes out of the way," she said, stopping to fluff pillows and kiss her granddaughter before hurrying downstairs. *She's so serious for a five-year-old,* she thought. *And so cute.* Abby enjoyed being a grandmother but seldom had the opportunity to have any of the children at her house one-on-one. Actually, the fast pace of her son's household seldom allowed visits at all.

Left alone, Molly luxuriated in the quiet room. "I wish I could stay always," she said aloud. No one heard her. She fell asleep.

The next two weeks with her Nana and Grandpa passed far too quickly.

Saturday, just before noon, Molly heard the sound of her father's car pulling into the driveway. Her heart suddenly began to hurt. She went to the door to greet her parents, as she knew she must. There stood the one person she didn't want to see.

"Mom had to show a house, so I came with Dad," Jeremy gloated, giving her a hug that hurt. "Glad to see me? We're staying overnight because Dad has tomorrow off."

Nana noticed a lonely look in Molly's eyes. Her "Little Miss Sunshine" looked anything but that. *She almost seems afraid*, she thought momentarily. Springing into the role of conscientious hostess, she overlooked that flicker of concern before it ever really surfaced into awareness. Her son didn't appreciate advice, anyway. *No need to make waves.*

Nana Montgomery always kept busy when she had company. Cooking, talking cleaning—always making sure her guests were comfortable.

While everyone else played cards after dinner, Molly went to finish the paint by numbers she'd started in her room. She liked being sheltered inside those four walls that danced with memories of tea parties and Nana.

At 9:00, her father's voice summoned her to the top of the stairway, "Time for bed, young lady."

"Can Nana tuck me in, Daddy?" Molly asked, her small voice hopeful.

"I'll do it, Dad," Jeremy offered, bounding up the stairs two at a time.

"How refreshing to see a brother who cares so much about his sister," said Nana, pouring coffee for her husband and her son. "Who wants to shuffle?"

* * *

"If one more person calls me a *cleaning lady,* I'll scream!" Analese Harper talked to herself as she unfolded the check in her hand. Few people knew that her rather exorbitant fee was but a small fraction of her former hourly rate. *On second thought, I chose this little adventure,* she reminded herself, chuckling at her private joke. She preferred her current role as a domestic to the monotony of office life.

This was the second morning she'd helped this particular client prepare for a party. And the client liked beginning at 7:00 A.M. Analese wasn't a morning person; Lucy Bakersfield, the client, was. "I love getting everything ready for a dinner party by noon!" Lucy enthused, inhaling the pungent aroma as Analese added an extra dash of cinnamon to the chutney bubbling on the stove.

"I think this is the last hors d'oeuvre," said Analese. "You can spoon the chilled chutney over Neufchatel and spread crackers around it this evening, just before your guests arrive. The miniature quiches are in the freezer;

everything else is on trays in the fridge. I've double-checked every room—I think you're ready," she smiled.

"No one else I know has a cleaning lady who is also a gourmet!" said Lucy. Clapping her hands with childlike anticipation, she added, "Tonight will be simply delightful!"

Drawing a line through the last item on a long list, Analese shrugged. "The caterer called. He'll be here at 5:00."

Shifting her red Fiat X 1/9 into second gear, Analese remembered her Harvard reunion. "I'm using my MBA every day—in as many homes as anyone could possibly want," she told her incredulous Business-school classmates. They thought she was eccentric to give up calculating debt to asset ratios in a prestigious brokerage for a certain declension into obscurity.

But Analese was having the time of her life. A few years of climbing the corporate ladder was all it took Analese to realize she'd rather wear designer jeans than designer suits. Cleaning houses freed her mind to analyze how people chose to live and why; scrubbing floors freed her mind to analyze speculative investments and even to savor some plain-vanilla S and Ps without the incessant interruption of jangling phones. She didn't miss the bond crowd—but she did feel sorry for old friends whose lives were dominated by bearish dives and bullish jumps.

Lately, her unorthodox work was based in Meadowbrook Hills, a neighborhood separated from the rest of the city by a guard and a gate. The guard knew the sound of her car and had the gate opening as she approached.

Instinctively, she steered toward it, glancing at her planner—opened, as usual, on the seat next to her. She noticed the reminder for Saturday at 1:00: #1 Briarhurst. "Oh, shoot!" she yelled to no one in particular. She'd forgotten that Babs Montgomery had switched to Saturday. Deftly, Analese made a U-turn and headed up Briarhurst Drive toward her least favorite client's home.

The Montgomery's house wasn't tougher to clean than any other, and they didn't complain about her work. It just seemed that their house wasn't a home. Sure, there was the usual clutter of a busy household, the sometimes-muddy hardwood floors, the occasional spots on the carpeting. But it seemed like everything was done for the sake of appearance. Analese always felt like putting a velvet museum rope around the living room after she'd cleaned it to Mrs. Montgomery's precise instructions.

Pulling her keys out of the ignition, Analese looked at the house. It was ordinary, really, compared to other houses in the neighborhood. Traditional in style, it was a large brick two-story Tudor with white shutters. The brick walk gave a feeling of warmth and charm that wasn't replicated anywhere inside the house. Each room looked like a staged interior design studio—too perfect to be real.

No one was home. That wasn't unusual; she had keys for all of the houses where she worked. As she inserted her key into the lock, she shuddered, remembering why she hated coming here. Jeremy. He gave her the creeps. She started cleaning this house last year, when she was 27; she guessed he was not even a teenager at the time—but he stared at her; he made her nervous. *I'm overreacting,* she scolded herself. *He's a kid.*

Analese started with the kitchen. One half-empty bowl of cereal was on the counter, exactly where Jennifer had left it the day before. Another was on the table next to the note pad where Babs had been figuring the perfect strategy for selling a new client's house. "Doesn't anyone in this family ever eat together?" she muttered.

She had a habit of making a checklist for her work. Instead, this time she did a brief mental analysis of each family member. *Mr. Montgomery: never see him; he's always working. Mrs. Montgomery ('Babs' is way too informal for this woman): she's not here even when her body is—the consummate professional woman. Jeremy: I'd rather not go there. Jennifer: nice, but rarely here, either. Molly: sweet, and I think she's scared of Jeremy, too. Wait a minute— it's ridiculous for me to worry about the Montgomerys—after all, it's the markets that are driven by fear and emotion, not me!* Forcing her mind to go somewhere—anywhere—else, Analese turned the radio on full blast and cleaned to the sounds of the top 40.

* * *

Babs awakened late that morning to the incredible luxury of a quiet house. The night before, she'd been with her clients far later than planned. "A delightful inconvenience," Babs reminisced, elated that they bought after seeing only five houses. Now, the morning she'd set aside to continue working with them was free, the first Saturday she could remember having absolutely nothing on her agenda. She lay in bed an hour longer, just letting that fact soak in. When the phone rang, she immediately tensed with an all-too-familiar adrenalin surge. "It's probably them, backing out," she muttered. "Hello," she said, forcing her brightest voice.

"Hi, Babs, this is Mitzie McWilliams."

"Well, hello," she said, relieved. "I hope Jennifer hasn't worn out her welcome," she joked. Although Jennifer and the McWilliams' only child had been inseparable since they met, it was their first sleepover.

"The girls are having a great time. In fact, that's why I'm calling—they're not ready to finish being together just yet. Both Raegan and Jennifer are begging to go over to the club for a swim after we eat a bite of lunch. I thought you might like to come along. I haven't seen you since we closed on the house," she finished. She wasn't really asking Babs to come; she was telling her to come, her inimitable style always assuming others would choose to do anything she suggested.

"I'd be delighted," Babs enthused, glad to schmooze with her best customer—the one who bought the eight-figure property she called The Crown Jewel.

"Can I meet you at the club at, say, one o'clock?"

"Perfect."

Popping a motivational tape into her cassette player, Babs reveled in the unexpected indulgence of using drive time for something other than planning.

"Your brain is hard-wired for a career where you can excel," the speaker was saying. It pleased Babs to think she'd chosen the field that was right for her. "Real estate—something everyone needs," she murmured, instinctively turning the car toward a familiar logo. Mitzie was still her client, albeit part of what Babs considered her "Goldilocks Group." All their houses had to be "just right," with mind-boggling specifications. During the interminable search for her perfect house, Mitzie had insisted on a stop here every day. And the payoff was definitely worth it. Running inside, inhaling the familiar aroma of coffee beans, Babs thought of another of her favorite maxims, "First-class clients give first-class referrals."

Back in the car, Babs felt a twinge of guilt. She'd forgotten to get a treat for Jennifer and her friend.

Raegan's nanny was in the water with the two girls when Babs arrived.

Looking for Mitzie, Babs waved to the girls. Finally she saw her on the terrace above the pool, engrossed in a book.

Babs handed her a paper cup. "Thought you might like a cappuccino," she said, cheerily.

"My favorite—how did you know?"

"It hasn't been that long, has it?"

"Five months."

Babs sighed, easing into a lounge chair. "Where does the time go? Sometimes I think I work too much."

"I know. Sometimes I think I'm on too many committees. I'm wondering why I ever agreed to chair the Fire and Ice Ball for the hospital auxiliary." She laughed lightly, changing to another topic. "Babs, that reminds me of something I've wanted to talk to you about. I've been thinking a lot about our girls."

"Is something wrong?"

"Oh, no, nothing like that," Mitzie reassured her. "More like something right. The two of them always have a marvelous time together. Since Raegan doesn't have any siblings, Tatyana—her nanny," she nodded toward the pool, "Tatyana thinks she needs someone to bond with. Since I have such an enormous responsibility with the Ball, she could get a little lonely during the next few months." She took a deep breath, plunging forward. "So I was wondering if you'd mind if our girls had play dates on a more regular basis?"

"I don't have a problem with that," Babs shrugged.

"To be perfectly honest, I really have a little more in mind," she continued, glancing at the girls in the pool. "What I'm hoping is that Jennifer could come over three— or even four—days a week to be with Raegan until school starts." Leaning toward Babs, she brightened, "Of course Tatyana would look after both of them. She is absolutely wonderful. She said she could teach Russian lessons to both girls—and they always do the cutest little craft projects."

"I'd have to think about it ... " Babs said slowly, her dubious gaze fixed on Tatyana.

"Forgive me for being so rude. I neglected to ask if your nanny would accept different arrangements. Perhaps my proposal wouldn't work for your other children—you have others at home, don't you?"

"Jeremy and Molly," Babs answered. "Jeremy takes care of his sisters, so we don't need a nanny. It's worked quite well so far." She paused. "But, lately, Molly has been a handful. Perhaps it would help her brother to have only one of them …," she said, trailing off. "Of course I'd pay your nanny for the extra trouble," she finished, warming to the idea.

"We wouldn't dream of it. You'd be helping us."

"Don't say anything to the girls just yet. I need to give it some thought."

During their drive home, Jennifer whined to her mother, "Why don't we have a nanny? Raegan always gets to do fun things. We never do fun things, because Jeremy is a mouse potato."

"Don't talk about your brother in that tone of voice, Jennifer Marie," Babs warned. "He doesn't sit in front of the computer all the time, and you know it."

Jennifer mumbled, "Yeah, right. The rest of the time, he's watching TV."

"What was that?" her mother demanded.

She knew her mother hated sarcasm unless she was the one delivering it. She changed her approach, using a saccharine tone. "I'm sorry. I was just wondering why we don't have a nanny."

"We don't have a nanny because we don't want a stranger living in our house."

"Tatyana isn't a stranger to Raegan's family. She's their friend."

"Hmm," Babs said.

Jennifer knew it was time to be quiet. Neither of them spoke until Babs pulled into their driveway. She turned to Jennifer with rare playfulness, startling her. "Would you like for Raegan's nanny to take care of you a few days each week this summer?"

"Yes, yes and yes!" Jennifer screamed excitedly.

"We might be able to work something out."

* * *

The hour drive home from Nana's seemed interminable to Molly. She fell asleep listening to her father and brother discuss how much better their golf course was than Grandpa's.

As the gate to their development swung open, Jeremy turned around and squeezed Molly's arm, hard. "We're home!"

Molly rubbed her arm and stared out the window, memorizing details of each house they passed. Her favorite was the house she called the *tiny cottage.* It was actually quite large, but she'd heard her mother say it "had the charm of an English cottage." She could see ducks swimming in the pond just behind it. Once, she'd seen Mrs. Terwilliger sitting on a bench by the pond, her gray hair pulled into a prim little bun. Molly noticed that the cottage had new curtains. *Maybe Mrs. Terwilliger is inside today,* she thought, intrigued by the gazebo in the side yard, with its copper roof and white wooden benches.

Every house was different in the neighborhood; each house was custom. Babs Montgomery had become a realtor so she could buy in Meadowbrook. It wasn't a neighborhood of multi-millionaires, but everyone was, as Babs liked to say, "comfortable." Filled with Volvos, Mercedes, and a few token American-made cars, all protected by round-the-clock security, it definitely looked safe.

J.W. kept talking, "They gave the right guy the model citizen award at your club meeting last month, Jer. Good work." Jeremy squirmed. He didn't want to talk about that night.

Molly held her arm, remembering the meeting. The whole family sat in the front row while Jeremy accepted his award. She was close enough to see Jeremy flinch when Mr. Sanderson handed him his plaque.

J.W. referred to Bill Sanderson as "the original model citizen," because he was the developer of their neighborhood. This club for future leaders was Bill's idea—and his early-retirement project. He'd spent months writing its mission statement: "Teaching young men to lead their community today, their world tomorrow." He said he owed it to his community to give back what he'd been given. He had the time to do it. His own kids were grown, and his wife kept busy teaching fourth grade.

A garage door automatically opened, and J. W. drove into one of his four garages. "Let's all help get everything into the house," he said, picking up Molly's suitcase and his own duffel bag. Jeremy carried his backpack and the cookies Nana had sent home with them. Molly carefully carried the shopping bag where she'd hidden Cotton.

When she repaired him, Nana hadn't asked how Cotton's neck had been cut. He looked matted and worn, which only made Molly love him more.

Chapter Three

Summer dragged on, each day a grim variation of the day before, with few happy exceptions. Now that Jennifer went to Raegan's house three days a week, Molly had to work harder to avoid Jeremy. She discovered every culvert near their home. She also made a new friend on the day she slipped into Mrs. Terwilliger's yard to hide. Sure no one was home, Molly was startled when she heard the hum of a voice. Looking toward the gazebo, she saw Mrs. Terwilliger—earnestly talking to what looked like a flowerbed.

Noticing Molly, she jumped. "Oh, my dear! You gave me quite a fright. I think I gave you one, too," she chuckled. Her eyes brightened as she studied Molly, liking what she saw. "You're the little girl from the big brick house at the end of the street, aren't you? I see you hurry by all the time. You look like a little rabbit, scampering here and there. What's your name?"

"Molly," she said, her face wearing the same serious expression it usually did.

"I'm Mrs. Terwilliger—and, goodness, gracious! I must have scared you half to death, out here talking away. I'm a little dotty, living all by myself," she explained.

Molly didn't know how to respond.

"My cat died two months ago. She's buried right here," said Mrs. Terwilliger, pointing toward the flower-covered knoll. It was marked with a hand-painted sign. "Patty, My Best Friend," she read aloud, her eyes misting. After a long pause, she added, "I miss her every single day." Then she laughed, her mood jumping tracks. "I've probably violated a few city ordinances putting her here, so it will be our little secret."

Molly cringed. She didn't like secrets.

"Oh, don't be scared. You won't get in any trouble for knowing about Patty's grave. What's wrong with me? I guess I'm a silly old lady, because I haven't even given you a proper welcome. Let's see," she said, scratching her chin. All of a sudden, her face lit up like the sky after a storm. "I baked some tasty ginger cookies this morning. What say we have ourselves a little tea party over by the pond?"

After that day, Molly liked finding flowers to take Mrs. Terwilliger for Patty's grave. Sometimes she found them in the woods, other times in her yard. She was always careful to take flowers only where there were enough others so it wouldn't look like any were missing. She didn't want to get in trouble. But, she felt good whenever she brightened up her friend's day. And Mrs. Terwilliger put all the pictures she colored for her right on her refrigerator, "Where I can see them all the time, you little sweetheart," she said. Sometimes Jeremy didn't even get mad after she went there, especially if she brought him some of "Mrs. Twigger's" cookies.

* * *

Soon summer ended, and the first day of kindergarten at Maple Elementary School began. Molly knew her parents always had important appointments at work, so she wasn't surprised when kindergarten orientation was delegated to her sister.

"OK, Molly, that's your classroom," said Jennifer, en route to fifth grade in the same building. "Your teacher is Mr. Mulligan, and he's a grouch. I don't know why you have to have him for your teacher. I thought he was supposed to retire. Just be real good and do what he says and don't try to be the teacher's pet."

Molly interrupted her. "What's a teacher's pet?"

"The kid the teacher likes best and the other kids hate."

Molly felt a familiar tightening in her stomach. She'd already worried about how she could sit still in school, especially after Mom told her she had ants in her pants and Dad called her a wiggle worm. They both warned her she'd be in a lot of trouble with her teacher if she didn't sit still. She looked around for an escape.

Jennifer gave her arm an affectionate tap and took off down the hall, "Remember, the KidzVille bus will pick you up at noon," she called over her shoulder. "See you at home later."

Left alone, Molly hesitantly walked into her new world. Twenty-three other kindergarten students were milling around six tables, trying to find their names, printed on cards set at each place.

"Please sit in the chair closest to your name," Mr. Mulligan said as the students scrambled to sit down. Two girls shared the name *Hannah*; he had to guide both of them to their seats. Molly was relieved that she didn't need help.

As he welcomed his class, Mr. Mulligan's eyes rested on Molly, who was nervously twisting her hair and unconsciously chewing on a long, blonde curl. "Now, class, we will have a break at ten o'clock for snacks every day, so none of you needs to eat your hair like this little lady is doing."

Some of the students laughed, and Molly felt every eye bore into her head; she flushed crimson. She wanted to run, to go somewhere–anywhere–else.

Every life has its bright spots, and Molly's had Kate. The bubbly redhead had found her standing alone on the playground during their first kindergarten recess. "You can call me Kate, but my name is really Katherine, but I like Kate. What name do you like better?" Before Molly had a chance to answer, Kate continued, "I chew on my hair sometimes, too, and I don't think it was nice that they laughed at you. I didn't laugh. And your hair is pretty. Yellow is my favorite color."

For the first time all morning, Molly relaxed a little. "I like your hair, too, Kate," Molly smiled. It matched her personality, tumbling helter-skelter to her shoulders, each red curl choosing its own direction. *She's nice*, Molly thought.

"That snack wasn't even very good. I'm going to tell my mom to send cookies, because I don't like those kinder-garten crackers. They could at least have cinnamon crack-ers." Too quickly, recess was over, and they had to go back to the classroom.

Mr. Mulligan barked instructions as he passed sheets of paper to each table. "We'll be learning a lot this year, and I want you all to do your best work. Now then, look at the pictures on the bulletin board. I want you to draw any two of these designs on your paper. Raise your hand when you're finished."

He headed toward Molly's table ten minutes later. Mulligan smiled as he showed the class her paper.

She tried to smile, too, hoping he liked it.

"By the end of the year, we won't have any more of these wavy lines," he said, turning to be sure everyone saw her pictures. He continued talking to Molly, loudly, so everyone could hear, "We'll give you some extra work on your fine motor skills, little lady." He returned the offensive

paper and held up Molly's seatmate's paper, displaying it
for the class to admire. "Soon all of your work will be nice
and neat like Amanda's," he said.

Molly quickly turned her paper over. She hated school
already.

When the morning ended, Molly was the first one out of
the classroom. Kate caught up with her as she tried to find
her bus to the day care center.

"Molly, I'll see you tomorrow. What are you going to
wear? I'm wearing my new jeans and yellow top and
probably a yellow bow in my hair. Will you wear a ponytail?
I will, too. 'Bye!" Before Molly could answer, Kate was
waving happily and climbing into a mini-van packed with a
shaggy dog and what looked like a lot of people talking at
once. The van door shut behind Kate, sealing off the sound
of happy voices. Molly walked on to her bus, which was
already full of noisy kindergarteners. She felt alone.

* * *

At 5:45, Jameson Montgomery spotted Molly across the
room at KidzVille.

She brightened at the familiar face.

"Hi, Molly, how was school today? Your first day, isn't
it?" He took her hand without waiting for a response and
strode confidently toward the door, nodding briskly to the
workers. He glanced at Molly as he pressed the remote to
unlock her car door. "Well, you certainly look beautiful
today," he said. "I'm sure all of the little boys wanted to play
with you at recess! And what is your teacher's name?"

A small voice answered, "Mr. Mulligan."

"Fine, fine." J. W. boomed, happy that he had connected
with his youngest daughter. He was already thinking of how
he'd describe the moment to his colleagues. The women
always enjoyed personal anecdotes.

Chapter Four

Mr. Mulligan seemed to savor Molly's failures, and she soon became so nervous in class that she really couldn't do anything right. She lived for recess and Kate. Even when she wasn't at school, she liked to dream about the fun they had together.

Molly awakened early on her birthday, October 12, and lay thinking in her bed, still holding the stuffed pig Kate had given her at school the day before. "We're best friends and I picked this pig for your sixth birthday present to make you laugh because I'm sorry you can't have a friends' party for your birthday," she said, unwrapping the gift herself. "Here, Molly, I'm giving it to you a day early," she beamed. "I'm going to tell my mom she needs to have a party for you next year because your mom always has to show houses. The pig's name is Lulu. Don't you think she's funny?" Molly fell asleep with one arm around Cotton and the other around Lulu.

Molly wished she could say everything right. Everything came out wrong when she tried to sell Kate's idea that evening. "Guess what, Mom?" she'd said, trying to sound enthusiastic. "Kate said she'll have a birthday party for me next year since you always have to show houses."

"Tell that little busybody that we Montgomerys have a family tradition of eating out on birthdays. Just wait; we'll have our own party for your little school friends next year. You can be sure of that. We know how to do the right thing."

* * *

Molly watched the door handle turn. This time, she was ready. "I'm six today," she stated, surprised by the resolve in her voice, "and Nana says I am a big girl, and I won't let you come into my room anymore."

Jeremy began to laugh, until he noticed the look of determination on his little sister's face. He grabbed her arm savagely, and clamped his other hand across her mouth. "Shut up." Jeremy took off his belt and wrapped it around her neck, lifting her face slowly toward his. He breathed heavily. "I could really hurt you if I wanted to," he said. He slowly slipped the belt off of her neck and threw it aside, letting her flop back toward the bed. "Don't you *ever* talk back to me again or I'll kill you. And, I'll kill Jennifer if you ever tell her–or anyone else." Small bruises were already forming on her arms. Noticing them, he softened. "Come on, it won't hurt you to help me out here."

He left the room as quietly and quickly as he'd entered it, while Molly wept softly on her bed. She didn't hear her sister knock.

"Molly, what happened to you?" Jennifer gasped. "Are you OK?"

She grabbed her sheets to cover her naked body. "I fell out of bed, that's all," Molly lied.

"You have bruises all over your arms—I see them, Molly! Tell me what happened. You've got to tell me what happened." Jennifer started to cry.

"Nothing, Jenn."

"I'm getting Mom and Dad."

"You can't!" Molly was terrified. "It's no big deal, I just fell and got bruises, you know?"

"Nobody gets bruises like that from falling out of bed. Tell me—or I get Mom."

Nausea rose from the pit of her stomach. "I can't," Molly mouthed.

Starting to stomp out of the room, Jennifer tripped on something; she reached down to pick it up. Leaning over Molly's bed, she demanded, "What is Jeremy's belt doing here?"

"I guess he forgot it," Molly whispered.

"Why?" Jennifer waited for Molly to speak.

"I can't tell. He'll kill you," Molly said softly.

"Nobody's going to kill me."

Whimpering, whispering, Molly admitted what had happened that day—she didn't tell about any other days.

Jennifer knew she couldn't make up a story like that. "I have to tell."

"Jeremy will kill you. He said he would."

"He's not going to kill me," she insisted, her jaw tensing. "Besides, they need to know. OK?" she said, brushing a strand of hair from Molly's eyes. Jennifer let her little sister cry, then dug through her dresser to find an undershirt and panties. "I'm here for you," she said, giving them to Molly.

Molly pulled them on under her covers, feeling hopeful for the first time in two years.

They both heard their mother at the same time, and breathed a sigh of relief, realizing she was headed down the stairs and not toward Molly's bedroom. But they knew she'd be back soon. Her daily ritual never varied. Up and in the shower at 6:00 AM, coffee, cereal and a cigarette with the morning paper at 7:00, and backing out of the driveway by 7:35. On birthdays, though, she always remembered to say "happy birthday" before she left.

"Let me wash your face before she comes back," Jennifer said. When she went into Molly's bathroom, Molly slipped out of bed to find something to wear. She chose the white sweater Nana Montgomery knitted, holding it to her nose, wishing she could still smell Nana's perfume. It was soft and fuzzy and even had Molly's initials monogrammed on the front. Molly ran her fingers across the tiny red flowers surrounding the letters, and then pretended to get a hug from Nana as she pulled the sweater on.

Soon, their mother stood in the doorway, digging for her keys while she talked.

"I'm off, girls, but I want to say 'happy birthday,' Molly." Finding the keys, she glanced up and noticed that Molly was dressed. "Looks like you two got an early start."

"Mom ..." Jennifer tried to speak, but her mother was already gone.

"Got an 8 o'clock meeting," she called back. "We'll go out for pizza with the Wendhams tonight. There are doughnuts on the counter. Don't be late for school, kids." The garage door opened and she was gone.

"I'm getting Dad," Jenn said, seconds before they heard his car backing out of the driveway. She was not to be deterred. "Tonight, Molly, I'm telling them."

Downstairs, Jenn glared at her brother.

"What's *your* problem?" asked Jeremy, gulping milk from the carton.

"As if you didn't know," she shrieked. "I found your belt in Molly's room—and I'm telling Mom and Dad what you did!"

"As if they'd believe you," Jeremy snickered, pinching her arm. "You just go right ahead and try."

She wrenched away from his grip.

That evening, the family gathered for their typical celebration at Giuseppe's Italian Ristorante with their neighbors, Sheldon and Lauren Wendham. They had no children of their own and were like an aunt and uncle to Jeremy, Jennifer and Molly. They always came to birthday dinners at Giuseppe's.

Pretending to have a good time was such hard work that Molly could barely eat one piece of pizza.

"Happy birthday, Molly," the Wendhams called cheerfully, getting into their car. "Great time, everyone."

Molly, her face solemn, held the doll they'd given her to the window, helping it wave goodbye.

She and Jennifer rode home with their dad. Jeremy rode with his mother. In their father's car, dinner smiles faded into ominous silence—a silence that increased in volume when they pulled into their garage. They filed, one-by-one, into the house, tense, waiting. Everyone seemed to know it would only take one spark for the day's kindling to erupt into a blaze of anger.

When her parents were alone in the kitchen, Jennifer lit the match. "Dad and Mom, please listen to me. I'm so scared ...."

Her father stared at her, incredulous. "Your brother called my office today and said that neither you nor your sister appreciates his leadership."

Babs interrupted. "He called me, too, to tell me that ridiculous story you concocted." Her eyes blazing, she continued, "Watching too much TV? Did you get this idea on a talk show? Big brother hurts little sister," she sneered.

"Molly has bruises shaped like fingerprints all over her arms," Jennifer begged, forgetting the personal ramifications of crossing her parents. "His belt was in her room ...."

They didn't let her finish. Babs grabbed Jennifer's arm with a guttural cry, "You little brat!" At first, it seemed as though she was going to shake her. She stopped abruptly, forcing herself to remain calm, since she was a staunch opponent of child abuse—in any form. Both she and J.W. prided themselves on their involvement in social issues; in the last election, in fact, they had campaigned for the candidate with the child abuse platform.

Babs glanced at an open window, wondering if the Wendhams were on their deck, glad both houses had big lots separating them. She closed the window, congratulating herself on her ability to quickly regain composure and self-control. "I truly hoped you'd forget your foolish lies, Jennifer Marie," she said, gazing at her daughter with what she was sure was genuine sorrow. "Sit down and listen up! Don't mention this again—ever. It's high time you realize that all Jeremy does is sacrifice his time and his social life for you and Molly." Pointing for emphasis, she concluded her speech. "You're grounded for the rest of this week."

Jennifer tried to argue, but her mother stopped her. "Drop it!"

Babs and Jameson wordlessly began depositing presents into three shopping bags. Opening the kitchen door into the garage, Babs tossed the bags next to the garbage cans. "This makes our point nicely, don't you think, J.W.?"

Jennifer watched them, too nervous to move, too scared to speak.

Her mother glared at her. "Jennifer, where is your sister?" she barked.

Staring sourly at the floor, she shifted her weight in the chair, frantically wishing she could find a way to protect Molly.

"Our oldest daughter seems to be a deaf mute. Come on, J.W., let's get this over with," Babs said, frustrated that, once again, she would miss the first segment of the ten o'clock news. She stormed off to find their youngest child. He followed.

Molly was in the basement, huddled behind the furnace. She knew the party at the restaurant was a show put on for the Wendhams' benefit. The silence in the car had frightened her. She'd heard her parents yelling at Jennifer. Scrunching her body into a ball, she tried to disappear.

Babs stood over her. "Look at me when I talk to you," she raged. "I hope you'll always remember how you ruined your sixth birthday by lying." Grabbing Molly's shoulders, she held her terrified little face close to her own, for the moment forgetting all about composure. "Start treating your brother with respect. And don't repeat any more of your hideous lies." After pausing to catch her breath, she continued in measured tones, "We're taking back your birthday presents." She glared at her daughter with disgust. "Go to your room. I can't stand to look at you."

Molly looked at her father. "Help me," her eyes said.

Retrieving a magazine from the recycling bin, he flipped pages without looking up.

As she stumbled upstairs, Molly wondered if she'd get to keep the miniature china tea set that Nana and Grandpa Montgomery had mailed to her a week earlier. It had four china cups and saucers, a teapot, a sugar bowl, a creamer and four little plates. Everything was decorated with delicate blue birds inside a matching circle of flowers. Nana knew Molly's favorite color. She'd even sent everything needed for a perfect tea party—a tin of butter cookies, tea bags, fancy napkins and a box of caramels, Molly's favorite.

Moments later, her door burst open to reveal her mother; her voice jolted Molly back to reality. "Grandmother Montgomery is on the phone," she said, releasing the mute button and handing the portable phone to Molly. Her father stood a few feet away, his hand covering the mouthpiece on the hall phone.

"Hi, Nana." Molly managed a weak smile.

"Molly Dolly, I thought about you all day today. I'm so sorry we're in Florida and couldn't get back for your birthday."

"Me, too, Nana," Molly whispered. "I like the tea set."

"Maybe you can have a tea party tomorrow."

"I'd like that. What are you going to do tomorrow?"

"Start our trip home. What else did you get for your birthday?"

J. W. and Babs glared at Molly, insisting on a perfect performance.

"Oh, I got some nice other presents, too. Mom and Dad gave me two new outfits. One is a green sweat suit and the other is a red skirt and sweater. The sweater has a black Scottie dog on it. And they gave me a book–no, two books–and a game. And, Jennifer gave me a dress for my doll. And Grandmother Finster sent me a comb and brush set because I'm in kindergarten now and I can brush my own hair. And my friend Kate gave me an orange pig."

She struggled to find an answer to her grandmother's next question. "Oh, Jeremy, um, gave me some colors." The bruises were colorful, sort of an ugly green and purple. "Thank you, Nana. Love you, too." She paused. "Miss you," she whispered.

She didn't make a sound when she was shaken awake at midnight.

Chapter Five

J eremy Montgomery had his own problems, the least of which was surviving junior high school. He was almost fifteen; he looked twelve. He felt like he was twenty, except when he was with Bill Sanderson. Then, he didn't know how he felt.

* * *

The first time Bill touched Jeremy was after a Future Leaders' Club meeting two years prior. He'd asked Jeremy to stay behind the others, to help put away chairs. "Hey, Jer," he said, giving his new recruit a manly pat on the back. "Good to have you in the group. You're a great addition. In fact, I'd like you to be my personal assistant this year."

"Thanks," he said, warming to the praise, not used to hearing that from anyone besides his mother. Jeremy flushed under the honor of being singled out by his idol.

"I've had my eye on you. You're going places." Bill stopped short of his next thought. "Hey, same time, same place next week, OK?"

Jeremy's smile spoke for him.

Week after week, Jeremy cheerfully stayed after meetings to help Bill. For the first time, he'd found an adult who cared.

Bill, too, knew he'd found exactly what he was looking for: And he knew exactly when to pounce.

It was a few months later, at the end of a particularly tough week for Jeremy. First, he had exams, then he was rejected by the only girl he'd had the courage to ask to the Valentine's dance. "I know how you feel," Bill empathized as they put chairs away after the Future Leaders' meeting. "Jer, you know, I've found something that really helps me handle stress like this."

"Yeah?"

"Let's take a drive." He paused, smiling. "Need to call your folks?"

It was already 9:30 PM. "I'd better. How late will we be?"

"Hey, I have a great idea. We'll have an overnight at my cabin. It's just twenty minutes away and would be a great break for both of us, time to relax and talk ...." When Jeremy nodded his assent, Bill reached for his cell phone. "I'll give my wife a quick call."

"Ingrid, one of the guys in the club and I are going to do some high-pressure planning at the cabin tonight." He winked at Jeremy. "I think we'll just stay over so we don't make you wait up too late." He paused, waiting for her to answer. "OK, love you, too."

"By the way, I have an extra toothbrush and anything else you'll need out at the cabin," he said, handing the phone to Jeremy.

His call lasted less than thirty seconds.

The two hopped into Bill's new SUV like two teenagers on an adventure. Jeremy lay his head against the leather seat and tried to forget his miserable week.

Soft shadows danced lazily over the incandescent landscape. Like silent sentinels, empty tree branches cast shifting images on the road before them. Jeremy didn't see anything, nor did he notice that the drive took an hour.

Bill pulled up to Mirror Lake, letting Jeremy absorb the spectacular moonlit view. "Hey, in the summer, we can take my boat out. You ski?" He pulled into the driveway. "We're here."

The word *cabin* didn't begin to describe the sprawling structure. Perched close to the lake's edge, it was designed skillfully around nature, with trees and rocks left as integral features of the interior decor. The focal point of the living room was an enormous boulder, which Bill had brought in from Colorado. It was obvious why Bill had consistently won awards for his architectural innovations.

Jeremy stood in front of it, gaping sophomorically. "Wow, I didn't know you could put a rock like this in a house."

Bill laughed easily. "With the right kind of money, you can do whatever you want. Come see the rest of the place."

Jeremy followed.

"After working in the industry for a couple of decades, you learn what works, what doesn't." He paused, waiting for Jeremy to be adequately impressed. "Like this room," he said, leading Jeremy into a spacious den. "I told my people I wanted inlaid wood walls, and they told me the cost would be out of sight. I said, 'not out of mine. If you can't see it, you'd better get your vision tested!' They finally figured out it was 'my way or the highway.' They wanted the work, so they figured out how to do it right." He laughed, bringing Jeremy into his world. "I always build the best. Don't you think that's the only way to go?"

Jeremy nodded in awe.

"Hey, Jer, why don't you pick a few CDs while I throw together something to eat?" He showed Jeremy how to use the sophisticated remote. "You're going to enjoy this. It's state of art, top of the line, with a thousand-CD capacity. Take your time; make sure we have the music *you* like. It's time to do something nice for *you*, don't you agree?" He laughed, giving Jeremy a playful whack on his shoulder. "Tonight's your night, man."

Jeremy liked the way Bill spoke to him, like they were real friends. He liked Bill's CD collection, too.

An hour later, sitting on the comfortable leather sofa, the two sampled pizza, almond-crusted Brie cheese and crackers, as well as "private collection" chocolates Bill ordered from Europe. Then, Bill let Jeremy sample liquid fruit from his bar.

Jeremy, for the first time experiencing the beginning twinges of inebriation, laughed as he felt his body relax. "Now I get it," he said.

"You mean about the stress? This is OK, Jer, but it's nothing compared with what I really want to show you. Are you ready for something you've never felt before?" He motioned for Jeremy to follow him to the master suite.

"Did we see this before, Bill?

"No, Jer. I always save the best for last."

They walked through the bedroom, bath and dressing room into a spacious glassed-in spa that featured a diamond-shaped Jacuzzi. Swirling waters were surrounded by palm trees and flowers of every imaginable color and size; the music Jeremy had chosen earlier piped into the room via an unseen speaker.

Let's get comfortable, man," Bill said, casually unzipping his jeans and placing them on a wicker chair.

No one but Bill had ever called him a *man*. Without embarrassment, he stripped down, feeling only a twinge of discomfort when he noticed Bill watching. Then he climbed down the marble steps into the foamy water beside Bill.

Bill had the uncanny ability to sense Jeremy's feelings. He kept the conversation light and funny, and Jeremy let himself relax completely. They talked like old friends ... and when they didn't talk, the silence was soothing.

"OK, now I see what you mean, Bill," Jeremy said at last, his voice barely audible above the sound of bubbling water. "This is the most relaxing thing I've ever done."

Bill's response was a quiet, reassuring laugh. "Jer, there's more. Come with me."

Bill stepped quietly out of the Jacuzzi and reached for the *off* switch in one motion. On a nearby peg were two soft, white terry robes. Bill put one on and held one out to Jeremy.

Suddenly, without knowing why, Jeremy blushed as they walked down a wide hallway into another room.

A welcoming fire was already crackling in the fireplace.

Bill took off his robe and sat in a massive leopard-upholstered chair. He motioned for Jeremy to sit next to him.

"Hey, man, I'd better get some sleep," Jeremy protested, trying to keep things light. He tried to back up, but Bill pulled him toward the chair. Bill smiled with his mouth, but his eyes were cold.

The smile was gone when he dropped him at home the next morning. "Here's some pocket money," he said, thrusting a fifty-dollar bill into Jeremy's palm. "Go treat yourself."

* * *

Molly didn't know about her brother's pain; she only knew her own. After two years of struggle, she couldn't remember life before the torment began.

First grade was even worse than kindergarten. Molly quickly discovered that Mr. Mulligan's influence reached far beyond the walls of his classroom.

Mulligan believed in helping new teachers. "I'm only one year away from retirement, so you'd better glean all you can from me now," he told his colleagues, only half kidding. Eileen Trent, Molly's rookie first-grade teacher, gladly came under his tutelage. Molly Montgomery became her test case; Trent scrupulously studied the copious notes in the file Mulligan lent her. After several weeks—and a one-day ADD seminar she took that summer, she felt confident in her diagnosis. By the time she actually met Molly, she was amazed to see how closely she fit the profile. Fidgety, distracted, tuned out. With such a solid two-parent family backing her, she concluded that Molly's problem was chemically based.

She couldn't wait to see Mr. Mulligan for their daily coffee break in the teacher's lounge at the end of her first week.

A narrow, cramped room next to the janitor's closet, the teacher's lounge was the place where all-knowing teachers made pronouncements that sealed the fates of their unwitting students.

"Molly is one of those rare children who probably can't be helped by conventional methods," Mulligan intoned philosophically. He closed his eyes. "You'll agree, I'm sure. By all intents and purposes, she should, at the very least, be above-average intelligence. Case in point, look at her parents. Both professional, well educated." He paused, reflective. Nods around the room confirmed the prognosis. His disciples sipped coffee, thoughtfully.

Mulligan knew he'd nailed this one.

Enjoying her proximity to genius, Eileen jumped in. "So, then, how do you recommend that I proceed?" She listened wide-eyed, anticipating her first major verdict.

"Extensive testing, start there. Dr. Barnes can administer the psych profile. Your next step: develop an IEP." He paused patronizingly, rolling his eyes. "You do know what that is, don't you, Trent?"

Eileen very nearly discovered the terror he invoked in students; her pride stopped her just short of feeling it. "Individualized Educational Plan. Any Education graduate knows that," she retorted smugly.

Mulligan's voice increased in volume. "I rather imagine you'll need to put her in a special education classroom several days a week. You might be able to put her in the one-day program, though. The tests will determine that for you. Might take awhile, but the process is quite forward, really."

* * *

Amanda didn't like being desk mates with Molly; she'd had enough of her in kindergarten. On her birthday, she bragged about the cookies ("my favorites") and ice cream bars she was going to give their class. That afternoon, she conveniently gave away all of the treats by the time she reached Molly—except the ones she'd kept for herself. Turning her back to Ms. Trent, she handed an empty napkin to Molly, folded to look like something was in it. In a cutting voice intended only for Molly's ears, Amanda said, "You don't really belong in first grade, so I didn't bring any for you. Too bad." With that, she took her seat opposite Molly, eating a cookie with obvious relish.

Molly put the napkin on her lap, her face devoid of emotion.

Sitting across from her, Jacob watched the exchange. When Amanda stood to be crowned Queen of the Day, he passed his ice cream bar across the aisle to Molly. "Here's mine," he said.

Without another word, he began eating his cookie, leaving Molly no choice but to eat the treat he'd given her before it melted.

Amanda turned around in time to see. She was furious.

Molly couldn't imagine why Jacob would want to help her. As she picked up her backpack after school, she caught his eye.

"Like it?" he asked.

"Thanks," she murmured, stunned by his kindness.

The next day, her feet swinging in front of her desk, she was still puzzling over that wonderful event.

"Molly Montgomery, this is the third time I've asked you to quit wiggling in your chair," Ms. Trent said, clenching her teeth. "Recess, everyone," she said, motioning them with forced cheeriness. "Molly, stay here."

As the other children eagerly filed outside, Molly waited for her punishment.

"You are a distraction, Molly, and I'm not going to put up with it," Ms. Trent said, angrily. "Follow me. This is where you'll be—until we can get you tested."

Molly stood, watching her teacher struggle to lift the desk, which probably weighed more than she did. Giving up, exasperated, Ms. Trent pushed it through the door, knocking over her "What Is a Family?" display on the way. "Perhaps you'll learn to listen now—and sit still," she said. "We'll leave the door ajar so you can follow along."

When the children returned from recess, Amanda began the loud refrain, "Once a dummy, always a dummy; nobody can help, you're just too funny!" Some of the other children laughed with her, repeating the chant as they filed into class.

Dr. Pearson overheard them as she walked down the hall. She surveyed the scene before her, glancing at the prodigal student and glaring sternly at the others. Molly stared at the floor. Her peers fell silent, their eyes trained on Ms. Trent, who had become suddenly engrossed with organizing her desk.

Back in her office, Esther Pearson wondered what sort of situation exiled such a diminutive student to the hallway. She wasn't at all happy with what she saw as she scanned Molly's files. "How have I missed this?" she scolded herself.

In the teacher's lounge the next day, Ms. Trent was holding court with several other faculty members. "Well, I finally had to put her desk in the hall. At least I don't have to watch her fidget now." Her back to the door, she failed to notice that Principal Pearson was standing in the doorway. The laughter abruptly ceased.

"Am I to understand that you removed a student merely for your own convenience, that no disciplinary infractions have occurred and that, furthermore, you have a decided bias against this student?"

She didn't pause long enough for an answer.

"I have observed you allowing students to ridicule this pupil, and that, Ms. Trent, will simply not be tolerated. What do you have to say!" It was a demand, not a question.

"Dr. Pearson, this child presents continual behavioral problems in the classroom," she said. "I've been trying to schedule psych. testing, but ..." Looking across the teacher's lounge at Mulligan, she gathered courage. "She distracts other students. They don't like her because she interferes with their education."

"It seems to me that *you* are interfering with Molly Montgomery's education. Have you informed her parents of your concerns?"

"Repeatedly. They do not respond."

"Hmm. We'll see about that."

Without another word, Esther returned to her office and asked her secretary to place a call. "On second thought," she said, uncharacteristically changing her mind, "Please call Miss Montgomery to the office."

This was a new experience for Molly. Although she had frequently been in trouble with her teacher, she had never been sent to the principal before. Her legs trembled as she walked down long corridors wondering what she'd done.

Esther Pearson was as kind to needy students as she was tough on teachers. She personally escorted Molly into her private office and then took the chair next to her instead of behind her massive desk. "You're not in trouble, dear," she said, seeing Molly's terror.

Most children would have cried, but not Molly. She sat mutely beside Dr. Pearson, still waiting for judgment.

"How can I make school more pleasant for you?"

Molly couldn't speak. She didn't know what to think.

Dr. Pearson looked down, scanning Molly's file for the third time that day. Frowning, she closed the folder. *Nothing in her folder makes any sense!* she thought. She turned to Molly, "Do you like school?" she asked kindly.

"No," she whispered, instinctively trusting this woman.

"Why not?" Dr. Pearson leaned forward so she could hear Molly speak.

"I always cause trouble. Everyone laughs at me."

"There are two sides to every sheet of paper," the principal mused aloud, tapping a pencil against her desk. "See?" she asked Molly, holding a blank sheet before her. "Don't let someone else write your story, dear. Their false impression isn't who you are."

Not understanding, Molly squirmed in her chair.

The pencil continued its rap-tap-tap as Dr. Pearson sat still, deep in thought. With a wistful smile, she put her hand lightly on Molly's shoulder. "Do you have one friend at school?"

"Kate," replied Molly, her voice barely audible.

"Hmm." Again she opened the green folder, turning pages briskly until she found the one she wanted. "Kate ... that would be Katherine Johnson?" Observing Molly's solemn nod, she continued. "I see you were in class together for kindergarten ... but not this year." She paused, almost seeming to forget Molly was in the room with her. "Will you wait here a moment or two longer?"

Molly stared at the bright posters around the room, trying to figure out what they said. The words were too hard for her to read, but she liked the vibrant pictures. They were happy. Her heart quit pounding, and she sat back in the chair, eager to see Dr. Pearson again.

When she returned, she was smiling. "Molly, I'd like to try putting you in another classroom for the rest of the school year. Is that all right with you?"

Molly quickly found her voice, "Yes!"

"Come with me, then." They walked back down the long hallway, but turned away from Molly's old classroom. Soon they were walking into a different room–Kate's room!

Molly didn't know how to accept this astonishing change of events. Dr. Pearson even had her coat and books brought to the new room.

Molly's new teacher, Brooke Warren, wasn't anything like Ms. Trent. Even so, Molly still lived in fear.

After a couple of weeks, Miss Warren began to call on her in class, hoping to gently draw her out. "Molly, can you tell the class your favorite color?"

Molly stammered, unable to think of an answer.

"There are so many colors, aren't there, dear?" interjected Miss Warren. "It *is* difficult to decide." With that, she opened Rien Poortvliet's masterfully illustrated book, pointing to various colors as she slowly turned pages depicting the animals of Noah's ark. "This fox is incredible, isn't it? What a beautiful color!" She looked questioningly at Molly, who still couldn't summon the courage to reply. Without pausing, she drew the entire class into the discussion. "Oh, look at this! I think I see every color in the rainbow in this scene." Turning to the next page, she continued, "This is my favorite." She looked at Molly, smiling with encouragement, waiting.

Molly smiled back and met her eyes. "Mine, too," she said. "I like blue."

Miss Warren continued reading, her beaming face all Molly needed to make her heart soar.

Chapter Six

➜❖❮

On the last day of school, Molly lingered in her first grade classroom.

Startled, Miss Warren looked up from her desk. "Hello, Molly," she said, smiling. "I didn't know you were still here. Everything OK?"

Her voice constricted by emotions, Molly took a deep breath.

Miss Warren walked around her desk and took Molly's hands in her own. "Thank you for being my student," she said. "It has been a delight to have you in class. I wish you'd been here all year."

Tears glistened in Molly's eyes. "So do I," she whispered.

"You are special, Molly Montgomery," she said, looking kindly at her student. "I hope you'll come see me when you're a second grader."

Earnestly nodding her head, she promised, "I will, Miss Warren, I will."

Brooke Warren felt a vague disquiet when Molly picked up her monogrammed book bag and headed to the playground. Through the window, she saw her sitting on a swing, her head pressed against the thin metal chain.

* * *

It was summer, and Molly remembered all the places where she could slip under the fence to get into the forest bordering their neighborhood. She had to time it right. Jeremy and Jennifer both slept late, so she thought she'd be safe if she left when her parents went to work. She thought wrong.

One early morning–just a few days after summer vacation began–Jeremy was waiting in the back yard, planning to quietly follow her. Crouched next to a towering blue spruce tree, he was a pitiful sight. The automatic sprinkler had already surprised him, and his damp jeans were clinging uncomfortably to his legs. His big toe was bleeding from where he'd stubbed it as he ran. Training his eyes on the back door, he rubbed his scratchy face.

Molly sensed his presence before she saw him. She turned and ran–not to the house or toward the forest but directly toward her favorite cottage-house down the street.

"She's hiding at Terwilliger's!" he muttered, cursing.

Molly kept going, pretending she'd planned this all along, even though she knew it was too early in the morning to visit.

Jeremy went back into the house and peeled off his jeans. Climbing into bed, he pulled his down comforter over his shivering frame, quietly crying as he glared at the vent on his wall.

As soon as the coast was clear, Molly headed to the woods. Tensing at every sound, she forced herself to think, to look. A branch caught her hair, and she reached for it, pulling herself into the big old tree. "I'm like a cat," she whispered. "I can be very quiet, and I can climb." She felt a sense of triumph as she peered down from her leafy fortress.

Hours later, her growling stomach reminded her she'd forgotten to bring anything to eat. "Tomorrow, I'll bring snacks."

When Jeremy called Mrs. Terwilliger's house that afternoon, he discovered Molly had never been there. His confusion deepened his determination to find her.

Jennifer was in the kitchen with a friend when Molly came home that afternoon. They'd just ordered pizza.

"Hey, Molly. Want some?" Jennifer asked.

Jeremy walked in. Tersely, he motioned her to follow him.

She didn't move.

He spoke—his jaw set, his voice firm. "Mom called. She's going to be late, but she said to give you some jobs. Come on, Molly, it's time to get busy."

"What jobs?" Jennifer demanded.

"She has to clean her room. Now."

Like a prisoner walking to her execution, Molly followed her brother upstairs.

He pretended not to hear Jennifer tiptoe after them. "Mom said to pick up your toys," he commanded Molly, in his best imitation of their mother's no-nonsense voice. "I have to check my e-mail. Come tell me when you're done so I can inspect your room."

He waited in his doorway until laughter drifted up from the kitchen, confirming that Jennifer had returned to her friend.

Summer was a fog for Molly, a dizzying blur of sneaking food, hiding and— inevitably—facing her tormenter. Resisting Jeremy was futile. The more she tried, the worse it got.

But he never did find the tree. Even once, when he was standing right under it, he still didn't see her. Barely five feet above him, Molly felt her heart beating, pounding so loudly that she was sure the sound would betray her. But he'd stomped off, yelling loudly at her, at everyone, even at Bill Sanderson, his club leader.

Molly grew even quieter and more serious that summer. Always slender for her age, now she seemed smaller. The eyes that once held childish laughter now contained something distant, imperceptible and dead.

Chapter Seven

"**K**ate, what's wrong?" her mother asked, concerned. "Oh, Mama, today was Molly's eighth birthday, and I think she's sad, and she has to go out to eat, and I don't even think she likes doing that. Her mom said she could have a party last year, but she didn't get to. I think she forgot all about it. I didn't forget, though," she added, "but Molly won't talk about it. And today when she passed out birthday treats to our class, she didn't even smile."

Her mother paused. "I have an idea," she said, smiling.

Kate looked puzzled.

Mrs. Johnson called Molly's mother to ask if Molly could have a sleepover Friday with Kate.

Babs was relieved. One less kid around would simplify the bridge party she'd been planning for Friday night. "That will be fine," she said. "I'll send her things to school with her."

All week at school, the two second graders lived for Friday. Kate's enthusiasm bubbled at every opportunity. "I can't wait, Molly, this is so much fun. Tell me again what you're bringing."

"I'm bringing my new pink suitcase–the one Nana gave me for my birthday–and my jeans and a sweatshirt and my comb and brush.

"And don't forget pajamas and your swim suit!"

* * *

The Johnsons' van was waiting in front of the school when Kate and Molly appeared on Friday afternoon.

Pulling a wide-eyed Molly into the van with her, Kate enthused, "Hi, everybody, did you have a good day? What's for snack, Mom? Did you call the pool? Is it open tonight? What's for dinner?"

Kate's mom calmly kept up with the steady barrage of her daughter's questions. Laughing, she asked, "Katherine, aren't you going to introduce your friend?"

"Oh, Mom, this is Molly, and she's my best friend. And, Molly, this is my brother, Peter. He's seven, and he's in first grade."

"Hi, again," Peter said. "I'm almost eight. Kate and I are only ten months apart," he said with a gap-toothed grin.

Kate rushed on, "Oh, I forgot—you already met him at school! This is my sister, Sarah, and she's four. And this is our baby sister, Mary. She's one year old. Peter and I are the only ones who go to school, and Sarah and Mary get to stay with Mom all day. I wish you could come to my house every Friday." She paused to take a quick breath, then added, "Mom, can we go out for doughnuts today?"

The doughnut shop was on their way home and soon everyone was happily talking between mouthfuls.

Mrs. Johnson smiled at Molly, trying to draw her into the conversation. "I understand your dad works at Prime Security Bank, Molly."

"That's where we go, and when we go to the drive-through bank they always give us suckers," said Peter.

"I like prupple ones best," Sarah said.

"That's purple," corrected Kate, giving her sister an affectionate tap. She turned to Molly and asked, "Do you ever get to go to your dad's bank and help him?"

Molly paused to remember, "Once they had an open house, and I got to walk inside the vault," she said.

"What's a vault?" Sarah asked.

"Where they keep the money!" Peter said. "Molly, did you take some home?"

Molly laughed. "No, I think it was all locked up in little metal boxes."

"Maybe some of our money was in there," said Peter. "I'm glad you left it there, then."

"Time to head home," Mrs. Johnson announced when everyone finished eating.

The drive to the Johnsons' house was noisy, and Molly couldn't keep up with the banter. She wasn't used to this much conversation. She liked it.

Sunny yellow chrysanthemums nodded a welcome by the back door of the Johnsons' rambling older home. Framed photographs wallpapered the entrance. Molly might have lost herself in them for hours if she hadn't been distracted by something wet on her hand.

"Don't mind Fred," Kate reassured her. "He does that to everyone he likes. Down boy," she said, loudly. Taking Molly's hand, she said, "Come on, I want to show you my room!"

Minutes later, the girls had spread dolls over Kate's bedroom floor. "Come on, honey, I know you can do it," said Kate, holding a doll and talking for it. "Try that flip again."

Her doll spoke in a voice not unlike Kate's, "I can't. It's too hard." Kate, herself again, encouraged, "Here, let me help you." The doll turned head over heels and Kate enthused, "Good! You did it! I knew you could!"

Molly silently studied the braided hair of the doll she held.

"Your doll needs to do a trick, too, Mol. Remember? They're at gymnastics class."

Molly dutifully turned her doll over.

"Good somersault! Now you need to talk for her, Mol," Kate said.

"What do I say?" Molly asked.

"It's easy. They just say what they're doing, how they like it, stuff like that." Seeing Molly's discomfort, Kate reached over to help, flipping her own doll and engaging Molly's doll in conversation. "Hi, my name is Isabelle, what's yours? Why don't you do a flip? It's not hard. You can do it." Her doll's high voice sounded kind and compassionate.

Molly followed Kate's example. She gently turned her doll over. "OK, Isabelle, I'll try. My name is Emily." She spoke in her new doll-voice, looking at Kate shyly. "Is this OK?"

Kate smiled, nodding. "I like having you here, Molly."

Molly smiled back.

Brandon Johnson pulled into the driveway as his wife, Kelly, and Peter finished hanging a banner in the dining room. Kelly, a former gymnast, lightly jumped from her stool and back up again, adding a quick flourish of pink paint under the letters of Molly's name.

Peter ran to the car to meet him. "Dad, we're almost ready!" he said.

Brandon walked into the dining room and hugged his wife, then turned to Peter. "Nice banner. You help make it?"

"Think she'll like the bugs I drew on it?" he asked, grinning.

Kelly switched gears. "Make any stops on the way home?"

"Was I supposed to?"

"No!" She looked worried. "You didn't forget, did you?"

"It's in the car. Just wanted to see you sweat."

Kelly, sitting cross-legged on the floor while she wove streamers through the rungs on the "chair of honor," reached over and gave Brandon's shoelace an unraveling tug. "Not funny," she said, trying to restrain her smile. Just then, the dog crashed into the room. "Fred. Rug," she ordered the dog as he knocked over Mary, a roll of tape stuck in his tail. "And, Peter, please get the cake from the car and put it on the kitchen counter."

Helping his wife make a salad, Brandon asked, "Why hasn't Kate invited Molly here before?"

"We've tried since they were in kindergarten, but first she was too busy to come, then I was pregnant with Mary and feeling lousy, then it was all the activities, not to mention having a new baby." She sighed, "I'm glad they finally connected." Her voice trailed off, "She's really a sweet girl. I hope Kate lets her get a word in; she's really quiet."

Brandon laughed. "I'm sure that's why they get along. Kate barely stops talking long enough to breathe."

Kelly carried a pan of steaming lasagna to the table, nearly losing her balance when Peter blew past her into the dining room. "Cake's delicious," he said, licking his fingers.

"You didn't!" his mother exclaimed.

"Relax. He didn't even open the box," Brandon chimed in.

"You're your father's son."

Sarah interrupted, "Now may I call Kate and Molly, please, please?"

Lighting the tapered candles at the center of the dining table, her mother said, "OK," standing back to survey the scene. Clusters of pink balloons hung from the chandelier. A rhinestone tiara sat in the center of Molly's plate, sparkling in the candlelight. The aroma of freshly baked bread filled the air.

Peter heard them coming, "Let's yell 'SURPRISE' when they walk in—now! Kate smiled and hugged her friend, clapping her hands together and smudging the purple polish she and Molly had just applied. Molly was bewildered.

"This is your UN-birthday party, Molly!" Kate exclaimed. "Just for you!"

Molly still didn't understand, but smiled as if she did. The attention overwhelmed her, and she fidgeted awkwardly.

"Sit here, Molly, sit by me," Sarah said, pulling Molly's arm and guiding her to a chair between hers and Kate's. "Mom said I could sit by you."

"Hi, I'm Mr. Johnson, and I'm glad you're here," said Kate's dad. His wife, carrying a pitcher of iced tea, began to fill glasses. "Let me help," he said, taking the pitcher out of her hand.

"I could get used to this," she said, pulling the rubber band from her ponytail and releasing a mass of chestnut curls before she collapsed, exhausted, into a chair.

"We ought to do this more often," he said, taking his place at the other end of the table.

Suddenly, the room became quiet. Even Kate grew quiet as she and Sarah took hold of Molly's hands. Molly flashed back to an Easter with Grandmother Finster. But this prayer was different—and they weren't even at church. First, Mr. Johnson thanked God for His love, for the food, for taking care of them all day. Then, he prayed for every member of his family by name–and he even prayed for Molly. He talked to God like He was a family friend. Kate and Sarah dropped her hands, and the flurry of activity whipped up again, much too soon for Molly.

"Can we eat breakfast in the dining room, Mommy?" Sarah shouted over the commotion.

"It's nice, isn't it?" agreed her mother, smiling at her as

she passed food. She turned to Molly. "How's our 'unbirthday' girl doing?"

Molly's attention was focused on Fred, who was winning her sympathy by tapping her arm gently with his paw.

"Fred, you go out to the kitchen and sit on your rug!" Mrs. Johnson said.

Fred slunk unhappily away.

Molly liked Fred. In fact, she liked everything about this household.

Seizing a brief a lull in conversation, Mr. Johnson asked, "Have you ever been to an 'unbirthday' party, Molly?

"Um, no," she responded, hoping not to offend her hosts.

"We haven't either," offered Peter.

Molly smiled, relieved.

"Since we couldn't be with you for your real birthday, we decided to have a special party on a day that isn't your birthday. And that's why we called it an 'unbirthday' party," explained Kate. "Aren't you glad?"

No one noticed that Mrs. Johnson had slipped away until she emerged from the kitchen carrying a rose-colored cake rimmed by eight candles. Kate jumped to her feet and began singing. Her family joined her. "Happy unbirthday to you, happy unbirthday to you, happy unbirthday, dear Molly, happy unbirthday to you."

Molly couldn't speak. She looked around the room, wondering why they were doing so much, just for her.

Kate broke the silence, "Blow out the candles, Molly, and wait for a blessing!"

Molly's eyes reflected her question.

With wax melting on the cake, Mrs. Johnson hurried to explain, "Instead of making a wish, we all ask God to take care of you in a special way."

After Molly blew out the candles, Mr. Johnson looked

around the table, smiling. "Who wants to give the first birthday blessing?" he asked.

Kate raised her hand, "You mean UN-birthday blessing! I do, I do!"

She quickly bowed her head in prayer and began, "God, thank you for Molly, my very best friend. Please make this party special for her and give her a good unbirthday."

Mrs. Johnson continued, "Thank you, Lord, for this dear girl. Show her how much You love her."

Molly had never felt so surrounded by love, not even at Nana's house. By the time everyone had prayed and cake was served, she was almost too happy to eat.

Kate yelled, "Oh, no, we forgot something!" Without another word, Kate, Peter and Sarah jumped up from the table and ran out of the room.

Molly could hear them scurrying from room to room upstairs. She stared at her plate, afraid to move.

Mr. Johnson broke the silence. "This house is a little crazy. Sorry about the commotion. I'm sure they'll be right back."

Just then, Molly heard them thundering down the stairs. They were pushing each other, each trying to be the first one downstairs.

"Slow down, kids!" their dad called.

The train of children screeched to a stop at Molly's chair.

"I painted this for you," Sarah said shyly. Showing her work to Molly, she explained, "This is you and Kate playing dolls—and here's my doll, Maude. I painted dolls because Kate said she was going to play dolls with you." She pointed to a blend of colors in the corner of the page. "This is Mimi—Mary's doll."

Molly studied every detail; Sarah beamed.

Peter handed her another picture. "I drew this with my new colored pencils. Know what it is?" When Molly hesitated, he continued, "It's the swimming pool at the Y, where we're going tonight for the rest of your party. See?" he asked, "That's all of us swimming in it!" He gave her a second gift, wrapped in a paper napkin. "This is a rock I found."

Molly unwrapped the smooth black rock, smiling.

"I thought you might like to start a rock collection," Peter offered simply.

"Thanks," Molly said, pleased. Her eyes sparkled.

Kate gave Molly her package, which was wrapped in last week's slightly crumpled Sunday comics. "Guess what it is, guess!" she interrupted as Molly carefully tore off the paper. "It's something you can have always. It is just like mine, and it is my favorite book and it's the best book in the whole world and it's for every day, even un-birthdays!"

When Kate paused for breath, Molly studied the cover of the book and read aloud, "The Children's Bible." She looked up, "Thank you, Kate."

Kate said, "Do you like it? Did you already have one?"

Mr. Johnson smiled at his daughter. "Kate, let Molly answer!"

"I don't." Molly smiled at her friend, "Thank you, Kate."

Mrs. Johnson broke the momentary lull in conversation. "Who wants to go swimming?"

The children bolted upstairs to find swimming suits and towels.

Two hours later, happy and tired, everyone quietly munched popcorn in the den, listening to Mr. Johnson read a bedtime story.

"OK. Bedtime, everybody," the two parents said in unison.

Suddenly energized, the Johnson children asked if they could stay up and play games. "Nope, it's bedtime," their parents said. "Maybe tomorrow, before Molly goes home."

Molly shivered, terror washing over her face.

"Don't you like games, Molly?" Kate asked. Although Kate moved at the speed of a hummingbird, her ability to sense people's emotions was keen. "We could play outside instead. Or maybe ... ."

Before Kate finished speaking, Peter interrupted, "The park, the park, let's go to the park!"

Laughing, Mrs. Johnson said, "What time do you need to get home, Molly?"

Molly didn't hear the question.

Mrs. Johnson gently repeated, "Molly, what time did your mother say we need to bring you home?"

Molly couldn't remember what her mother had said; that world seemed so far away. She forced herself to think, to picture her mother speaking to her. She looked at Mrs. Johnson and said, "10:00, I think."

Peter and Kate groaned in unison. "That's too early!" Kate groaned. "Won't your mom let you stay 'til after lunch? We need more time to go to the park. Let's call and see."

Molly's heart froze; her mother didn't like her orders challenged. She quietly but insistently shook her head. "Mom said 10:00."

Mrs. Johnson threw Molly a lifeline, "We need to respect Molly's parents, kids. Why don't we have waffles for breakfast?"

Molly's early departure time was quickly forgotten.

Brandon and Kelly lay in their own bed talking after they'd tucked the last child in bed. "That sweet little girl seems paralyzed; do you think it's because of all the hubbub at our house?" Brandon asked.

"I haven't had time to think about it," Kelly said. "But, did you see her face when the kids talked about playing games?"

"She seemed to relax after that ..."

"... until I asked her when she needed to get home."

"Well, I hope she and Kate continue to be good friends. I think she needs one."

When Molly walked into her kitchen at 9:55 the next morning, she felt like she'd stepped out of an imaginary world and back into the real one.

"You're late," her mother complained.

"You said ten," she answered quietly, the light fading from her eyes.

"You're calling me a liar?" her mother screeched.

"I, uh, I thought you said ten," Molly stammered, wondering what she'd done wrong.

"What kind of people would bring you home an hour late? The nerve!" Molly watched her lips move, but she couldn't hear the words she was saying.

Chapter Eight

Molly didn't know her mother had asked that she and Kate be put in separate classes for third and fourth grade. She could hardly believe her eyes when she started fifth grade and saw Kate's desk across the room. They'd rarely seen each other for two years.

Kate had already spotted her. "Molly, I can't believe it!" she yelled, running. "I've missed you!"

"Me, too," Molly said.

"We called your house about a hundred times," Kate said. "But I never got to talk with you. Your mom always said you were busy."

Molly didn't know Kate had called. She thought she'd forgotten her.

"I thought you didn't want to be friends anymore," Kate said.

"I thought you didn't."

"I'm sorry," they said in unison, hugging each other.

A few weeks later, Kate invited Molly on a picnic with her family to the Hidden Sunken Gardens.

Molly waited nervously, trying to figure a way—any way—to keep her mother from saying "no" to the invitation.

She never would have guessed that Jeremy would turn the tide in her favor.

Her mother was distracted and stressed that day after work. "Jeremy, what are you doing next Saturday?" she yelled up the stairs. Not hearing a response, she ran halfway upstairs, "I need you to baby sit Saturday."

"Mom, you know that's the day of the forensics competition," he said, poking his head out of his bedroom door. Noticing her frown, he added, "I can't get out of this, Mom. We leave at 6 AM."

"Of course," she said, remembering the new laptop she'd bought to "give him an edge." She raised her voice, "Jenn, get in here."

Jennifer sauntered into the kitchen. "What?" she asked.

"I need you to watch Molly next Saturday."

"Can't. Fall camp out, remember?" Appealing to her mom's checkbook, she added, "You've already paid my registration."

Molly walked into the kitchen at that moment, oblivious to the discussion. *It's now or never,* she thought. "Mom, Kate asked if I could go with her and her family all day next Saturday to the Shrunken Gardens," she said, summoning all her courage. "May I?"

Relieved that her dilemma was solved and bemused by her daughter's childish mispronunciation, Babs burst into laughter.

Molly quietly went to her room, her hopes dashed.

Jeremy was waiting. A high school senior, he was now six feet tall. Weight lifting and football practice had bulked out his body so that the seventy-pound diminutive fifth grader was hardly in a position to resist. But Molly had given that up long ago.

When he left, she got up from her bed and threw up in the bathroom. Molly brushed her teeth over and over again, and gargled with mouthwash. Then she went back to her room and lined up her stuffed animals beside her on her bed. The lion always went by her head.

* * *

Babs Montgomery believed that a woman should continually grow and learn. She'd read an article at the beauty shop about the importance of quality family time and had decided then and there that her family would follow the article's suggestion. "It's time to change things around here," she'd told everyone that morning. "We're going to start eating dinner together once a month, and Family Night starts tonight. Dad and I have clear schedules, and you kids do, too. Don't make any plans."

By 7:30, everyone was finally accounted for, and waiting for Family Night to begin. Everyone but Molly.

"I told you this Family Night idea wouldn't work," muttered Jameson, crossing his legs and opening the Journal.

"Molly isn't feeling well," Jeremy quickly volunteered.

Glaring at her husband, Babs said, "Jeremy, honey, you go get her. She was fine after school. She's just being lazy again. She needs to come be part of this family," she said, scratching her son's back softly as he left the table.

When Jeremy poked her shoulder, Molly recoiled. It had been less than an hour since his last visit.

"Mom says come for dinner," he said.

Molly pulled on a sweat suit and stumbled downstairs to the kitchen. The rest of the family was already eating Chinese food when she walked in.

"Tell your father where you want to go Saturday," said Mrs. Montgomery, trying to keep a straight face.

Molly was having trouble waking up.

"Molly. I asked you a question."

"Um, a picnic?" Molly said, slowly, afraid she'd say something wrong.

Babs was irritated when Molly failed to give her joke a punch line. "No, stupid, where did you ask me if you could go earlier?"

Flustered, and unsure of the right answer, Molly said nothing.

Mrs. Montgomery turned to her husband, "Molly said she wants to go to the *shrunken* gardens," she laughed. "Isn't that hysterical?"

Jameson Montgomery had never appreciated his wife's humor, and he wasn't in the mood for mind games. "What did you want to do, Molly?" he asked, impatiently.

Molly looked directly at her father and delivered the line she'd practiced, "May I please go with the Johnsons on a picnic at the, um, Gardens Saturday?" She blushed, still afraid she couldn't say it right.

Babs surprised everyone when she said, "… of course you can go to your little Gardens. Just tell those people I'll have to drop you off early, because I have three open houses that day."

"And I'm going on my camp out," added Jennifer.

"And I have my speech contest," Jeremy reminded his dad. The last thing he wanted was to miss a chance to spend all day on a college campus, especially the one where he planned to be next fall.

Jameson shook his head and shrugged, at last understanding his wife's reasoning. "Free babysitter, Babs?" he asked cynically.

"I don't hear you coming up with any ideas," she retorted, washing down three aspirin with a shot of brandy.

Babs glared at Molly, "Well, aren't you going to eat?" she said.

Molly didn't feel hungry, but she woodenly lifted her fork to her mouth. Suddenly she realized that her mom had agreed to a day with Kate. She began eating with more appetite than she'd had in weeks.

Babs noticed. "Molly, make up your mind. Which is it? Are you sick or not?" Turning to her son, she joked, "What is this, PMS?"

Jeremy blanched.

Molly was used to being called names at school. "Chicken Legs" was the current favorite among the girls who ruled the back of the bus. But "PMS" was a new one. She wondered what it meant.

On Saturday, Molly was dressed and ready before dawn. She was wearing new yellow shorts and a matching shirt that was covered with daisies. She looked in the mirror, admiring the flowers but oblivious to the signs of her changing body. She pulled on her expensive yellow leather sandals and frowned, remembering the day two weeks before when she'd last worn them. "These go with your new outfit," said her mother, handing her a shopping bag. "My daughters aren't going to be looked down on by anybody."

Jennifer had hated the green sandals their mother had chosen for her, but Molly liked her yellow ones. Both girls had looked perfect—and felt miserable—for the end-of-summer party at the country club.

The all-too-familiar click of her door handle broke Molly's daydream. She waited like a trained animal, her back to the door.

Jeremy grabbed her shoulders, turning her to face him.

Confused, Molly searched his eyes for some clue of what he wanted before he hit her for responding too slowly.

Jeremy's eyes were cold. "You're too old to play our game anymore," he said. "Hope you're not too disappointed." It was time to stop, he decided, before he was put in the impossible position of explaining away a pregnancy. "Why so quiet?" he added, laughing. "You don't want to stop, do you?"

Molly looked down, not knowing what else to do. When she looked up again, he was gone. Like one emerging from a coma, she struggled to focus on the day ahead.

Downstairs, a storm was brewing. "Mom, why am I the only person whose mother always forgets to send treats?"

Babs glared at her older daughter with carefully controlled anger. "Because your mother has a life," she said, tossing her several bills. She laced her words with sarcasm, "I'm sure you can find some kind of suitable treats for your little club with that."

Jennifer pocketed the money, grabbed her sleeping bag and designer duffel and left without saying goodbye. She jumped into her friend's car. "Hey, guys!" she said cheerfully. "Is it OK if we run past Madeline's Cookie Shoppe?" Jennifer was a true Montgomery, her bright face betraying no hint of the rage roiling inside.

Babs was still fuming as she and Molly left, wondering why she hadn't tried to call someone–anyone–to watch Molly at the house. They drove in silence. Needing distraction, she turned on talk radio.

It was easy to find the Johnsons' neighborhood, since her job took her all over the city. 402 Elm Street. Not a bad part of town. A lot of college professors live in this university neighborhood. She turned to Molly, "What does your friend's father do?" she asked as they neared Kate's house, clearly the standout on the street.

"I think he's a teacher at the college."

"He teaches? What does her mother do?"

"Um, I think she stays home."

"You're kidding. Grandma and Grandpa must have money," she laughed derisively.

Babs appraised the exterior of the house with a trained eye. Beautiful landscaping. Excellent exterior color scheme. Quality window treatments. About 100 years old but in mint condition, a spacious two-story. Easily 4,000 square feet.

She began to second-guess herself. Maybe these people weren't so bad after all. She'd formed an instant opinion when Molly came home from their house two years ago, saying that they gave her some sort of blessing. Molly was always misrepresenting the truth.

Kate had been watching at the window for an hour already, so her mother was glad when she heard her squeal of delight as she bolted through the front door, "Molly's here, she's here!" Kelly Johnson left the kitchen and followed her daughter outside to meet Molly's mother. All that greeted her were exhaust fumes. Babs wasn't one for mushy goodbyes.

Brandon joined his wife outside and greeted Molly. "You look like one of the flowers we're going to see at the Sunken Gardens today," he said exuberantly.

A cloud passed over Molly's face, lifting only when she saw Mr. Johnson's smiling eyes and realized his words were complimenting her, not teasing her.

* * *

"That little Molly looks like she's afraid someone is going to bite her," Brandon mused to his wife later that day.

Years later, Kelly remembered his comment.

* * *

As the Johnsons and their guest began the half-hour drive to the Hidden Sunken Gardens, it was apparent that Kate hadn't lost her gift of gab. "We went to Sunken Gardens last year, and there were so many flowers you couldn't even count them," she said. "And there are fountains and pools, and the gardens are called hidden because there are trees all around them and you can't see them from the road."

Peter was a mature ten—"almost eleven," he preferred— years old, and he wanted to be sure his sister didn't forget any of the explanation. He jumped in when Kate paused to breathe, "... and the gardens are in a valley, so they're really lower than the road. You have to climb down a long stairway to find them. That's why they're called *sunken*."

At last grasping why her mother had laughed at her, Molly felt stupid.

"There are about twenty million stairs," interjected Sarah. "I bet you could count them all, Molly, because Kate says you're the smartest girl in the class."

Molly didn't hear her.

The Johnsons' van pulled into a parking lot next to their destination, and everyone tumbled out. Mrs. Johnson reached into the back of the van. "Kate, you and Molly can carry the iced tea and lemonade thermoses. Peter, will you help me with the picnic basket? Sarah, here's the table-cloth, and Mary, will you please carry the potato chips?" Mr. Johnson followed the procession down the long descending pathway, carrying their youngest child, one-year-old Grace.

"... eighteen, nineteen, twenty ..." Kate and Molly led the children in counting the stone steps as they wound their way down to the sunken gardens. "Forty," Kate shouted triumphantly as they jumped down the last one. She turned to Molly, "Don't you just love it here, Molly?"

"Yes," Molly quietly agreed, gazing at the colorful flowers dancing around her.

"The picnic area is right over here," Mrs. Johnson said, pointing toward a shimmering pond. "We'll take the three little girls with us and meet you over here by the Reflective Pool in an hour or so. OK?"

"OK," Peter, Kate and Molly agreed. Peter took off running toward a large frog he'd spotted. Kate looked at

Molly. "Let's go exploring!" she said. Molly took Kate's proffered hand and they walked together toward a waterfall. The two girls watched in wonder as three spires of water changed simultaneously from fountain to waterfall that cascaded down a jagged rock-covered hillside into a crescent-shaped pool. The sound of crashing water drowned out Molly's thoughts and fears and replaced them with the simple wonder of being alive in the midst of such an awesome place. She looked beside her and noticed innumerable flowers lining both sides of the waterfall. Beyond them were huge stone planters full of cascading flowering vines that tumbled like laughter into the general merriment of color.

They continued down a stone pathway to yet another fountain. This one was different from the last one; it looked like it was made of thousands of tiny stones. Myriad rivulets of water arched up and over a statue of a woman perpetually pouring liquid from a large stone jug.

Peter caught up with the girls. "I bet she's carrying water for her thirsty brother," he teased. Peter always asked Kate to run and bring him drinks when he was playing softball in their yard.

Hearing the word "brother" reminded Molly of Jeremy. She couldn't fight the urge to run.

"Hey, wait for me," Kate shouted, dashing after her. "Where are you going, Molly?"

Molly shook herself. Skipping at a slower pace, she called out, "Over here."

Kate caught up with her, and both girls stood together, trying to count how many colors were in the flowerbed next to them …. "five shades of purple, four reds, two yellows, nine different blues." Most were flower varieties they'd never seen.

Peter called to them from somewhere nearby, and they stopped counting and followed the sound of his voice.

"This is fun, come look into the Reflective Pool—you can see yourself," he said, making a face at his reflection.

Kate stood on the other side of the lily pond, looking down. "I don't see anything," she said, perplexed. "Just my shadow."

"The sun's behind you there. Come over here," Peter said. "It needs to be in front of you."

Kate walked around to the other side of the pool to stand next to Peter, and Molly stood next to her. "There it is!" she exulted.

Peter asked Molly, "Isn't this great?"

"Yes," she said, staring into blackness. She only saw Peter and Kate's reflections. Not her own.

"OK?" Peter asked, tugging at his sister's arm. "Come on, I'm getting hungry."

They had walked full circle to the picnic area at the base of the staircase. "Look where we are now!" Kate called, running ahead. A stone walkway bordered the pond and led them right to Kate's parents and sisters.

While Kate's mom set out the picnic, Mr. Johnson carried Grace on his shoulders and walked with the other children around the pond, pointing out names of the flowers that bordered the picnic area ... marigolds, petunias, cone flowers, geraniums, baby's breath, chrysanthemums ... and "hmm, do you know what these are?" The children laughed when they saw the strange plants he'd found. Towering above all the other flowers, five feet high, were dozens of giant plants, their thick furry stems topped by huge white blossoms.

"Monster plants," shouted Sarah. The name stuck. For the rest of the day, everyone tried to find more monster plants in the rest of the garden, but apparently these were the only ones.

"Want to see a flower talk?" asked Mrs. Johnson, putting a snapdragon between her thumb and index finger, talking for it. "It's a flower puppet," exclaimed Mary, awestruck.

"Let's eat," shouted Peter, running toward the picnic.

"Whoa, mister, aren't you forgetting something?" asked his mother.

"Oh, yeah, we need to pray."

"And wash your hands," she said as she gave out disposable washcloths.

Molly felt protected and safe when everyone's head bowed to pray before the meal. Her thoughts quickly turned to other things as everyone passed food around the picnic table and began eating. Potato salad, sandwiches and fruit soon disappeared, and it was time to continue exploring the sunken gardens. This time, everyone walked together.

"Did you notice the large evergreens surrounding the garden?" Mr. Johnson asked the children.

"We noticed them last time we were here, Daddy!" Sarah explained.

"And did you know they're called *conifers?*"

"Why?" Mary asked, posing her favorite question.

"Because they propagate themselves by growing cones. In those cones are the seeds of new life. That's how new evergreen trees begin."

"What do you mean?" asked Sarah.

"Honey, do you remember last year, when Mama was pregnant with Grace?"

Sarah looked bewildered, so her father continued, "With people, God has a different way of beginning life. Babies are nurtured inside their mamas until it's time for them to be born." Brandon paused and looked to his wife for help, his look conveying that he wondered how he'd managed to get himself into *this* subject. Kelly continued for him.

"Within each plant, God has designed a way for more plants to grow. That's what the seeds are for." She pointed to a nearby sunflower. "These seeds at the center can be planted when they are mature, and new sunflowers will grow from them."

"If somebody doesn't eat them first," said Peter, whose favorite snack was sunflower seeds.

Brandon picked up a pinecone on the pathway and returned to his earlier thought, "Inside this cone is the beginning of a new tree." He broke the cone apart so the children could look at the pine nut inside.

"I see it!" shouted Kate as her brother and sisters crowded near to see, too.

Kate turned to Molly. "Did you know Daddy is a professor of agrr ... ?

"Agronomy," interjected Kelly.

"Right, ag ... oh, Mom, I'm too excited to say it right!" wailed Kate.

"Let me help you," volunteered her father. "Let's sound it out."

In just a moment, Kate was saying the word with the confidence her parents continually instilled in her. She continued her explanation. "Where he teaches, everybody calls Daddy *Dr. Johnson*," she said proudly.

"Well, is he like a doctor people go see when they are sick?" Molly asked, confused.

"I'm a different kind of doctor. That title just means I've gone to school for a very long time ... you can still call me *Mr. Johnson*," he smiled, hoping to reassure her.

But Molly was already somewhere else, her eyes transfixed on some unseen point.

Chapter Nine

Days, months and years blurred into forgotten yesterdays, with little observation of all that was disappearing with them. Jeremy was away from home, already in his sophomore year of college. Jennifer was a high school senior, with a job at the mall that kept her out late most nights. Molly was in seventh grade—and had the house to herself every day after school.

When she came home on her thirteenth birthday, she saw an envelope propped next to the computer on the kitchen desk. *Maybe a birthday card from Dad,* she thought, her heart surging. Then she noticed it was addressed to her mother. For a split second, she considered peeking into the envelope; she was sidetracked by Jenn's copy of Cosmo instead.

Curling up on the couch in the den, she flipped pages she barely saw. Her mind drifted to California. She could still see the long moving truck in front of the Johnson's house and the procession of men carrying out Kate's bedroom furniture while she and Kate watched glumly from the hammock where they lay side by side, fingers entwined. Molly rocked there for hours after they left, knowing she would never be back. But she often returned in her mind.

It was October; three months had passed since they moved away. Imagining their street, with tree branches arching gracefully over it to form a hidden, safe place, an unbidden tear slid down her cheek.

The phone rang, yanking Molly from her reverie. "Hello, Montgomery residence."

"Guess who?"

"Oh, Kate, how did you know I was thinking about you right this second?"

"Because it's your thirteenth birthday, silly, and we're best friends! What 'cha doing? I know what I wish I were doing ... *anything*—as long as it's with you. How do you like being a teenager?"

Before Molly could answer, a chorus joined Kate: "Happy birthday to you, happy birthday to you, happy birthday, dear Molly, happy birthday to you!"

Kate was so excited she could hardly talk. "Peter and Sarah and Mary and Grace wanted to sing to you, too. Can you hear everybody?" She began giggling and couldn't stop.

Molly smiled. "I even hear Fred barking," she said, her voice wistful. "Oh, I miss you all so much!"

Kate continued, "OK, you guys, I need to talk to Molly now; privacy please?"

Molly heard Kate's mom in the background shooing everyone from the room. "So, what are you doing to celebrate?" Kate asked.

"Probably eating out. Nobody's home yet, so I don't know."

"Then fly out to California tomorrow for another unbirthday party!"

Molly's smile flickered. The unbirthday party seemed like a different lifetime.

"How's school? Who's in your classes?"

An hour passed in animated conversation, then Kate said, "I hope you like the way I wrapped this present!"

Laughing with her friend, Molly said, "Oh, Kate, the only present better than this would be for us to be together. Seventh grade is lonely without you."

"It's hard being in a new school without you, too."

"Have you found new friends?"

"Nobody like you."

Molly felt herself smile from the inside out. She hadn't been replaced!

"But there are some cool kids in my church youth group."

"Jenn works at the mall now," she changed the subject. "She sells shoes," Molly said after a moment's silence.

Once Kate had counted thirty pairs of shoes in Jennifer's closet. "What store does the Queen work in?"

"Ten Two You."

"If anyone could convince someone to buy five—or even ten— pairs of shoes, the Shoe Queen could!" she laughed. "Tell Jenn I'm glad she found the perfect job!"

It was always hard to know which of Kate's remarks to answer, since they tumbled so quickly on top of each other. Molly let herself remember the times Jennifer had taken them with her to the mall, bringing Kate back to their house to bake chocolate chip cookies afterwards. Typically, Jenn taught them the fine art of makeup application before they merged to the kitchen. There, as the three of them laughed and talked, Molly stirred up a bowl of cookie dough, with three soupspoons jutting out so they could bake, eat and talk some more. Kate provided a bridge, somehow connecting the sisters with laughter.

"I just thought of something," said Kate. Molly snapped to attention. "Remember when we gave Jenn that permanent after she bleached her hair?"

Remembering the green hair, Molly and Kate fell into another round of convulsive giggling.

"When Mom found out … ." Molly burst out, unable to finish her sentence.

Kate had the talent of being able to talk and laugh at the same time. "Remember the wig she wore the next day?"

"The red one that was even brighter than *your* hair?" Molly teased.

"You should see my hair now. It's totally frizzy! Hey, whatever happened with Jennifer's boyfriend?"

"He thought the wig was some kind of joke. He never asked her out again."

The two friends jumped from subject to subject for another half-hour, until Kate's mom came back to the phone, "Happy birthday, honey. We all miss you."

Molly tried to swallow the lump in her throat. The only times she'd ever experienced "family" was with the Johnsons. Suddenly, she wanted to run away to beg them to adopt her. "I miss you, too," was all she could choke out.

Kate got back on, "Well, I have to go now. You can call me on my birthday … don't forget, it's December 12th! For two whole months, we get to be the same age—then, I get to be older than you again!"

Molly laughed. Kate could always make her smile. "You're my best friend forever, Kate."

* * *

Molly hadn't heard a car drive into the garage and was surprised to see her mother at the kitchen table. It was an even bigger shock to see her sobbing. She'd never seen her mother cry.

Chapter Ten

B abs froze when she saw her daughter. The house was
quiet when she arrived home, so she assumed she was
alone. Her demanding day was forgotten when she saw the
envelope from Jameson waiting on her kitchen desk. She
could hardly remember the last time she'd received a note
from her husband, although she never forgot the first one—a
hastily scribbled invitation that he'd handed her in their
college cafeteria.

Barbara Finster had been mortified when the handsome
lacrosse player had spotted her in a hairnet, replenishing the
salad bar. "Does that lovely uniform come with pockets?"
he asked, exchanging smiles with his friend. Barbara, not
sure what to say, took the postcard, which was embossed
with the Greek letters of the most elite fraternity on campus,
and put it in her pocket.

Like Cinderella, she transformed herself in borrowed
clothes for the party that night. Jameson Montgomery liked
what he saw and had the means to make sure his new girlfriend was never seen working for food services again.

Wondering if Jameson were trying to rekindle the old
spark, Babs reached for the note.

Barbara-

I doubt you'll be surprised to read this, since our marriage has been a sham for years. All we share is a house and three kids, and I need more than that.

You can keep the house—it's your dream house, anyway.

I'll be sending the divorce papers to your office for you to sign tomorrow. I wanted to give you some time to process this information first. Please don't embarrass either one of us by doing or saying something stupid. Let's keep this process civil. Money shouldn't be an issue—we both have enough. But, I'll be generous.

I imagine you'll want custody of Jennifer and Molly, and that's fine. Of course I'll see them occasionally, but I see no need to traumatize them by drawing up formal visitation papers.

Don't try to tell me this isn't the right thing to do. You know it is.

I've moved into my apartment today. You probably didn't even know I've had one for nearly one year. And, yes, there's someone else.

Jameson

She quickly crumpled the note and shoved it into her purse when she saw Molly. Blinking back tears of rage, Babs stood, her back to Molly, and walked to the sink. She scrubbed her hands frantically, buying time so Molly wouldn't catch on.

"Hi, Mom. You OK?" The Montgomerys didn't discuss each other's personal lives, but seeing her mom cry forced Molly to break convention.

"I'm fine, dear." She smiled a bright smile. "Just a little bad news. Don't you have homework to do?"

"Yes, but … well, I thought we were going out to eat."

"I'll just order in."

The phone rang, and Babs dashed for it, hoping it was

J.W. "Babs Montgomery here," she said in her most professionally pleasant voice. She was not going to give him the satisfaction of her sorrow.

Overhearing her mother, Molly's confusion increased.

"Absolutely—of course!" she enthused into the phone. "We were on our way out the door ...." Her motions forced, she turned to Molly, her face set in a strained smile. "Well, Molly, it seems we have a birthday to celebrate. The Wendhams are waiting for us at Giuseppe's. Where the heck is Jennifer?"

"At work, Mom."

"It's the two of us, then."

The silence in the car was palpable.

Babs muffled the quiet with thoughts of revenge.

Sheldon and Lauren Wendham were waiting in the lobby of Giuseppe's.

"Happy birthday, Molly!" Lauren spoke first.

Peering beyond them, Sheldon asked, "Where's the rest of the family?"

Babs tried to sound calm, but her voice was nervous and high-pitched. "You remember, don't you? Jeremy desperately wanted to get home for tonight, but you know how it is—he's a busy college student now. And didn't I tell you that Jenn has a fantastic new job at the mall? Her boss wouldn't let her off."

"Maybe Jameson hit traffic," Lauren said, glancing toward the door.

"Of all nights, he had a commitment he couldn't get out of," Babs lied.

"Our gain," Sheldon said. "We'll have the birthday girl all to ourselves," he continued, playfully squeezing Molly's arm.

Molly pulled away, relieved to hear the hostess call their name.

"I'll just duck into the ladies' room for a minute," Babs loudly announced, "Meet you at the table." Instead of walking toward the restroom, she walked to the lobby and punched her security code into the ATM machine to begin draining their joint account.

She counted thirteen twenty-dollar bills, one for each of Molly's years, and put the rest in her purse. Noticing a customer leaving with a doggie bag, she turned and walked briskly to a waitress to ask for a bag for "leftovers." After hastily stuffing the twenties into it, she stopped at an empty table to scrawl, "Happy birthday, Molly. Love, Mom," a few inches above the face of a smiling dog. She paused, then added "and Dad" to her signature, knowing that Sheldon and Lauren might wonder if the gift were only from her. Babs smiled again, thinking, *After all, he contributed.*

She caught the waiter's attention as soon as she sat down. "Bring me an Old Fashioned–and make it a double," she laughed. "We're celebrating my daughter's thirteenth birthday!" Suddenly Babs was in a great mood. "Molly, you want a Shirley Temple, don't you?"

The waiter added it to the order. The Wendhams glanced at each other, slowly sipping white Zinfandel while Babs handed Molly her unusual gift.

"Well, Molly, happy birthday! I'll bet this wasn't what you expected!" The volume of Babs' voice increased with each phrase.

Molly hesitated.

"Open it, silly," she laughed, insistent.

Molly saw the crisp bills inside the bag.

"Come on, read your card," her mother cajoled, relieved that the waiter had arrived with her drink. This wasn't working as well as she'd hoped.

Molly stared at the bag, this time noticing her mother's message. "Thanks, Mom," she said uncertainly.

Babs tried to speak playfully. "Can you guess what you get to do with your gift?"

Molly grasped for an answer, her cheeks reddening with embarrassment. "Uh, I don't know," she said quietly.

The Wendhams joined the guessing game. "I know!" Mrs. Wendham exclaimed. "Molly's going somewhere, and the bag represents her suitcase!"

Mr. Wendham joined in. "Foreign or domestic?"

Babs gulped her Old Fashioned, feeling the warm glow of relaxation creep through her body. No one was more surprised than the giver when she uttered her next words, "Molly, this money is to put toward a ticket to go visit your friend Kaitlin!" She laughed, continuing, "In California. Take it out! Count it!"

Molly could hardly breathe. Never in her wildest imagination did she dare to hope that her mother would let her visit Kate. She paused, remembering the last time her mother had seen her friend.

That day, Jennifer, Molly and Kate were baking cookies when their mother unexpectedly arrived home early from work. "What a mess! What do you kids think you're doing?" She yelled at them before she saw Kate. "Oh, I didn't know you had a guest," she said. "Well, girls, we do have dinner plans, so your guest will have to leave now. Bye, Carla. So nice to see you again."

"Her name is Kate, Mom," Jennifer said, indignant.

"Jennifer, you drive her home," Mrs. Montgomery said, not missing a beat. "We're in a time crunch here." She looked at Molly, waving toward the door. "I guess you can ride along. Hurry."

Dinner turned out to be pizza in front of the TV. "Some *plans*," Jennifer protested.

Her mother's words jerked Molly out of her reverie, "I said, count it!"

Molly slowly removed the crisp bills from the doggie bag and counted to thirteen.

Her mother was ebullient, "One for each year!" She looked at Sheldon and Lauren to be sure they were observing.

All of a sudden, Molly realized what was at stake. Boldly she asked, "When do I get to go to California, Mom?"

Babs spoke loudly, ebullient with her gift's success. "How about for Christmas?"

"Can I call Kate and ask her tonight?"

"Of course!" She spoke to the Wendhams, her voice grating. "All right, it's settled then. A California hol-i-day for the birthday girl!" Babs was on her third Old Fashioned and was beginning to be incoherent. She was the only one who didn't notice.

Everyone ate dinner quietly–except Babs. After she finished off a fourth drink, Sheldon whispered to his wife, "I think you'd better take Babs home. She's in no shape to drive. I've never seen her like this."

Babs rode in the front seat and Molly in the back as Mrs. Wendham drove their car home. Babs talked nonstop. Molly, oblivious, was already imagining her trip.

While the Wendhams helped her mother inside, Molly ran upstairs and dialed Kate's number.

Sheldon and Lauren walked her into the kitchen, with Babs laughing, then babbling with manic energy. "Wanna know where J.W. really was tonight?" She stumbled as she leaned toward them, her whisper conspiratorial. "Ssh!" she said, "I can't tell the kids yet, but I can tell you, because you're my *dearest* friends in the whole world." After fumbling in her purse for the note, she handed it triumphantly to Sheldon. "Read this. It tells all. More than you'd want to know. More than I ever knew. Big news." While Sheldon read, she kept talking. "That fool doesn't know I'm going to drain his accounts. I'll fix him. He won't know what's hit him."

Sheldon had seen the first draft of the letter the week before when he and Jameson met for lunch. Making a mental note of Babs' last comment, he said only, "Lauren, why don't you help Babs get to bed?"

"Oh, I'm perfectly all right; in fact, I'm happy as a clam," Babs, insisted, slurring her words. She practically pushed them out the door. "I have my pride," she said. "Don't patronize me."

The Wendhams walked silently into their house next door. Not knowing what else to say, Lauren asked Sheldon if he'd like a cup of decaf.

"Sure," he said absentmindedly, going into the den that doubled as his office.

When Lauren joined him ten minutes later, he was hanging up the phone.

* * *

Kate answered the phone but didn't recognize Molly's excited voice at first. Finally, identifying her, she screamed, "Molly!"

"Kate, you aren't going to believe what happened tonight! My birthday present is the best. I still can't believe it!"

"What? Tell me—what is it?"

"My mom said I can come see you!"

"You're kidding, right?"

Suddenly Molly realized she'd just invited herself to her friend's house. "Oh, no," she said.

"What's wrong?" Kate asked, concerned.

"I'm so sorry, I shouldn't have invited myself to come visit you."

"Are you kidding? We've invited you to come anytime. So when are you coming?" Kate was laughing.

Molly spoke in a quiet, fearful voice, "Is Christmas OK?"

Kate didn't answer. Instead, she yelled to her entire family, "This is so exciting! Molly's coming for Christmas! It's OK, right, Mom and Dad?" There was only a brief pause, then Kate exuded, "They say it's great!"

"Thanks, Kate." She heard her mom coming up the stairs. "I'd better go. I'll call again sometime."

Kate's enthusiasm was unmistakable, "Don't forget!"

"OK. Bye!" Molly quickly ended the call when her mom staggered into her bedroom, a drink shaking precariously in her hand.

"How's the little birthday girl doing?"

"Um, OK," Molly set the portable phone on her dresser. Her mother didn't notice.

I'm going to my room to watch TV. Night, night."

As her mother teetered down the hallway, Molly had a sinking feeling that she'd already forgotten about the trip, that she wouldn't really let her go, after all. She had to think of a place to put the money, in case her mother decided to take it back. She threw away the doggie bag and folded the bills into her sunglasses' case. The teen line rang as she slipped the case under her mattress.

"Hello, Montgomery residence." Beaming at the sound of the familiar voice, she replied, "Oh, Nana, thank you! Yes, I've had a great birthday! The best! Guess what, I get to go see my friend Kate in California!" They talked awhile, then she said, "No, Dad's not here. I think he had a meeting. Mom, uh, isn't feeling very well. Do you want me to get her?"

No, we called to chat with you, Molly Dolly," said Grandpa Montgomery. "The worst part of our move to Florida is missing you and your brother and sister," Nana added. Unaware of their son's recent decision, the senior Montgomerys continued conversing with Molly until a distraught Jennifer entered her room.

"Get off the phone, Molly. NOW!" Jennifer ordered.

Molly was used to her sister demanding to use the phone line they shared, but Jenn didn't look like she wanted the phone.

Bye, Nana and Grandpa. I love you, too. Thanks for calling. And thanks for the new outfit you sent. I'm going to wear it tomorrow."

Molly set the phone down and looked questioningly at her sister.

"Where's Mom?" Jennifer asked, on the verge of tears.

"In her room," Molly said. "At least I think that's where she is."

"Did you see this?" Jenn demanded, brandishing the letter Babs forgot to pick up after Lauren set it down. "This was on the kitchen table when I got home from work."

Molly took the note, dimly comprehending it was the one she'd seen earlier. She read aloud, "To Barbara," and handed it back. "I can't read this. It's not for us."

"You have to see what Dad told Mom," Jennifer ordered. "It changes everything."

As Molly read aloud, Jenn sobbed, "How can he do this to us?"

Molly couldn't respond, suddenly realizing why her mother had been so odd. The paper fluttered from her hand to the floor.

Jennifer stooped to pick it up, then paced with it, back and forth. "We have to do something!" she said at last. Her face had the same determined look her mother's often wore. "I'm going to talk to Mom."

Molly could hear her mother screaming at her sister all the way down the hall. "How dare you? It's my name on that letter, not yours."

"I didn't see the name. I thought maybe Molly had a boyfriend."

"You know what your father's handwriting looks like."

"Mom, what are we going to do?"

"Quit the hysterics, Jenn," she said, tossing a box of tissue at her middle daughter. "Nobody died."

Chapter Eleven

B abs slept little and woke early. The master suite seemed even more empty than usual. She fumbled for a pill to combat her headache. "I am staying in control as of this minute," she said to her bleary reflection. She hated weakness.

She was used to waking up alone; Jameson often slept in his office when he worked late, or crashed on the couch in front of the big-screen TV. She looked around their expansive room, as though noticing it for the first time. In the corner was a small table for two, right where she'd insisted it be, in front of a stone fireplace that had never been used. The loveseat in the bay window had become a clothes rack. A few pictures of Babs and Jameson dotted the built-ins, none of them taken within the past ten years. Babs leapt to her feet and turned them face down.

It was strategy time. Sitting at the elegant desk her husband had given her when she passed her real estate exams, she totaled the funds in their various accounts, noting which she could access with each of her three ATM cards. She took a quick shower, eager to launch her attack. With a practiced hand, she made sure her makeup was perfect, her hair, flawless. She smiled. "Excellent," she said. "No one could believe I'm almost forty-five."

Babs did look more like thirty. Her long slender legs exquisitely complemented her shapely body; three workouts at the gym every week made sure of that. Carefully, she pulled a magenta cashmere sweater over her head, and then turned to contemplate the full-length mirror. "What man would turn anywhere but right here," she said, patting her ample bosom. Her words slapped her in the face; Jameson had stopped trying to touch her years ago. "This is nonsense," she spoke firmly to the mirror, carefully pulling on panty hose so she wouldn't snag them with her perfectly shaped nails. She willed herself not to cry. "There will be no pity parties here." Looking back at the mirror, she recited her life philosophy aloud, "Deal with it and move on." After removing her new black suit from its hanger, she added painstaking finishing touches to her ensemble. Elegant silver brooch, pinned on her jacket just so. (It took three tries to get it right.) Diamond earrings—but not the ones he gave her; the ones she bought to celebrate selling The Crown Jewel. Her eyes glanced briefly at her left hand, then, pained, looked away. The two karat-emerald-cut diamond wedding ring mocked her. Hot tears welled up. "Stop it," she said, slapping her face and glaring at the trembling form in the mirror. "That's enough." Babs wasn't one for regrets. She checked the mirror again, turning to admire her sleek updo. "Jacques got the color exactly right this time." She patted her platinum hair and strode confidently into her day.

She greeted her daughters with determined cheerfulness, "Good morning."

Jenn gasped in astonishment.

"Look kiddo, this might seem like a lousy hand, but I know how to turn things around."

Babs left the house, whistling on her way to the nearest ATM.

Two hours later, Babs was pounding her fist on the seventh ATM she'd tried. All said the same thing: "Insufficient funds."

She jumped back in her car and drove to the downtown bank. Although Babs seldom stopped to see her husband at work, she had no problem finding a place to park. Her car slid smoothly into the spot right next to J.W.'s, the spot reserved for his senior vice-president. Her thoughts turned to speculate where he'd spent last night—and who had been there with him. Always efficient, she shifted mental gears, taking her cell phone from her purse to let her secretary know she was running late. The phone was back in her purse by the time the elevator doors opened. She planned to deal with J.W. just as quickly. He was merely a problem to be solved. "He's going to be *extremely* sorry to see me," she fumed as the elevator took her toward the bank's mezzanine-level executive suites.

As she walked toward J.W.'s office, he and his secretary walked out of it, his arm around her slender waist. They both saw Babs at the same time; instantly, his arm dropped. Jameson's momentary panic was rapidly replaced with a gaze of calm determination.

Babs avoided his eyes, mentally appraising the woman who had taken her place instead. It took her less than ten seconds to decide that J.W. was in the middle of a bizarre mid-life crisis. She glanced down at her own custom-designed suit and perfect body, a smug smile her face. It was only a matter of time, she knew, before he'd come to his senses, begging forgiveness with a velvet-covered box.

His voice cut into her thoughts, "What brings you here, Barbara?"

"As if you didn't know," Babs delivered each word with a hammering blow. "Let's go into your office a moment," she said, staring coolly at his companion. "Alone."

"Fine, then," he held his office door open for his wife and turned to his lover, "This won't take long."

You're acting like a hormonal adolescent, Jameson," she screamed, not caring who heard her.

"So *now* you'll finally call me Jameson. You've known I've always hated *J.W.*," he said quietly, bluntly.

"I've never heard you say that," Babs spat back.

"You haven't heard half of what I've told you," said Jameson, suddenly sounding fatigued.

Babs changed the subject, seeming not to hear him. "Where is my money?"

"*Your* money?"

"You know perfectly well what I mean. All our accounts are drained. If you think you're going to pull that one over on me, you've got another thing coming!"

"Isn't that what you'd planned to do to me today?"

Babs didn't remember telling Sheldon. She couldn't believe this disgusting turn of events.

"There's a daily limit on cash withdrawals from linked deposit accounts, anyway," he said, enjoying her silence. "Or did you forget that I'm the one who knows money?"

She was speechless with rage.

Jameson continued, his voice measured and firm. "I don't need your money, Barbara. I simply want to make it crystal-clear that you are not going to control me. I've already deposited your share of the money in a new account." He picked up a folder on his desk and handed it to her. "Here's your new checkbook, with a brochure explaining the account's features. You can sign the signature card and leave it at the New Account desk on your way out." Stepping aside, he opened the door for her to leave. The interview was over.

With lightening speed, Babs walked over and shut it. "Don't patronize me! I'll open my own new account, and it won't be here." She conveniently neglected to mention that most of last year's real estate profits were already squirreled away in an account at a competitor's bank.

Babs blew out of the bank like an arctic wind.

A ripple of quiet laughter accompanied her stormy exit. (For months afterward, the office gossips delighted in embellishing her Waterloo.)

She stepped out of the elevator into the parking garage, planning a way to win the next round. As she reached her car, she paused to admire it, glad the title was in her name. Tapping red fingernails against the steering wheel in staccato rhythm, she enumerated her achievements, her possessions. The job: owner of the real estate company with highest metro sales volume last year. The house: custom-built, with every feature she wanted. Money: enough capital to retire early. Family: three kids—and the husband her college roommate had described as "way out of your league, Barbara." She ran her hand slowly across the leather seat, seeking comfort. Unbidden, Jameson's words reverberated in her mind.

* * *

Beth felt the chill of Babs' presence long after she left.

The last time she'd seen Jameson's wife was at the office Christmas party. She'd even talked with her. A polished, sophisticated woman. Obviously wealthy, beautiful, impeccably groomed. Beth was intimidated. Terrified, actually.

She started working for Jameson just a little over a year ago. That was the month she planned to begin her master's program. But, that month she had taken a temporary hiatus from school—the third one so far—to earn enough money to continue. She expected good pay and good hours. Not an affair.

Her thoughts spiraled downward, her mind in anarchy. *How can I long for him so much that nothing else matters?*

But he's married! He's the man I've always wanted. But I don't want to be a home-wrecker! Beth hardly fit the home-wrecker profile. Sensible. Quiet. Conservative. *This is going to kill my parents.*

Beth's parents were real, born-again Christians. She had gone to church with them until she left home for college. Suddenly their faith wasn't relevant. She considered herself an intellectual who preferred mental pursuits to spiritual ones. Sometime during her sophomore year of college, she'd finally admitted to herself that she'd never believed the way her parents did. They talked about a personal faith, but she couldn't buy the idea that Jesus was the one way to God. It seemed too exclusionary, too narrow-minded. But she couldn't argue with their lives. They were kind, good people. She knew all they'd wanted for her was what was best, so, although she rejected their faith, she followed their advice about sex for a long time, all through her undergraduate years—resisting her friends' suggestions to "live a little" more times than she could remember. Until January.

"Wait until you're married, honey," her parents had lovingly explained time and again. "God designed sex to be something beautiful for you to share with the man He has for you." She'd heard it since she was ten. Boyfriends had told her she was frigid, that she'd never get married. She staunchly held her ground, privately terrified of getting a STD. She hadn't counted on the powerful effect Jameson Montgomery would have on her, or the force of the attraction between them.

Jameson hadn't interviewed her for the job. The bank had a personnel department for that. She hadn't even met him until her first day at work. His last executive secretary had taken maternity leave and then abruptly decided to stay home with her baby when her leave ended. The bank had to scramble to find someone with the right background for the position. Beth's summer job at her hometown bank and her business courses had prepared her perfectly to work for a bank president.

At first, working for Jameson was pleasant–nothing more, nothing less. Beth was preoccupied, wishing she could have started the fall semester at the university so she could get on with her life. And she was busy just learning her job. Gradually, though, she realized what a wonderful man she was working for.

The first snow, in mid-November, had set her heart in motion. Going into his office to deliver the day's mail, she stopped—as she often did— to gaze out his window. The business district had been transformed into a crystalline wonderland of softly descending snowflakes. "Isn't it beautiful?" she whispered.

The wistfulness of her voice made Jameson stop to look at her, not the snow. "Yes," he said, slightly taken off guard.

He joined her at the window, where both of them stood silently watching for several minutes.

He spoke first, "Did you play in the snow as a child?"

"Oh, yes," Beth said. "My brother and I used to make igloos, snow angels, and have snowball fights ... ." She paused, remembering, then asked, "Did you?"

"I was pretty serious. I mostly read books." Jameson was intrigued. Most people stayed away from him, intimidated by his position and his lack of words. He wanted to talk with people, to get to know them, but he never knew what to say. And his job was important to him; it always had been easy to become absorbed by it and oblivious to everyone else. But Beth exuded a quiet calm he found alluring. Her work was impeccable, her appearance elegant, yet soft and approachable. So far he had maintained his professional decorum around her, but he knew it wouldn't take much to melt his resolve.

Usually Beth wasn't impulsive, but there was something in his pensive expression that overrode her cautious reserve. "Come on," she said, surprising even herself with her boldness.

He looked at her quizzically, "What?"

She smiled, "Your ten o'clock meeting is about to start."

Jameson didn't catch on until she walked across his office to his closet and handed him his wool topcoat. Laughing, enjoying the sense of unexpected adventure, he put on the coat and followed her lead.

As the elevator carried them downstairs, he helped Beth into her coat, both of them smiling with a sense of anticipation. Disoriented, Jameson fumbled for the appropriate rules to follow, the right role to play, blissfully unsure of himself, yet more carefree than he could ever remember feeling. Stepping out into the new snow, he laughed, liking the sound of his voice.

She threw a soft snowball at him and he gently volleyed a handful of snow at her feet, careful not to hurt her.

His gentleness disarmed her.

Beth's amber eyes were framed in the darkest, longest lashes he'd ever seen, and he wondered how he could have missed noticing them before. Now they were smiling, laughing, dancing. With him.

It seemed natural to take her gloved hand in his. Was it trembling as he held it by his side? Or was he shaking? He was almost fifty, but he felt fifteen.

"Mr. Montgomery, shall I serve the coffee?" Beth said, donning her best British secretary's accent.

"Yes, I think this conference is at a good break point," answered Jameson, finally in on the joke.

In a nearby coffee house, their latte sat untouched while they gazed into each other's eyes, letting the rest of the world fall away.

After an hour, Jameson glanced at his watch, startled that so much time had passed. "I have a meeting," he said, pushing away from their table with obvious reluctance.

A block before they reached the bank, he dropped her hand. As they stepped into the revolving door, both of them tried to pretend nothing had happened. Beth, flustered, took a sharp left turn. "I'm going to check on something at payroll," she called back.

Embarrassed by her impetuous behavior, she became extremely professional and exceedingly busy for the rest of the day. It wasn't until months later that she let her guard drop again.

* * *

It was Friday—the day after the office holiday party. After tossing and turning all night, Beth gave up and decided to go to the office early, to get a jump-start on her work before anyone else arrived. She knew the night guard would let her in.

After reviewing voice-mails, she walked into Jameson's office to leave the list of messages for him. She jumped when she noticed him asleep on the leather sofa behind his desk.

He awakened, and sat up, smoothing his rumpled slacks and tucking in his T-shirt. "Oh, hello, Beth. What time is it? I must have overslept."

"No—I'm really early—oh, I'm so sorry," she began, embarrassed, backing out the door of the massive office.

"No, wait," he said. "I'm the one who's sorry. Please forgive me for startling you," he smiled, motioning her to sit by him.

Beth tentatively sat on the opposite end of the sofa.

"This is the first time I've stayed here in a long time," he said, shrugging. "It didn't work out to go home last night." Noting Beth's confusion, he continued, "My wife and I had a little disagreement."

Beth said simply, "I'm sorry." She suddenly understood why he kept a suit and dress shirts in his office closet. And why the adjoining bathroom had its own shower.

"Don't be. That's a common event these days. Our marriage is sterile."

"But, I thought, I mean, don't you have children?"

He smiled, amused by her question.

Realizing her mistake, Beth blushed.

Obviously more of a morning person than she, Jameson laughed easily and kept talking. "Don't be embarrassed. My marriage is a sham. We never talk, we never share ideas. I've shared more with you than … ." he stopped abruptly, afraid to say too much. He reverted to his earlier description, "We do have three children, but that's all we've shared lately."

Beth didn't want to know what he meant. All she could think about was their day in the snow together, the latte … . She felt herself getting hot. Then, for a brief moment, she forgot caution and looked at him.

His restless night had left his hair tousled, adding to the look of a vulnerable little boy. Without thinking, Beth slid toward him and slipped her fingers through his silver-tipped hair, trying to return it to its usual impeccable state.

Tears filled his eyes at her tender touch. He reached up and touched her glossy chestnut hair, then leaned over and tenderly, lightly kissed her cheek.

His overnight growth of whiskers startled her. She laughed softly.

"What?" he asked.

"Your whiskers tickle." It was the first time she'd been kissed by a man in the morning—the second time she'd been kissed at all. She pulled back and stood, sensing that she was standing on the brink of a massive mistake.

He was frustrated. He wanted her more than he'd ever wanted anything, anyone. But, he, too, suddenly realized who he was and where he was; he checked his impulses. "I'd better get ready for the day," he said, resuscitating his brisk, formal demeanor.

She busied herself at her desk just outside his door. People began coming in to the office, and he was tied up in a stream of meetings all day. Their paths barely crossed.

* * *

Beth left work at 5:00, eager to escape. "I'm leaving now," she said, pressing the intercom. "See you Monday." She was relieved when he didn't respond to the terse message.

She let a blur of billboards and lights fill her consciousness from the suburb to the city, thankful for the distraction as she rode home. After leaving the train, she stopped for cappuccino at a noisy corner coffee house, hesitant to be alone with her thoughts. She still couldn't stop thinking about Jameson. She felt his presence, remembering how his hand had held his coffee mug that November day, how perfectly his fingers were shaped ... how his eyes held hers so strongly, so longingly that she felt one with him. Forgetting her nearly full cup on the table, she hurried away, hoping to outrun her thoughts. Her steps were quick, firm and determined, taking her back to the haven of her building. Her key stuck in the lock, and she looked up, realizing she was on the wrong floor.

Safe inside her own apartment, Beth felt the usual surge of relief at being in familiar surroundings. Comforted, she thumbed through the day's junk mail, purposefully clipping coupons she knew she wouldn't use. Just as she was about to launch into the night's event—organizing closets—the buzzer rang. She walked several steps from the bedroom door, pushing the button that connected her to the lobby.

"Surprise." A voice came through the metal plate in her living room.

"Yes," she said, but her mind couldn't comprehend who

it was. Few people ever came to see her, so she knew it probably was a mistake.

The buzzer rang again, jarring her thoughts. "Are you there?"

"What are you doing here, Jameson?"

Beth paused for a second that felt like years, then pressed the button that would allow him to exit the lobby and come upstairs. "I'm in 310," she said.

"I know," he responded.

During the moments it took him to come upstairs, Beth lectured herself, trying to believe that she could help him–and his marriage–by being his friend. Like the mantra she used when she was skiing, she told herself to stay in control. After quickly checking her hair in a mirror, she responded to his gentle tap on her door.

"How did you know where to find me?"

"You work for me, don't you? I checked with personnel." He was laughing.

"I don't believe you're here." She was smiling.

"Are you going to ask me in?"

Dressed in a navy cashmere sweater and jeans, Jameson looked fabulous. He pulled a dozen long-stemmed yellow roses from behind his back.

She pressed her nose into them, relaxing in the fragrance. "What's the occasion?" she asked.

"I wanted to thank you for being the perfect secretary."

"You came all the way into the city for that?" she laughed.

"I hadn't ridden the train in a long time. I needed a change." His confidence allayed her fears, yet Beth was frozen in place. "May I?"

His shining eyes melted her indecision; she opened the door with a flourish.

Walking into her living room, he seemed totally in control—and more happy than she'd ever seen him. "Beth, I was hoping you'd go to dinner with me," he said. "I know it's last minute, but it's a perfect night."

She hesitated. He gazed at her, and the tenderness she saw in his eyes rendered her incapable of coherent thought. She turned away to force herself to think calmly.

Buying time, she asked, "Would you like a cup of coffee?"

"Great. Fabulous!" he said.

With shaking hands, she poured water into the coffee maker, trying not to notice his eyes following her every move. She didn't have to ask how he liked his coffee.

He ambled into the tiny kitchen as she searched for two mugs without chips and stood beside her as she poured. "Thanks, it smells great," said Jameson, taking both mugs from her into the adjacent living room.

"Seeing you—I, I feel like I should be preparing your board report."

"We're off work tonight," he said, setting his mug next to hers on the antique trunk that doubled as her coffee table. The love seat was the only place to sit in the compact living room, so they sat down together.

Feeling uncomfortable and at a complete loss for words, she reached for her mug.

Jameson reached for his at the same time, and they awkwardly bumped heads.

"Are you OK?" they asked in unison, dissolving in laughter like two self-conscious teenagers.

He stared at Beth again, and this time she didn't look away. Suddenly she was warm, and she stood to take off her suit jacket.

He helped her, his hand brushing the softness of her silk blouse as he lifted the jacket gently off her shoulders. He wanted to take off her blouse, too, but he kept himself in control, only touching the sleeve—with a faint lingering pressure that sent shivers through her body.

One look at her eyes told him she'd felt the touch the way he'd given it.

He was quite familiar with the feelings surging through his body, but Beth was entering uncharted territory. Suddenly, she was terrified. Part of her wanted to tell him to get out; part of her wanted him to stay–forever. She blushed, embarrassed at the torrent of intense physical feelings.

As though reading her mind, he stepped back. "Where shall we go for dinner?" He knew he no longer needed to ask her if she wanted to go with him. Consent was written in every line of her body.

Beth hesitated for less than a second, "Surprise me? Just give me a second to change clothes."

She disappeared into her bedroom and quickly put on her new black dress. It had been hanging in her closet for weeks, ever since the day it came in a surprise box from her mom. "I know you won't splurge on something for yourself—so I'll send a few early Christmas gifts—with hopes you'll have a special party to attend," her mother's note said. Beth checked the mirror and left her mother's wishes behind her.

"All set," she announced, reaching for her coat and scarf. Jameson held the coat as she slipped into it—and into his arms. She coughed, trying to break the intensity of the moment.

"Race you downstairs!" said Jameson, sensing her mood.

A cab carried them past Lake Michigan, glimmering with the lights of the city, mirroring their bliss.

The lighting, the food, the music—everything about the restaurant Jameson chose—was perfect. Everything about their time together was perfect, too—except that he was married. Both Jameson and Beth tacitly accepted the delusion that they were meant to be together. For long moments, they simply gazed at each other, reveling in their simulated intimacy born of secrecy.

The two strolled along Michigan Avenue after a

leisurely dinner, until the chill of the wind forced them to find shelter. It was after 2:00 AM when they arrived back at Beth's building. She tensed.

"I should go," he whispered, backing away. "I respect you too much to expect you to ask me in." He knew exactly where he was going and was willing to take his time.

* * *

The next time Jameson came to Beth's apartment, he found the buttons on her blouse. Finally she felt loved. Finally her life had passion. One by one, each warning ringing in the recesses of her mind was muted and, by degrees, fell silent. Her beliefs about the sanctity of marriage went the way of other childhood ideals.

The following day, after Jameson left to return to his family in the suburbs, Beth was so overwhelmed with guilt that she threw up. Pausing to think, she vowed she'd never repeat the previous night's behavior. But the next time he touched her, she didn't ask him to stop at all.

Jameson's only regret was that it took him ten months to decide to sever legal ties with his wife. He wasn't worried about his kids. "They're resilient," he told his parents, explaining the pending divorce. "They're going to be happy just knowing their mother and I are happy." He took time to mull over his future, confident Beth didn't want commitment any more than he did. It never occurred to him that he had missed his daughter's thirteenth birthday.

Chapter Twelve

It was Saturday, Analese Harper's favorite day to get ready for the next week. After filling her teakettle, she left the kitchen to play through Debussy's *Passepied*. Knowing her proclivity to get lost in music, she filled the kettle with extra water to keep it from boiling dry. It had been whistling insistently for several minutes before she finally tore herself away from the piano that had become her therapy. Even then, it was only sheer determination to tackle the job at hand that forced her to move.

"Why do people insist on making such messes of their lives?" she asked Rupert, her Cavalier King Charles Spaniel. He peered at her woefully, and then lay his head down with a loud sigh. She filled a bone china teapot with boiling water, deciding on Earl Grey—the tea she always chose as an antidote to inner turmoil. She emptied the now-preheated teapot and spooned a generous amount of tea leaves into it before filling it once again with steaming water. While the tea steeped, she set a timer for four minutes—she liked her tea a bit stronger than some—then set out cream and sugar. Reaching up to the cupboard, she moved mugs around until she found the china one her grandmother had given her seven years earlier to celebrate her graduation from Oxford. She smiled, remembering the fun she had showing her grandmother the way to make proper tea. Her eyes filled with tears. "I wouldn't have stayed in England that summer if I'd known it would be our last," she told Rupert.

Her thoughts traveled to yesterday's events. She couldn't shake thoughts of the Montgomery family and the particularly embarrassing situation she had stumbled upon.

In her nicest voice, Mrs. Montgomery had wheedled, "Just this one time, please change your cleaning day for me; I want to host a little party that evening." As requested, Analese had arrived, precisely at 12:30 PM. She began her work upstairs. Apparently, Mrs. Montgomery was not expecting her after all.

The large master bedroom was part of a suite; adjacent to it was a mirrored room, the principal feature of which was a hot tub big enough for two. Just as Analese began to dust, she caught a reflection in the dresser mirror of four feet poking through bubbles. The sleepy Southern accent she overheard confirmed her suspicion that they did not belong to Mr. Montgomery.

She stepped backwards, hoping to slip away, unnoticed, but unfortunately, Mrs. Montgomery had heard something, too.

Afraid that one of her daughters had come home early, Babs quickly toweled dry and slipped into a long silk robe. She softly closed the door behind her and followed the footsteps that preceded her down the stairs. There she found Analese reaching for the front door.

"Oh, Analese," she'd said, visibly relieved. "I thought Jennifer was home."

Analese smiled weakly, unable to stammer out a reply.

Babs found one for her. "But, of course, you're here to clean, and I completely forgot when my 'event' was changed from evening to afternoon. How silly of me." She laughed at her hilarious joke. Although she didn't feel a need to justify her actions, she also didn't want to lose her domestic. "My husband and I have begun divorce proceedings," she stated flatly. "It seems he has found another bath partner, so I'm merely following his example." She'd laughed again, hoping to ease the tension.

"Shall I come back another day?" Analese asked, finally finding words.

"We can wait until next week, at your regular time," Babs said, laughing giddily, "but I'll pay you extra for today's little inconvenience, and I'll try not to give you any more surprises." She laughed again, prancing back up the stairs to the hot tub, confident she'd taken control of the situation.

Analese couldn't get away fast enough. She shifted from first gear to second and then to third, all within the first block.

After arriving home, the same questions kept tumbling over and over in her mind, *How could a mother forget to set a good example for her daughters? How does she rationalize away such disgusting behavior? And why is Mr. Montgomery abandoning his family?* She sat in her favorite chair, a floral wing back, and sighed as she lifted her feet onto the needlepoint footstool, last winter's stress release project. Ordinarily she felt comforted when she studied her finished artwork, but now the scene on the needlepoint merely jeered at her. Its focal point was a dove.

Peace had always eluded her. Perhaps she was really more of a philosopher at heart than a businesswoman. Lately, while she cleaned houses, she analyzed the dynamics of the people who lived there. But nothing could explain a family like the Montgomerys. "I care more about their wood floors than they care for each other," Analese told

Rupert. He gazed at her with empathy and climbed onto her lap when she asked him, "Is everyone so thoughtless?"

She began to weep for them, her thoughts wandering once again to her family, as they seemed to more and more. The tears came faster as she began crying for everyone who had missed the love of family she had known with her own dear parents and her grandmother. An orphan since she was ten, she had been raised by a kind grandmother. Because she had inherited money from all three of them, she could buy more than most people twice her age—but owning things didn't inspire her. She wished she'd known her other grandparents and began to grieve that loss, too, her thoughts quickly turning to Rupert's heart murmur and the inevitable loss of her best friend.

Analese never allotted more than ten minutes for a good cry; she glanced at the cuckoo clock on the wall and saw her time was up. Picking up her teacup and pouring fresh tea on top of that which was left to restore it to the right temperature, she scratched Rupert's Blenheim spot, sipping contentedly while carefully, purposefully pursuing another vein of thought. "Now I shall remember families I have known who are unlike this one that troubles me so, Rupert," she said, failing to notice that the dog had left the room. Her mental journey continued, and she smiled, remembering a family who had meant almost as much to her as her own. "How could I possibly have lost touch with them?" she scolded herself. Immediately, she picked up the phone.

None of her clients would have dreamed she could begin to afford such a luxury as a private secretary. Analese liked keeping her life a mystery. It sometimes even made her laugh to herself while she worked, especially when one of the wealthy women magnanimously handed her a twenty dollar bill and told her to "go do something special." And that was precisely the reason she wanted to contact the people who had now been brought to her mind. It was their lives she emulated when she squelched her pride and graciously said, "thank you."

The phone rang only twice. Her secretary was diligently at work, preparing the week's financial statement. "Harper Enterprises," she answered calmly.

"Erica, can you add one more thing to your day?"

"Sure, what's up?"

"I need you to locate a couple I knew years ago. Their name is in my Rolodex in the storage room, but I haven't talked with them for four or five years, so they could have moved. I'm pretty sure I have an address but no phone number."

"No problem. I have a computer disc that has addresses and phone numbers for just about everyone who has a phone," Erica laughed. Analese had hired her because nothing rattled her.

"Great. Do you know the Rolodex I mean? Not the circular one—the smallish one from grad school."

Erica had switched to the portable phone so she could search while they talked. "Got it. What's the name?"

"Lewellen."

"OK, it's here. Ken and Debbie?"

"That's it! What's the location on the card?"

"There are five, no—seven—different addresses."

"Is there one in Russia?"

"Yep, that's the one scribbled in the corner. It's hard to read."

"Still hoping I'll update the addresses?" she kidded.

Erica laughed, "I'm not holding my breath," then was back to business. "You want me to try to locate them in Russia, right? What are they doing there, anyway?"

"They do emergency relief work all over the world."

"I guess so—what a list! Afghanistan, Somalia, Hungary, Haiti, Mozambique—and Montana?"

"They worked at an Indian reservation in Montana. That's where I met them."

"When were you in Montana, Analese?"

"The summer after my grandmother died. I decided to work on the Indian reservation when I noticed their ad for summer interns."

"And ... ."

"Well, Erica, it was either that or have a summer-long pity party. I knew I had to think of someone besides myself or I'd go crazy."

"What about the Lewellens?"

"That year, they were teaching summer school to the children–reading, math, crafts, basic health care–various subjects. They taught me more than I taught any of the children." Analese was at an uncharacteristic loss for words. She was shocked to find herself incapable of describing the people who had given her hope during the darkest time in her life and showed her that God cared. She cleared her throat and became the boss again to sidestep further discussion. "So, um, Erica, try to locate them for me, OK?"

Erica knew when to be quiet. "I'm on it."

"Thanks. I knew I could count on you."

She hung up the phone and began rummaging through bookshelves, trying to find the book Debbie Lewellen had given her that summer. It was on the bottom shelf, right next to *War and Peace*. "Erica wouldn't like my book cataloging system, either," Analese smiled to herself as her hand grasped the one she wanted. *The Lion, the Witch and the Wardrobe*. Years ago, it had helped her untangle some of the thoughts riddling her mind when she lost her beloved grandmother. She'd been hurt and confused when she asked Debbie how a world filled with pain could have been designed by a good God. Debbie had simply handed her the book and said, "Sometimes an allegory helps me understand that things aren't as they seem. See what you think of this."

She went to the kitchen and found an apple before she sat back in her favorite chair, this time to read. Analese didn't often allow herself the extravagance of what she dubbed a Riotous Reading Day, but when she did, nothing else mattered. Today, she needed to read, to get lost in Narnia, rediscovering the truths that had helped her during that other troubled time.

She ignored the phone and munched her apple as she read. Traveling through the pages, she remembered. It was Aslan, the book's Christ-figure, who had given her a new picture of a loving God. He was willing to give everything he had, even when he'd been betrayed.

Analese wondered how she could begin to understand such sacrifice. As she often did, she changed her own subject. "I'm a selfish pig, Rupert," she said aloud. Rupert was snoring loudly, one of the unfortunate symptoms of his heart condition.

For a reason Analese didn't understand, all she could think of was Molly and the sadness haunting her eyes. She recognized Molly's loneliness. Although she could do nothing to heal her own pain, she vowed to find some way to ease Molly's.

Chapter Thirteen

The Montgomery household settled into a dull routine. Jennifer and Molly knew better than to mention their father's absence, and soon each day blurred monotonously into the next.

As December approached, Babs was finally forced to mention her ex-husband. "Girls, your father called," she said with clipped speech.

Both girls looked up from the TV expectantly. "Yeah?"

"He wants you to come to his place for Christmas Day," she continued.

"Why the sudden interest?" Jennifer said, hurling a pillow toward the empty place where his desk had been.

"That's enough, Jennifer Marie. He's still your father, even if ...." Babs paused, unable to continue. With clenched jaw, she said at last, "He wants you to meet *Beth.*"

"Is Jeremy coming?"

"No, he's going home with his girlfriend for break."

"I don't want to go, either," Jennifer said. "Jeremy doesn't have to."

"You're going. And that's final."

Molly kept quiet throughout the argument. For weeks,

she'd been trying to find a way to talk with her mother about the promised trip to California. She knew it was now or never. Tenuously, she began, "Mom, I can't go to Dad's for Christmas."

"What in the world are you talking about?" Babs said, incredulous at her audacity.

"Remember, for my birthday, you gave me a trip to California to see Kate ... ." Molly's voice was quiet, but firm. She wanted this trip enough to risk her mother's fury.

"Now I've heard everything! There's no way I'd send a thirteen-year-old alone to California, much less pay for it!"

"You already did," she whispered.

Fortunately, her mother didn't hear her, because she undoubtedly would have forced Molly to relinquish the money, having zero recollection of her own ludicrous present. She laughed. "Whatever possessed you to think I'd let you go see that weird family is beyond me," she said. "Next subject, girls."

It had been a long time since Molly let herself cry. That night, she whimpered quietly until she fell into a fitful sleep, her birthday money still tucked away beneath her mattress. The hope of seeing her friend had sustained her through the collapse of her family unit; now that was crushed in the wake of her family's never-ending storm.

No one noticed the circles under her eyes until after school the next day. Analese was still cleaning when Molly arrived home.

Ever since the hot tub incident, Analese had carefully arranged her weekly cleaning times for late Friday afternoons, giving her at least a few minutes to talk with Molly. Mrs. M had been unusually accommodating, a hopeful sign that she retained some shred of a conscience.

Molly was rummaging through a cupboard trying to find something to eat when Analese came in carrying a mop.

Molly was momentarily startled, even though she knew Analese was there.

"It's just me, Molly. Don't worry," Analese said in a calm voice.

"Hi. Good to see you," Molly said sincerely. Although she couldn't verbalize it, she always looked forward to seeing Analese.

"So, how has your week been, Molly?"

"OK."

"What kind of an answer is that?" Analese teased her into giving more information.

"Well ..." Molly stalled.

"Let's see, did you dissect any strange creatures in the science lab, did any boys carry your books, did you wear a blue wig to school, are you driving the school bus yet, are you going on any exciting trips?" Analese wouldn't give up.

They both knew the script. After a few questions and a few silly replies, the two usually shared a laugh. This time, though, Molly surprised even herself with her response.

Analese always tried to stay lighthearted and was careful not to pry into Molly's personal life. Today was different, though. It was obvious that Molly's heart was breaking. She reached over to hug her, and Molly returned the hug—just for a second—then struggled valiantly to keep her emotions in check.

"Can I help?" Analese asked, handing Molly a paper napkin from the kitchen counter to dry her tears.

Finally, Molly spoke–softly, carefully. "Today is the first day of December, and I was supposed to go see my best friend Kate this month. Now I can't go." Molly looked out the window, distracting herself to keep from crying.

Analese's mind was racing, trying to follow Molly's thoughts. "You were going to go to California?"

"Yes. My mom promised me I could visit Kate," she explained.

Analese remembered the redhead well. She was the only friend she'd seen Molly bring home.

"She gave me money for my birthday. But now she says I'm making everything up. But I'm not," she said, shredding the napkin in her hand. "I still have the money she gave me for the ticket."

"Does she know that?"

Molly's voice was agitated. "No! If I told her, she'd just take it away from me and say I stole it."

"Hmm. You do have a problem." Analese paused. "Is there anyone else who knows about this gift?"

"The Wendhams do, but they wouldn't help me. Mr. Wendham is the last person I'd go to for a favor."

Analese decided not to pursue that angle further; the problem was big enough without adding to it. "Why won't your mom let you go to California?"

"She says I'm not old enough. But I think she doesn't like Kate."

Analese listened, thinking. Finally, she spoke. "Molly, your mom is going through a tough time. She's probably having trouble getting through each day." Analese almost gagged at having to defend someone she found utterly reprehensible.

The conversation was interrupted by the sound of the automatic garage door opening. Seconds later, Molly's mother breezed into the kitchen, obviously satisfied with her day. "Girls, I sold not one, but two houses today!"

"Congratulations," Analese said, trying to sound more enthusiastic than she felt.

"Molly?"

"Great, Mom!" She gave her two thumbs up.

"Well, looks like I interrupted something," Mrs. Montgomery said, eying the mop with more of an order than a question.

"I'd better finish up here." Analese spoke the command

she'd been given. It was obvious she'd overstayed her welcome.

Molly left the room with a quiet goodbye. She folded what was left of the napkin, then carefully put it into her jeans pocket.

An hour later, Analese backed out of the Montgomery's driveway, venting her frustration out loud. "Of all days, Mrs. Montgomery came home early today. And Molly really needed a friend today! Instead, I mopped alone in the kitchen while she moped alone upstairs." Flashing red lights in her rear view mirror interrupted Analese's monologue. "The perfect ending to a perfect day." She quit talking as she rolled down her window.

"Do you know what the speed limit is here?"

"Uh, thirty-five?" She looked up at the officer and felt beads of perspiration forming on her nose. His face was kind but resolved.

"Try thirty. And you were going?" A rhetorical question.

"Um ... forty?" She handed him her license and registration before he had to ask.

"Try forty-five."

"I'm sorry, officer. I was distracted ... by a problem a friend of mine is having."

Officer Bob Clark didn't doubt her sincerity, especially when he observed the tear coursing slowly down her cheek. People had tried tears on him before, but they were usually more overt. He could tell this one was trying to hide them. He looked down and began writing.

"Try not to drive when you're under emotional strain. I won't give you a warning next time."

"Yes, sir. Thank you, sir."

He handed her license back, then waited for her to downshift into first so she could continue her drive. It seemed like people under stress always had trouble shifting gears on those little sports cars. Back in his patrol car, he did something no one ever saw him do. He prayed. As he drove, trying to protect the citizens of his micro-world, he kept asking God to guide and protect Analese Harper and whomever it was she was concerned about.

She knew he should have given her a ticket. Forcing herself to concentrate on her driving, Analese kept thinking about Molly. By the time she'd turned into her own driveway, she hit on a workable solution. Immediately she dialed her cell phone.

"Aunt Elizabeth?"

"Analese? I can't believe it's you," replied her elderly aunt. "How long has it been?"

"I'm sorry I haven't called. I—well, you know. I keep pretty busy."

"I just hope you're calling to say you're coming to visit," her aunt replied.

"Actually, I was thinking of Christmas," she answered, relishing the surprise.

"Of course!" she said with delight. She paused to speak to her husband, "Ed, Analese is coming! For Christmas!" She returned to the phone, "Do you have your reservations yet?"

"I'm not sure what day I'll arrive. Can I let you know in a week or so?" They talked awhile, then Analese hung up, wondering why she didn't call them more often.

Step one completed, Analese turned to her planner for step two. After finding the number, she dialed, rehearsing her lines in her mind. The phone was answered on the first ring.

"Montgomery residence," the voice said crisply.

Analese wished she'd made notes. "Hi, Mrs. Montgomery, this is Analese Harper, and I wonder if I could talk with you a minute."

"Yes, but I'm expecting a call from a client shortly," replied Babs.

"I'll be brief, then." Analese could be the busy executive, too. "I'm planning a trip to California for Christmas and was wondering if Molly could go with me. You see, I really don't like to travel alone. I'll be staying with relatives, visiting Disneyland, going to the ocean," she paused, judiciously deciding not to mention Molly's friend Kate. "I could give you a complete itinerary, of course, and ...."

Interrupting her abruptly, Babs said, "I'm afraid that would be out of the question, Analese. Molly already has plans for Christmas." She made no attempt to conceal the irritation she felt at having the help offer to take her daughter on a trip.

Analese thought fast. "Actually, I would like to leave the day after Christmas," she said, straining to cover her own annoyance. "I don't want to leave any of my clients in the lurch before the holidays."

Babs began to silently reconsider. A week ago, her latest boyfriend had invited her on a cruise. They were leaving for the Caribbean on December 25. It would be a relief to find somewhere for Molly to go during that time so she wouldn't be beholden to Jameson and his "little tramp." Babs hadn't mentioned her trip to anyone yet, not before she'd ironed out every detail. "Analese, let me give it some thought and get back to you," she said noncommittally. Never one for small talk, she simply hung up.

Analese fumed—until she realized that Babs hadn't said "no," either.

Babs weighed her options. She knew Jennifer could stay alone while she was out of the country. She was older, and she'd spend most of her school vacation working at the mall, anyway. But, it wouldn't look right to the neighbors for Molly to be left alone all day every day of the two-week vacation. Ignoring Analese's offer, she decided the Wendhams would baby-sit Molly. They were the only friends she trusted. All that was left was finding the right time to tell them. She decided to take them out for dinner.

Later that evening, Babs was slowly sipping Zinfandel with the Wendhams, happy they'd been available to meet downtown. Waiting for a lull in the conversation, she casually mentioned her need for the stress release of a cruise, confident they'd understand and offer to watch Molly. Instead they began talking about their upcoming trip to Europe. Babs feigned excitement as they rattled on–incessantly–about their extensive travel plans, which happened to coincide exactly with her own.

"What are the girls doing for Christmas?" Sheldon asked.

"Oh, they'll be with me Christmas Eve—and with their father on Christmas Day," Babs answered as breezily as she could. "Jeremy won't be able to get home this year."

"When does Molly leave to visit her friend Kate?" Lauren hadn't forgotten the unusual gift.

Babs knew she'd been drunk on Molly's birthday. But, until that moment, she didn't know how badly. Thinking fast, she responded, "You won't believe what has worked out! I'm simply delighted Molly won't have to make the trip to California alone. My darling little cleaning gal, Analese, is going to fly out with her. She has family in the area, and she'll visit them while Molly is with her little friend. I believe they're leaving on the 26th." She felt quite relieved that she hadn't asked Wendhams to baby-sit after all.

Her after-dinner call to Analese took less than a minute. "Oh, Analese, I'm calling to let you know that Molly would be delighted to fly with you to California. I should tell you, though, that she'll be visiting a little friend of hers while she's there. OK, then. I'll have my agent check the flights and get back to you. Ta, ta."

Analese didn't know whether to be ecstatic or furious. "That woman has some gall," she said to Rupert. "She didn't ask me if the 26th were OK, and she's even taking over my flight arrangements!" Her dog stared alertly. "I suppose she thinks I don't have an agent." Then she had a good, long laugh, with Rupert at her heels. It finally occurred to her to celebrate. "An extra dog biscuit is in order, my friend."

Babs casually popped her head around Molly's door. "You should give your little friend a call and see when she expects you,"

"What do you mean?" Molly asked, almost asleep.

"Aren't you planning to go to California later this month?"

"I, uh, well, I thought you said no," Molly whispered, baffled by her mother's change of heart.

Babs pretended not to hear. "Of course you are going to California, so give Candy a call and let her know that you're coming on the 26th. It's two hours earlier in California, so you might as well call her tonight. My travel agent should get back to us about your flights tomorrow, but we need to let her know what airport is closest to them. By the way, Analese is going to go with you."

Molly lifted her head, staring numbly at her mother. Even when she left, slamming the door behind her, Molly didn't move. She couldn't. She was sure her mother would come back and spring the joke. Instead, she heard her voice calling down the hallway, "Molly, have you made that call yet? Hurry up!"

Molly's hands continued to shake as she punched in Kate's number.

"Hello, Johnsons!" Kate answered, exuding enthusiasm that was contagious.

Molly smiled, feeling a hint of excitement. "Kate, it's me."

"Oh, Molly! You're still coming, aren't you?" Kate knew about the Montgomery's recent divorce. Weeks before, her parents had cautioned her not to be surprised if Molly's plans changed.

"Is the day after Christmas OK? I have to go to my dad's."

Kate screamed with excitement. "Mom and Dad say the 26th is great! Wait a minute, OK? Mom wants to talk with you."

Mrs. Johnson took the phone. "Hello, Molly Dolly," she said warmly. "We're so glad you're coming. May I speak with your mother to confirm travel plans? Then you and Kate can talk some more."

"OK," Molly said. Her heart pounding, she walked to the den and handed her mother the phone, reluctant to let go of it. "Kate's mother wants to talk with you," she said simply.

Pacing back and forth in the hallway outside the den, Molly listened in.

Babs turned her professional charms on high to convince Mrs. Johnson she was absolutely thrilled to talk with her. "Yes, Burbank is marvelous! I wouldn't want to face LAX the day after Christmas, either. I'll fax the itinerary to you tomorrow," she said, adding a note to her Palm Pilot as she talked. "Great, then. You have a wonderful holiday." Mission accomplished, she handed the phone back to Molly and went upstairs with an armful of catalogues and her wallet.

Molly tiptoed to her room to finish the conversation, still afraid something could happen to ruin her plans. She fell asleep hours later with the phone cradled in her arm.

Chapter Fourteen

Jennifer complained all the way to her father's apartment on Christmas morning. "It's pointless to get up at dawn," she grumbled.

"It's 8:00 AM," Babs said, smiling. She was considerably more cheerful than usual. "Jennifer, we've discussed this. Adjust your attitude. Just think about all the great gifts you'll get."

"I still don't want to go," muttered Jennifer.

"Well, I do and my plane leaves in three hours," she babbled on. "Deal with it."

"Why are you spending Christmas with Tim? You and Dad are barely divorced."

"That's enough, Jenn! Get out of your dream world and face reality." Babs replaced her anger with the practiced smile she planned to use on Jameson.

"Molly–you have your tickets?" she asked, turning to her other daughter.

"Yes." Molly was even more subdued when she was excited. And today she was more excited than she'd ever been in her life. The visit with her father and his girlfriend was merely a stepping-stone to take her to Kate.

Babs parked in front of Jameson's building, irritated when she looked up towards his penthouse. Then, uncharacteristically reflective, she noticed her daughters and wondered if they, too, were dreading this encounter. She quickly pushed that thought aside, repeating her internal mantra, *Deal with it and move on.* Lifting Molly's suitcase from the trunk, she said, "Too bad Jeremy couldn't be here."

Jennifer and Molly didn't respond.

She kept talking. "Girls, let's get moving. By the way, your father faxed me yesterday. Beth won't be here."

Jennifer and Molly wordlessly grabbed their duffel bags.

Babs turned to look at Molly as she hurried nervously toward the doorman. "Your father knows you need to check-in at the airport by eleven tomorrow morning, Molly. Remind him Analese is picking you up by ten; it's going to take at least forty-five minutes to get there in traffic."

"OK, Mom." Molly studied the lobby of her father's new home, counting the different colors of marble forming intricate patterns on the floor and walls.

Babs arranged her mouth in a confident smile. No one noticed her hand trembling when she pushed the elevator button.

"I still don't want to do this," Jenn muttered, tapping her foot impatiently.

As the elevator rushed upstairs, Molly's stomach tensed.

Their father greeted them with his own version of an animated smile.

No one knew what to say.

Babs filled the silence with phony enthusiasm. Peering beyond Jameson into the expansive white-on-white living room, she talked rapidly. "Beautiful apartment. About four thousand square feet?" She nodded assent to her own question. "Excellent view," she said, with near-manic intensity.

"Thanks," he said, trying to quiet her.

"A lot of room for one man," she said, an edge in her voice.

"I do some entertaining," he said, dismissing her.

"So I hear," Babs said, the veneer gone. "Why couldn't she be here?"

"Beth had other commitments," Jameson answered. He looked grim.

Not noticing, Babs said glibly, "I have a plane to catch. You all have fun–see you next week—or I should say, see you next year!" She laughed mirthlessly and turned toward the door, calling, "Merry Christmas and Happy New Year to all!" She was gone before they could respond.

As soon as her mother left, Jennifer glared at her father, "Thanks for abandoning us, Dad. Mom's been unbearable since you left us."

"She didn't seem unbearable today."

"That's because she's going on her stupid cruise with *Tim*," Jennifer said, venting. "You still haven't told us why you left."

"Jennifer, that's between your mother and me," he said testily. "Someday, when you're more mature, you'll understand how much better it is that your mother and I parted ways. But, I really don't think it's any of your business."

"None of my business? I don't believe you said that. We used to be a *family*," she said, eyes blazing.

"Hey, it's Christmas." Her father cut her off. "This is our family time." Picking up Molly's suitcase, he walked ahead of them toward the bedroom wing. "Why don't I take you to your rooms and let you get unpacked? How about it, Molly–Jennifer?" He turned to Molly, who was running to catch up and said, "I hear you're going to California tomorrow—this is your first time flying, isn't it? You'll like it."

Quietly, she said, "I flew to Florida last year to visit Nana and Grandpa Montgomery and to... ."

He laughed as though they were sharing a fond memory, "Oh, yes, of course." Pausing, he added, "Oh, girls, I forgot to tell you, Nana and Grandpa Montgomery's gifts came this week. They said to tell you they're sorry they couldn't come."

"There are a lot of things he has forgotten to tell us," Jennifer mouthed sarcastically to Molly.

"Your rooms are on either side of the hall," Jameson said, talking over her. "Unpack and get comfortable, then we can open gifts in the living room. Shall we meet there in a half hour?"

He went to the kitchen and gulped a third cup of coffee, wondering why he'd chosen Christmas to get together with his daughters. *Why are these kids so angry? They'll get over it when they grasp that Barbara and I are happier this way.* He sighed, relieved that Jeremy had decided not to come. Jeremy had spent Thanksgiving with him and Beth. That hadn't gone well, either.

Remembering Thanksgiving forced him to remember Beth, something he'd promised himself he wouldn't do. In spite of his resolve, his thoughts reverted to the conversation they had last week–and the real reason she wasn't with him for Christmas.

She'd missed work for days. "Stomach flu," she said. It kept her in the city all week, which wasn't like her. Ever since he'd rented this apartment, she always spent her nights with him. She said she was too ill to think of riding the commuter train back to the suburb to spend the nights with him. He finally decided to go into the city Friday after work to surprise her, and even remembered to take flowers to cheer her up. He'd forgotten his key, so she buzzed him in.

They'd kept her apartment to enjoy spontaneous weekends in the city whenever they wanted. Well, this was a weekend, and here he was.

She looked terrible. No make-up, hair a mess, the whole place a mess.

Genuinely concerned, he asked, "Beth?"

"I'm so sorry," she began.

"What, that you have the flu? Everybody gets the flu." He could be as understanding as the next guy.

"No, no, it's not the flu. I couldn't tell you on the phone. I went to the doctor yesterday. I'm pregnant."

"You're kidding."

"I'm three months along."

"No way. Things like this, people notice."

"I've been irregular for years. I didn't think anything of it until I couldn't get rid of this nausea."

"You didn't tell me anything," he said, his voice rising.

"I've tried to tell you I suspected," she said, softly.

He bristled. "Look, I've been busy with bank examiners all month. If you tried to tell me, you sure didn't get the job done."

She began to cry.

"Beth, we can take care of it. Don't worry," he said, softening.

"Take care of it?" she asked, confused.

"Absolutely," he said in his most reassuring voice. "Call your doctor and find out where you can get an abortion. I'll take care of all the fees."

She looked at him in stunned disbelief. After a long pause, she said firmly, "I don't want an abortion."

"Think logically, Beth," he said. "It's just a blob of tissue at this stage, so now is the time to be proactive." A frown had replaced her tears, so he tried another tack. "You don't want to lose your figure, do you?" He sat next to her, patting her patronizingly.

"Jameson, you tell me," she said, her voice rising. "You've had three kids. You tell me when they change from blobs to humans? I think … ."

Jameson interrupted, shaking with rage. "Look, you are in no position to have a child, and I definitely am not going to be bothered. You don't have any idea about the expense of a child's education, the … ."

"I've compromised just about every value I've ever had to be with you, Jameson. This one is non-negotiable."

"Where do you get this self-righteous rubbish?" he seethed. "You didn't talk about compromise when you became my mistress, did you?"

Beth felt like she was suffocating. "I thought you loved me," she said, her voice trailing off. He had never called her his mistress before. "I thought you loved me," she whispered.

"This can continue to be a nice ride–for both of us. Understand?"

Beth thought he was going to shake her.

He checked himself. "You were on the Pill!"

She looked at the floor. "I forgot a day or two one week when I left my prescription in the city. I didn't think it would matter."

"There is an extremely simple solution to this, Beth," he sighed, exasperated. "Just schedule the appointment. You'll hardly feel a thing this early in the game."

"This isn't a game, Jameson," she said, rapidly sounding older.

Softening momentarily, he reached for her hand. "You know I'm right."

"No. I don't," she said, pushing him away. She choked on the words, fully realizing what they meant.

"So you're willing to give up everything we have," he said, standing. "I'm deeply disappointed by your choice." By now Jameson was in the hallway, buttoning his overcoat with jerky motions. "One more thing," he added, pressing the elevator button. "Start looking for a new job."

* * *

Hearing his daughters' voices in the hallway, Jameson snapped back to the present. "Let's open those gifts, girls," he said, smiling as he walked briskly into the living room. "We'll call your grandparents in awhile, too."

* * *

The next morning, Analese picked Molly up ten minutes early. She was ready. In fact, Molly had been ready for hours.

Analese noticed the dark circles under her eyes. "Great to see you, Molly!" she said. "Sunny California, here we come!"

Molly smiled her first smile of the day. It had been hard to leave her dad. She missed him, though she didn't know why. They hadn't spent any time together when they lived in the same house, but she cherished a handful of memories they shared—reading the comics together, steering his golf cart—and longed for more. She longed for a real Dad, someone who listened to her, to care what happened to her, even to tell her "no" sometimes. The divorce pushed that hope even farther away.

Molly and Jennifer entered the kitchen for breakfast that morning as their father was taking cinnamon raisin bagels out of a shopping bag, "These are from a little bakery across the street," he said. Neither girl responded. "We'll all have to get together again soon."

"What exactly do you mean by 'soon'?" Jennifer replied caustically.

Jameson turned colder than Chicago's winds. "Jennifer, I would hope you're smart enough to realize I'm not the only one in this equation."

"I've left messages on your voice mail every time I've had a ballet recital … and *nothing*."

"Your mother hasn't made this easy," he replied, turning colder.

"You don't even return my calls."

"Jennifer, I think we covered this last night," he responded, pulling cream cheese out of the fridge. "Hey, let's try these bagels. They're really good."

Jennifer stomped out of the kitchen.

He turned to Molly. "Bagel?"

Not wanting to offend him, she took one and slowly picked at it.

He looked at Molly, his eyes begging her to understand. "I do care about you kids, but I have a lot of demands on my time."

Molly nodded, pretending to see his point.

Her father's words replayed in her mind as she and Analese wove through traffic. To lessen the pain, Molly concentrated on the sound of the car as Analese shifted gears, jockeying for the fastest lane.

"I like your car," she said. "What kind is it?"

"Thanks, Molly," Analese said, shifting her X 1/9 into fourth. "It's a Fiat." She slammed on the brakes as a Volvo pulled in front of them. "Hey, they say Volvos can turn on a dime. That one sure did." She laughed. "I hope you're OK, Molly."

"I'm fine." Molly laughed. She'd never ridden in such a tiny car but was already fond of this one. Even the sideways pull she felt each time they rounded a curve made it fun.

"Are you looking forward to getting your license in a few years?"

"If I could drive a car like this, yes!" Molly said, loosening up.

"I knew you were my kind of girl. I wouldn't drive anything else. I got this because it's like the car my dad drove. It took three years to find. Know what some people call these?"

Molly thought a minute. "Maybe a 'tiny' something or other," she laughed. She couldn't think of a name.

"You're close. They call them baby Ferarri's. Nuccio Bertone designed this model, and he even designed a few Ferraris and a lot of Lamborghinis."

Molly enjoyed sharing adult conversation. Very much.

Traffic was bad, which only added to Analese's enjoyment. She scooted through lanes, making it to O'Hare in record time. "I haven't had this much fun on a trip for a long time. It's nice not to be traveling alone," she said to Molly.

Although they hadn't planned it that way, both of them were wearing jeans and denim shirts. Both wore their long, blonde hair pulled back in chic ponytails. Both were utterly unaware of the countless turned heads they left in their wake.

The man behind them in the check-in line spoke for them all. "Do you live in Chicago?" he asked Analese, too eagerly.

"No," she replied crisply, glaring at his wedding band.

"Where are you from?"

"New England," she said, dismissing him.

"I'm from Chicago. You here on business?" he asked, sure he was standing behind two models on hiatus.

"None of yours," rejoined Analese, silencing him at last. "Come on, Molly," she said, handing the agent her ticket.

On their way to their gate a short time later, they saw him sidling up to someone else. "He's at it again," Analese said to Molly, laughing, and then abruptly turning serious. "You can't give that kind of guy the least bit of encouragement," she explained.

As their plane lifted off the ground, Analese looked down, transfixed, as everything became smaller and smaller. "This is my favorite part of flying," she said. "It puts life into perspective."

Engrossed in the downy carpet of clouds beneath them, Molly exclaimed, "It's so beautiful!" Turning to Analese, she asked, "Do you like to fly?"

"Yes, except for those excruciatingly long overseas flights."

"You've been to other countries?"

"When I was in college, and some before that, too."

"I didn't know you went to college. I thought ... ." Suddenly afraid she'd said too much, Molly blushed and grew quiet.

"It's OK, Molly," Analese said. "I clean houses because I like to." She paused, unexpectedly wishing she felt free to explain her life. Instead, she changed subjects. "Have you traveled much?"

"Well, I've visited my grandparents in Florida, and I went on a school choir trip to Washington D.C., last year."

"I remember going to D.C. with my parents," Analese said.

"Where do your parents live?"

"They both were killed in a car crash—when I was ten," Analese responded quietly.

"How sad. I'm sorry." Molly didn't know what to say.

"I miss them still," Analese said in a whisper.

"I miss my dad, too." The words came out before Molly could stop them. Her eyes filled with uninvited tears. She was mortified.

Analese touched her arm briefly, compassionately. "Hey, here comes breakfast," she said, breaking the tension. They studied their trays, laughing at the indistinguishable contents of the tiny plastic containers labeled *Bistro Beginnings*.

"This must be the grand finale," Molly said, picking up a shriveled croissant.

When the plane began its descent into Burbank, both Molly and Analese felt relaxed and rested. Laughing their way to California had been invigorating.

"I'll miss you this week, Analese," said Molly as the plane touched down.

"Me, too. Let's grab lunch on Thursday before we head to the airport."

The first thing they saw was Kate, holding a huge welcome sign. Pandemonium broke out as the Johnsons spotted Molly. Analese quietly slipped away to the rental counter.

The twenty-minute drive to the Johnson home transported Molly to another world. Although the house—an old Spanish-style home on a tiny lot—was nothing like the tree-canopied house they'd moved from, the atmosphere felt unmistakably familiar. Molly first noticed the scramble of fourteen shoes at the back door, then the smell of three-cheese lasagna—her favorite since she'd first tasted it at the unbirthday party. She ran her hand across the plaid couch, remembering the time she and Kate had transformed it into a secret castle. At the same time, she felt a warm wet tongue tickling her fingers. Her homecoming was complete.

Even though it was wonderful to see them all, Molly was glad when Kate told her family, "We'll be back in an hour or so, guys." Turning to Molly, she said, "Mom says my eyes start looking glassed-over when I need space." She smiled. "Your eyes looked that way, so I thought we could go to the park."

"Do they still?" Molly asked, worried that she might have seemed rude to her hosts.

"No, silly," Kate said, tapping her on the back. She took off calling out, "You're it!"

Molly let her run ahead.

Kate called back to her, laughing. "Hurry up! We're almost to the park." She jumped a low wall and began twirling, arms splayed, in a shallow pool.

Molly followed Kate through an ornate gilded gate, onto a brick walkway encircling a bronze fountain. She sat on the edge. There a stone cherub held a seashell that showered her with a fine mist of water. She laughed, drawn into the experience at last.

Kate twirled again, this time with her arms to the sky.

At the same moment, they both thought of the last time they'd been in a park together. "Sunken gardens," said Kate, reading her mind. "Remember how Peter teased us all day?" They dissolved in laughter.

Linking arms and meandering down the winding path toward a marble gazebo, they sat across from each other on stone benches. Six pillars formed an airy wall around them. "I feel like I'm in a castle, Kate," Molly said.

Although the late-afternoon air was warm, a hushed coolness hung in the space. "I wonder if this is how we'll feel when we get married," Kate responded. "Do you think we'll feel like our homes are castles and that we've married our very own Prince Charming?" She jumped up, pointing to the iron grillwork of the domed open roof. "Molly, quick—come here. I forgot to show you something."

Reluctant to move, Molly stepped outside, wondering what was so thrilling.

"Look at the pineapple on top of the roof," said Kate, standing on tiptoe and pointing. "Do you know that's what sea captains used to bring home when they went on far-away trips? In New England, they'd set one in front of their houses so people knew they could come visit them—sort of like a fruity welcome mat," she laughed.

"How nice for them," replied Molly—without enthusiasm.

"That's not what I meant, Molly. I meant we could use a pineapple as a sign of our friendship—get it? Whenever you see a pineapple, you can remember that you're always welcome at our house!"

Molly tried to imitate Kate's fervor. "Oh, a pineapple— that's great." She suddenly felt much older than her childhood best friend.

"I even had Mom make a salad with fresh pineapple in it for dinner, so you'd know how really special you are to us!"

Molly had to smile. Kate was still Kate.

"Molly, did you hear me?" Kate interrupted her thoughts. "Christmas with your dad—how was it?"

"Different."

"Different how?"

"I mostly listened to Jennifer yell." Molly didn't want to talk about her family. "Did you get anything good yesterday?"

"We opened presents on Christmas Eve." Waving her arms with excitement, Kate explained, "… because we have a birthday party for Jesus on Christmas Day—since that's the day we celebrate Him coming to earth for us. We make a cake, sing happy birthday to Jesus–like a regular birthday party, only it's for Jesus."

"You have a party for someone who isn't here," Molly said, cynicism evident in her upturned lips. "Interesting."

"Oh, He's here, all right," Kate said, eyes glowing. "He said, 'I am with you always.' He comes to live with you when you become a Christian."

Molly tensed. "Kate, let's not ruin a good time. I want a moratorium on this subject."

"Is mora-whatever-you-said a word for 'stop'?" Kate asked, trying to cut the tension.

"It is. And I'm not kidding," Molly said, her words strained. "You preach at me every time we're on the phone, too."

Groaning, she put her hand over her mouth. "I'm sorry, Mol. You're my friend—I don't want to annoy you. But, Christmas is His birthday, isn't it?" After hugging her friend, Kate cheerfully transitioned to relating the week's plans to visit Disneyland. "We go there every time anybody comes to see us," said Kate. "It's the best!"

The segue bemused Molly. As far as she was concerned,

Mickey Mouse and Jesus Christ belonged in the same make-believe world.

Back at the house, Molly was inundated by Johnsons. Such a squabble broke out over who could sit next to the honored guest at dinner, that the family had to draw names to decide. Kate sat on Molly's right, defending her action with, "she's my friend, you know."

Friday, Molly's second day in California, was spent with the Johnson family at Newport Beach. She sat on the sand, staring at the waves, and then let Kate pull her into them. Later, Peter offered to let Kate and Molly try out his new kite. Molly was nervous—it was her first time to fly one. She held the roll of string, afraid to let it loose, afraid she'd do something wrong. "Let it go!" Peter said. The string bobbed up and down, quickly unrolling into the sky, taking the kite soaring into the wind. Molly was afraid that she'd make it vanish. Then, Kate took her turn, letting it climb high above the beach, laughing as she ran.

After the day of fresh ocean air, Molly slept soundly and awakened early, both because of the time change and because she was excited to go to Disneyland. As hard as she tried to maintain her outward sophistication, inside she was as eager to visit Sleeping Beauty's castle as every other girl on the path. When she and Kate saw it, they broke into a run. They barely slowed down until they fell asleep, leaning on each other, in the van twelve hours later.

Sunday, though, she awakened with a headache. The Johnsons were excited about going to church, but Molly couldn't force herself out of bed. She lay stone still, trying to concoct an excuse. As she lay thinking, she heard a soft knock on her door. She pretended not to hear, but the knocking grew louder.

"Kate?" three-year-old Grace asked.

"I think she's in the shower," Molly answered groggily.

"Can I come in?"

"Uh, I guess so," Molly said, turning toward the wall.

Grace bounded onto the edge of the bed, "Can I snuggle with you?" As the baby of the family, Grace was used to being doted on. Interpreting Molly's silence as an invitation, she climbed into the bed to give her a big hug.

Molly wasn't used to small children. She closed her eyes, pretending to sleep.

Grace tugged at her eyelid and asked, at full volume, her mouth a half-inch from Molly's ear, "Aren't you awake, Molly? Everybody else is. Please get up, I want to see you." She tugged Molly's arm, then dug her chubby fingers under Molly's armpits.

"I'm not ticklish," Molly said, trying hard not to open her eyes and laugh, but she couldn't help it. The simple affection of little Grace snuggled up next to her filled her with an unexpected sense of being loved.

"You're awake, you're awake!" Grace exulted. "Hurry up for doughnuts!"

By the time Kate was back in the room, Molly was ready to shower, her headache long forgotten.

Church wasn't as painful as Molly feared it would be. In fact, it wasn't anything like the experience she'd had at church with her Grandma Finster, with her mother breathing complaints in her ear. "I grew up with this droning nit-picker; I don't have to sit through it any more," Babs had fumed, while Molly stared at jewel-like stained glass windows, then fell asleep to the minister's voice. Here, there was singing, music, and a pastor who talked about God as though He was real. The people, some in dresses or suits, others in jeans or shorts, seemed strangely united in a shared experience of joy. That energy flowed over onto Molly who, despite her best attempt to stay detached, found herself tracking closely with the pastor who took the makeshift podium.

"Do you know that God made you, and He made you to become His child, to be part of His family?" he asked, looking out at the sea of faces. Molly felt his eyes on her when he said, "Read Psalm 139. It tells us that God designed each of us perfectly." She turned the words over and over in her mind, for the first time questioning her assumptions. A practiced actress, Molly knew the peace she saw around her could not be faked. The Johnsons, she saw, astonished, were not some happy aberration living in a fantasy world.

"Maybe God is real," she scribbled in the new diary Kate gave her as a welcome present. "Maybe Kate's right. How bizarre." She started a new paragraph, a To Do list she wanted to tackle when she got home.

All too soon, the week was over and she was back in Illinois. The constant activity of a happy, active home was replaced by the utter quietness of a nearly empty house. Jennifer, consumed with school activities, work and ballet lessons, was rarely home. Molly couldn't stand to be there alone, but she hated sharing her space with her mother even more.

Chapter Fifteen

➤◄

Packing her schedule with activities provided Molly the perfect escape.

The noise on the pep club bus was deafening "We've got spirit, yes we do—we've got spirit, how about you?" Perky cheerleaders yelled at the top of their lungs. "Come on, everybody, louder now! We've got spirit, yes we do ..."

Ten minutes into her first ride to a football game, Molly had decided to drop out. Her new friend Andrea, or "Andie," as she preferred being called, had talked her into joining. At first, Andie had reminded her of Kate. Cute and bubbly, with the incredible talent of talking non-stop, Andie had drawn Molly into her circle of friends the first week of freshman year, eager for proximity to the knockout blonde. When they weren't together, they were talking on the phone. The feisty redhead wouldn't take "no" for an answer when she'd asked Molly to join the pep club for Eastwood's first out-of-town game.

Molly had tried explaining, "I have to practice flute— my recital is in a month." She knew Mrs. Dennison didn't allow time off for good behavior. "My teacher expects at least an hour of practice time every day," she said.

"You've got to go with us, Mol," Andie insisted. "Friday's the time to cut loose."

Molly finally agreed, hoping this would help cement her friendship with Andie—and ease the loneliness she felt for Kate.

Once on the bus, Molly realized the similarities between Kate and Andie stopped at their red hair and gabbiness. "Did you meet Giselle Sullivan yet, Mol? She thinks she's so cool, but her clothes are a joke. She has absolutely no fashion sense—unlike you," she said with a smarmy smile. "And what do you think of Troy Barnett?" Andie brushed her hair as she talked, continually checking her appearance in a compact mirror. "He's been asking about you."

Listening, Molly felt lonely. It occurred to her that she'd never heard Kate be critical. Andie interrupted her thoughts, "Well, what do you think?" she demanded. "Is Troy going to ask you to Homecoming, or not?"

"I, uh, I don't know. Maybe," replied Molly, unsure of the question.

As the cheers grew louder, Andie poked her in the side. "Come on," she yelled, "Get pumped up!"

Molly was forced to cheer the remainder of the two-hour drive. On Monday, she joined the French club.

That night, Andie called. "Where were you after school today?" she asked, irritated.

"Working on the newspaper," Molly said.

"Mondays are Pep Club—I thought you'd remember," Andie whined. Her voice grew more insistent. "You'll have to quit the newspaper," she said. "That's for brainiacs who can't do anything."

"Actually, I like to write," Molly said, surprised that she could stand up for her decision.

"You're quitting the most fun club in school to work on the paper?" Andie asked, baffled. "I definitely shouldn't have nominated you for freshman representative today."

Molly pretended not to care when Andie snubbed her at school. She got involved in more activities, adding choir, forensics, and flute ensemble to French club and her other band activities. She kept busy working on the paper, too—busy enough to avoid thinking about anything but what she was doing.

Molly preferred being active to socializing—even more so after the disastrous experience with Andie—especially in the company of the boys who assumed she'd want to see them on weekends. Whenever conversations got personal, she expertly jumped tracks. "Just say no," she told herself when they called.

Chapter Sixteen

➔←

At the beginning of Molly's sophomore year, Jameson
Montgomery remarried in spite of himself. He was
frightened into monogamy and marriage when Chet
Hutchison, his long-time golfing partner, died of AIDS.
Chet had divorced twice, and slept around a lot. His last
months on earth were horrible. Jameson hadn't expected it
to be so bad when he'd gone to the hospital for their final
goodbye; his mind still recoiled when he remembered the
raw sores, the wheezing cough, his friend's emaciated body,
and—worst of all—the isolation. He wasn't going to die like
that if he could help it.

He owed a lot to Chet, actually. He never would have
met Mercedes if Chet's death hadn't inspired him to attend
an AIDs benefit in Chicago. By a strange quirk of fate, he
and Mercedes were seated next to each other. It didn't take
them long to discover they had a lot in common. He liked
living in luxury; she liked flaunting what she had. Both
liked living in the fast lane and were tired of driving it
alone.

The new Mrs. Montgomery kept her name, Mercedes
Mauritz. She'd married once, divorced once and had a

modeling career she told people she put on hold to take time to learn the ropes of being a banker's wife. That wasn't really the entire story. For the last few years, she hadn't been hired for anything but catalogue work, which she saw as an insult to her prestige in the industry. She'd been on the top of the heap for years and wanted to quit before she was put out to pasture.

Marriage gave her a good answer to her least favorite question: "Been on any covers lately?" But she missed the money—and the excitement. Being a banker's wife bored her. Desperate to fill her days with something that was both amusing and interesting, she decided to make Molly her next pet project.

Before she could start, Mercedes had to defuse the tension she'd created when she first met Molly. "I really don't know what I could have done to offend your daughter," she lamented to Jameson.

"Molly?"

"Do you think she resents my advice about her junk food habit? I was only trying to help," she sniffed.

He didn't respond.

Never one to agonize, she decided to fix the problem herself.

The next time Molly visited, Mercedes offered pastry for breakfast.

"New diet?" Molly asked, her voice laced with suspicion.

"Don't get edgy—I'm willing to admit my faux pas," Mercedes said, wearing humility like an uncomfortable pair of shoes. "Go ahead and eat what you want; I'll try not to be jealous that you never gain an ounce." Her lips curled upward. She was trying very hard—almost too hard—to make sure Molly understood. "I only want to protect you," she said, smoothing her hair, smiling at how silky it felt. "Most people destroy their complexions and their bodies when they eat junk food, but look at you! Your figure stays perfect, you don't need highlights and your complexion is simply flawless." She paused, trying not to spread it on too thick. "I don't have a single complaint," she said.

Molly's eyes narrowed.

Mercedes hurried to explain, "I really think you should be a model, Molly," she said. "You're perfect. If you've got it, flaunt it. Comprendé?" Mercedes loved using foreign words for emphasis. "You have cachet."

Molly blinked, tilting her head to clear her mind, fighting her urge to respond sarcastically. One nice thing about talking with Mercedes is that a reply was rarely necessary.

"I'm telling you, Mol, you have what it takes," she continued. "Your gorgeous blue eyes have an enigmatic look. The camera will absolutely love you!" Her own eyes glowing, Mercedes gushed, "I'd be willing to give you some pointers, and ...," she paused for emphasis. "I'll pay your way to the best modeling school in Chicago. That's how much I believe in you."

Molly flushed, feeling a dizzying surge of excitement on the one hand, a strange sense of apprehension on the other. The attention felt nice. For an hour, she listened to Mercedes talk about places she'd traveled and people she knew. Willing to go anywhere that would take her away from where she was, she decided modeling would be worth the risk.

* * *

She could hardly wait to get to her dad's apartment after school each Friday. Having a purpose in life beyond school helped her ignore the irritation she felt when Mercedes insisted she change her hairstyle or prompted her to sit up straight. At modeling classes on Saturdays, she applied the same perfectionism to learning her new craft that she did in every other area of her life. She even willingly underwent the hard work of having her book prepared, each pose custom-designed by the man Mercedes dubbed "the best of the best of Chicago's lensmen."

Early in the summer after her sophomore year of high school, she was called into the city for her first real shoot. She wasn't prepared to hate it as much as she did. She didn't like changing clothes in a room full of people, and she felt assaulted when photographers walked in and out, gawking at her body as though it were inanimate. To please Mercedes and her father, she stayed with it—and with them—all summer, dreading every day.

The one aspect of the modeling experience she enjoyed was analyzing the photographers' choices for each distinct pose. Neither that small perk nor the significantly larger check was enough to make her willing to continue the process. "I'll try it again later, another time," she explained to Mercedes. "I'm moving back with Mom next week; with the fall semester starting, I won't have time, anyway."

Anger erupted out of nowhere. "After all I've done for you … this!" Mercedes yelled, crumpling a letter that had just arrived and throwing it across the room. She stomped her foot, furious by the frustration that met her at every turn. "Do you have any idea how few girls your age—or how few women of any age—get the chance you've had?"

Molly kept quiet, her stomach tightening more with each word.

Her quietness reminded Mercedes of something she learned in a Communicating Your Way to the Top seminar. Following the script she learned in the advanced course, she added in a gentle tone, "I didn't mean to push you. It's just that you're so gorgeous, I want to show you off." Waiting as Molly fled the room, she quickly hid the portfolio that Today's Chic catalogue department had sent back to her and threw the rejection form letter in the trash.

* * *

Back in her mother's house, Molly faced a different barrage.

"I'm ordering in Chinese tonight, Molly. You and I are spending the evening together."

"OK," Molly mumbled, her mother's assumption pre-empting any excuse.

* * *

Babs Montgomery had decided not to remarry, though she'd had numerous boyfriends in and out of the house. She constantly denigrated them all, complaining about everything from their looks to their habits. Describing them to Molly gave her immense satisfaction.

That night, laughing at her own "hilarious observations" until tears ran down her cheeks, she lit into her current boyfriend.

Molly tuned out, her mind circling around to the flute piece she needed to practice later, her hands moving to the notes she remembered.

"I'll introduce you to him before he becomes a member of my Pathetic Band of Useless Rejects," her mother promised, a satisfied look playing across her face.

"Then don't spend time with men you don't like," Molly said flatly, practically asking to be sent to her room.

Babs shredded her with a contemptuous laugh. "Oh, Molly, you're so young—and so naïve," she said. "You'll understand some day." She paused to study her daughter. "In fact, it's high time I get you into the doctor." Pounding the table once for emphasis, she added, "You should be on the Pill by now–you're almost seventeen. Unless you're already on it?" She smirked, nudging Molly.

Molly edged away. "Not interested, Mom, really."

"What? Are you gay or something?" For a long time, Babs had suspected something, thinking there could be no other explanation for Molly's friendship with Kate.

"Mom, I don't want to have this conversation."

"No, we are having this conversation, and you are going to answer my questions." She stared, her derision obvious as she waited for a response.

"Just because I don't want to have sex doesn't make me gay, Mom," she said, incensed.

"I don't believe I'm hearing this. Most twelve-year-olds know more than you do," Babs replied, breaking a chopstick.

"And you're the relationship expert?"

"I'll pretend I didn't hear that," she said, her voice steel. "I'll make an appointment for you with my OB-Gyn whenever you're ready to come into this century."

"Don't hold your breath," Molly muttered, walking away.

* * *

Her junior year blurred into oblivion. While she focused on grades and activities, her family, one-by-one, laid out plans for her life. Her brother wanted her to attend his alma mater. He was a successful CPA by now—and his ex-wife enjoyed a hefty share of his profits. Her father tried to foist Mercedes' dream on her, knowing it was the fastest way to get her off his payroll.

One of the few people who didn't have a plan for Molly's life was her sister, Jennifer. She'd already dropped out of college to go abroad and find herself. "Wish you were here," was printed on the post card of Versailles she finally sent to Molly. She looked at Jennifer's scrawl on the other side, "Please don't wish you were here. This royal family was even more screwed up than ours. Miss you, Jenn." Molly wished she could ask Jenn for advice, but she didn't even have her e-mail address.

* * *

At least deciding where to spend summer before her senior year was effortless. Mercedes announced that she was planning a trip to Spain for most of July and August, and that Molly could have the apartment to herself. Winking, Mercedes added, "It can be your first solo adventure," promising to keep the arrangement a secret from her mother. Since the two households communicated solely by fax, Molly wasn't worried. But how Mercedes convinced her dad to go along with the deception, Molly never knew.

* * *

For months, Mercedes calculated every possible tactic to pull her "exquisite stepdaughter" back into modeling. Blinded by her own desperate desire to go back to the only world where she'd felt significant, she convinced herself she had only her stepdaughter's interests in mind.

By Molly's second day in the apartment, Mercedes could no longer wait to implement Part Two of her strategy. As soon as Jameson left for work, she set off for the deli across the street from their building. "You choose for me, darling," she said coquettishly to the teenager across the counter. "Something scrumptious." He returned her wink. The next hour was spent in the dining room, setting the stage for an elegant brunch. Like a spider, she waited, spinning words in her mind as she sculpted butterballs into flowers.

Oblivious, Molly read a new mystery novel in the bath, and then took time to blow-dry her hair and apply mascara. She hated makeup. But it was easier to wear it than it was to listen to her stepmother nag, "Now, don't take this as criticism, love, because it's not," words she invariably said within the first ten minutes of seeing Molly, "I simply want to see you enhance your natural assets." Frowning, Molly studied her closet, listlessly repositioning the hangers.

She detested dressing up and looked forward to living in sweats as soon Mercedes and her father left the country.

When Mercedes was quite sure that Molly had been up for at least an hour, she lured her into the dining room with freshly brewed coffee.

Molly emerged quickly, breathing in the heady aroma. "This looks nice," she said. "Having company?"

"You, Molly. I did this all for you. To celebrate the end of your junior year!" Mercedes smiled the smile of a gracious benefactress, but her eyes were scrutinizing Molly's response to the ambiance. "You have no idea how stunning you look—more chic than most people I know," she said, capitalizing on the moment. "Truly."

"Thanks," Molly said, relieved that she'd taken time to dress in her new jeans and a blouse Mercedes had given her.

"Hungry?"

"A little," Molly admitted, feeling her stomach rumble.

"Voilà!" Mercedes announced, lifting a linen napkin with a flourish to reveal croissants.

"Pan chocolät!" Molly gasped. "My favorite French pastry!"

"There's quiche in the oven, too. Be right back."

At first, they ate in silence, commenting only on the food. That was fine with Mercedes. She watched Molly's movements, trying to anticipate her desires. "More coffee?" she asked, pouring it.

"This is great," Molly said. "A nice end to an exhausting year."

"It's wonderful to see you slow down," she said quietly. There was an imperceptible pause while Mercedes searched her mind for a photographer's cue. *Open your eyes ... wider, wider. Part your lips—ever so slightly. Good, good. Now think sincere, think caring, ... you've got it!* It took her less than the click of a camera's shutter to arrange her face. "Your dad and I want this entire summer to be a relaxing time for you." She paused for momentum. "I also want to apologize for last summer. I've been giving it a lot of thought, and I think I've finally figured out why your first modeling experience was so unpleasant."

"Do you have any marmalade?" asked Molly, sending a clear signal that the subject was closed.

Mercedes pretended not to notice. "What happened was my mistake," she said, smiling shrewdly. "Will you just hear me out, ma belle?" Sensing encouragement from Molly's slight nod, she forged ahead. "I had you with the wrong agency!"

If Molly were at all encouraged by the epiphany, she didn't show it. She twisted her napkin as she spoke, "I don't know, Mercedes. I'm starting college in a little over a year, and ... ."

With this last objection, Mercedes lost all of the self-restraint she'd fought to hold onto. "You'll be bored stiff if you stay here alone every day," the older woman said, projecting. "You're going to need something to do. What would it hurt to try modeling one more time? You can go in when you want to, and–if, only if, you like it this time—you could continue part-time when you're back in school."

The cork had been removed from her champagne bottle of words.

Molly stared at the clock and coughed, desperate to change the subject.

Her tone firm, her jaw fluid, Mercedes was just warming up. "You'd meet a lot of interesting people, and you could do it for a few years, make a lot of money and then go anywhere you want to go. You hardly gave it a try—and you owe it to yourself to give it another shot. Molly, we really need to get you started now so that I can help you get going before your father and I leave for Europe in two weeks." She stopped abruptly, coaching herself: *Inhale; exhale; inhale; exhale.* Grinning, she deliberately changed her approach.

"It's a great way to meet men."

"I'm sure it is," Molly snapped.

"Have you ever had a boyfriend?" Mercedes asked, for the moment forgetting everything she'd learned.

"I have lots of friends," Molly said, scraping her knife against her plate, liking the grating sound it made. Her mother would have told her she was ruining the good china.

"I'm not trying to pry, love," she said, her eyes misting for effect. "Just last week, your dad told me he was worried about you, afraid you've never had a serious relationship."

"I'll know him when I see him," Molly said, setting her knife across her plate to close the subject. "Tell me more about modeling," she said. It was the only surefire way to derail the previous topic.

As expected, Mercedes launched into a nauseating recitation of her modeling career.

Molly blanked out until Mercedes abruptly jumped from her chair, startling her to attention.

"I have an idea!" she said. "I have to get shoes to wear to a benefit dinner tonight, and I don't want to spend the whole afternoon driving downtown. Isn't there a mall you like near here?"

"Uh, yeah. It's ten minutes from here," she said, starting to clear dishes from the table.

"Leave the mess!" Mercedes said. "I have someone coming in to clean today. We can go anytime you're ready." She held up her keys, "Want to drive?"

Molly had wanted to drive her stepmother's silver car ever since she first saw it, but her dad had warned her not to ask. As they rode the elevator down to the parking garage, she could hardly wait to get behind the wheel.

Mercedes didn't mind a one-sided conversation. "Not many people have cars named after them, do they? I've always wanted an SLK and finally decided I deserve it. From its oyster-colored leather interior and burled walnut shift knob to its perfect ride, my little Mercedes is my love."

Hearing this last pronouncement, Molly pictured herself wrecking Mercedes' prize possession. She started to hand the keys back.

"Quit being nervous," Mercedes insisted. "I'm a lousy driver, and I haven't hurt it."

The SLK worked better than any anesthetic Mercedes could have offered, each rotation of its wheels temporarily numbing Molly's resentment of her stepmother's intrusion into their lives.

* * *

Getting dressed for dinner, Jameson asked his wife, "Where's Molly? I thought she said she'd be here tonight."

"She's at the library–doing some kind of research for her school paper—planning ahead for fall or something," Mercedes whined. "I don't know why she doesn't get out at night and have some fun."

"Maybe if she did something useful during the day, she'd find something better to do in the evenings," he said, yanking his tie.

"We had fun shopping this afternoon," Mercedes said, avoiding his innuendo.

"She needs something productive to do," he continued.

"I can help," Mercedes beamed.

"What?" he asked, puzzled by her change of tone.

She was already punching familiar numbers, smiling into the phone, "Oh, Anson, Mercedes Mauritz here," she purred. "Hope I'm not interrupting. Yes, of course I'm married. I thought you knew I kept my name." Teasing, she continued, "You know that's not why I called. I simply want to touch base—and, dear boy, I do have a teensy little favor to ask."

Listening to him, her shrewd smile crept upward. "Yes, my stepdaughter did a bit of modeling awhile back.

She needs some work again this summer, and I thought your agency might need a stunning 5'10" blonde."

Hungry for his compliment, she leaned forward in her chair.

"Thanks, but I'm on hiatus. This summer, Jameson and I are taking the honeymoon trip we never had. Spain!"

She couldn't help smirking when he reminded her that he already had Molly's portfolio. It was she who had hand-delivered it to his agency the previous summer.

"How silly of me, Anson—I totally forgot you had her book."

She closed her eyes, concentrating, enthralled with every word.

"Absolutely, she can fill in at the last minute," she exulted. "You're right, she is a rare find. I'll have her there tomorrow morning."

* * *

Returning home from the benefit, Mercedes hurried to the intercom. "Molly, can you come to the living room? I have incredible news."

Curious, Molly rushed to them. "Hi. What function was it tonight?"

Mercedes set her evening bag on the table. "A little benefit dinner for the art museum," she said, appraising Molly with her eyes. "It's what happened before dinner that's really interesting."

"Oh?" Molly tried to be polite.

"Just before we left, I happened to speak with my old friend Anson—he's the one who owns the best agency in Chicago, the one where I worked for years," she said, running her hand through her hair. "This is so incredible, darling—he has an urgent need for someone exactly like you—tomorrow."

Her laugh rang phony.

"This never happens—isn't it amazing karma? I'm astounded that I happened to talk with him at precisely the right time. So," she finished with a surge, "I said you'd be there."

"I wish you'd asked me first," Molly said, irritated.

A pout expanded Mercedes' polished lips. "You told me just this morning that you'd try modeling again."

Molly sighed, knowing it was useless to argue. "When do I have to be there?"

"Eleven—and I'll be happy to run you in since I have errands to do in the Loop. That way, I can personally introduce you. You're going to love Anson. His agency is one of the best, you know."

Inside she was fuming, but Molly forced a smile. "I'd better get some sleep."

Mercedes called after her, "Come here, Molly. I have a marvelous idea. You can wear something of mine for your big day."

"I'm sure I have something I can wear," she said, not bothering to turn around.

"No, really, I insist. We'll put all my years of experience to work," she said, her sly smile contradicting her benevolent tone. "Let's get you into something a little more hip than usual," she continued, eyeing Molly's off-the-rack jeans. She spoke in rhythm with her brisk steps. "Come into my closet. I'll find something to make your look," she said with authority.

Molly bristled, resenting the familiarity, the orders and the expectations. But she followed her, mute, sheep-like, through the master bedroom and into the enormous custom-designed closet. She couldn't understand why standing in the middle of the innumerable organized racks of Mercedes' clothing, jewelry, shoes and accessories would make her feel sad. For some odd reason, it dawned on her that she was in the room that used to be the den—until Mercedes commandeered it for her first remodeling project.

This was the place where she'd last seen her sister. She hadn't thought of Jennifer for a long time, and it hurt to do so now. It was almost as though she could hear and see her standing across from her, screaming at their father. "You disgust me," Jenn had told him that night. "You and your self-indulgent lifestyle are exactly why I can't tolerate the status quo."

"Young lady, when you're my age you can talk to me about indulgence," he shouted. "Who do you think foots the bills for your life of leisure?"

Jennifer hadn't been back since.

As though emerging from a tunnel, she heard Mercedes clattering on. "You have to wear these jeans. This will be much, much better than showing up in last year's leftovers."

Mercedes thrust them into her arms. She wanted to walk out, hurt that Mercedes hadn't noticed her special effort to wear new jeans. Instead she stayed, stock-still.

"You'll be a knockout! Wear these sandals, too. They are my personal favorites—and they were only $300 at the spring sale." The actual price was $415, but Mercedes whittled dollars off all prices when describing them to Jameson. It was effortless to continue the habit with his daughter. She sighed, thinking how disappointed she was in Jameson. She had no idea he was such a tightwad when they married.

Oblivious to her treasure trove, Mercedes was cognizant only that she wanted more—much more—than she had. For the last two decades, her goal had been to own the best of everything, which she diligently searched for during her all-important spring and fall shopping trips to New York. That was the only place—the best place—to get the right styles. She was stunned beyond words when Jameson questioned her buying an $8,000 necklace at Saks

Fifth Avenue. That had been their biggest fight so far. "You are ridiculous," she'd shouted. "I always buy my casual jewelry at Saks, and I'm saving so much money I can't believe you'd question it! This accessory is a must this season."

He'd been so angry that she judiciously decided not to mention her plan to buy the South Sea Pearls at Kimoto's. She finally admitted to herself that $50,000 for a summer necklace was a bit beyond her reach. She scowled, remembering. "Here's a shirt, Molly," she said, trying to get her mind off her budget woes. "Go ahead and try on the outfit," she ordered, turning to rummage through her jewelry cabinet. "Now let's accessorize." She handed Molly a gold bracelet and earrings. "What you want is a sophisticated look that incorporates the new neutrals without being too obvious."

Molly wondered how Mercedes knew what she wanted without asking.

"This is it—you are stunning. Go gawk at yourself in my three-way."

"Thanks," Molly murmured. "It's great." She wanted to say that the jeans felt too tight and the shirt was too short. She went to bed instead.

Chapter Seventeen

>←

It was a beautiful day as they sped into the city. Molly gazed at Lake Michigan, letting it relax her. The feel of the ride in the SLK somehow reminded her of Analese—and their long-ago trip to O'Hare in her tiny X 1/9. *I miss her,* she reflected, closing her eyes and wishing her mother hadn't switched to a cleaning firm.

"You look like you're somewhere else, Molly. Care to share?" Mercedes asked.

Molly hated it when people pried into her mind, but she couldn't think fast enough to deflect the question. "I was remembering another time, riding in this same spot in a friend's Fiat."

"You know what 'Fiat' stands for, don't you?" Mercedes teased. "'Fix It Again, Tony'—they always break down, you know." She laughed, patting the console next to her. "But my little gem runs like a clock. It has to." She continued, obsessing on her favorite possession. "It was my present to myself just before your father and I got married. I can't depend on train schedules, you know. Never know what time I'll need to be in for work," she said, pausing to upshift into fifth. "I'll have to treat you to a ride with the hardtop retracted—a superb way to turn heads. Molly, are you listening?"

"Sure, that would be fun," she replied, on edge, smarting from the insult to her friend's car.

Mercedes kept up her incessant chatter. "You know what's amazing? Besides all its other perks, this car is environmentally friendly. I'm totally serious," she said, patting the steering wheel. "Xavier—my car dealer— told me that Mercedes was one of the first car manufacturers to use lead-free paint."

Molly let her mind wander away from the droning voice, trying not to be too critical of Mercedes for being on a first-name basis with her mechanic.

Mercedes switched subjects, her tone indignant. "Molly, do you have any idea how unusual it is to prance right into a job and skip the cattle call fiasco? In this business, to have both a booking and an agent on your first day is astonishing." Remembering her goal, she tried another tack. "I'm glad I was here to pull it off for you."

Molly noticed Mercedes' right eye, twitching. It always twitched when she was irritated.

"Thanks, Mercedes," she replied, adding a lilt to her voice. "I appreciate your help."

"Oh, I'm happy to help—all you needed was a door-opener. Anson doesn't usually recommend anyone for a shoot without a go-see, you know—but, he's one of the rare ones with enough connections to get you right into the industry. Anson and I go way back. Way back. His father was one of my best friends." She paused, unable to continue. When she spoke again, her voice cracked with emotion. "We knew each other before I knew your father. We had even talked of being married—but pancreatic cancer snatched him away from me—he only had three months after the diagnosis. Five years ago that seems like forever." She brushed a tear away, remembering. "Enough of that," she said, failing to notice that she had finally won a small portion of her stepdaughter's sympathy. "Today's your day."

* * *

Molly quietly studied the sign proclaiming *AG Models.* The emphasis was clearly on the initials *AG*, with stars punctuating the impressive golden script that was easily twice as high as the plain block letters forming the word *Models.*

Molly's cheeks were slightly flushed as they entered the studio, which only enhanced her natural beauty. Anson was tempted to whistle but shrewdly controlled himself. Instead, he spoke to Mercedes, "Hey, girl, long time no see. We've missed you." In her prime, Mercedes had been their highest grossing model.

"I plan to get back into the game this fall," she chortled. "Be sure and keep my agent's number handy."

"You bet," he said, hugging her, noting how much she'd aged since he last saw her. *No amount of Botox will save that face now,* he thought.

It was no wonder Mercedes wanted his help. Anson was not only the youngest agency owner in Chicago; he was one of the most successful. It helped him more than a little to inherit the agency from his father, Anson Greeb, Senior.

Anson II—he had an aversion to being called "Junior"—still remembered the months she was with his father; all the time he secretly wished she weren't fifteen years older than he. If her stepdaughter knew how to work a camera, she'd be at the top of the heap in no time. "Happy to have you on board, Molly," he said as Mercedes introduced them.

He glanced at Mercedes and understood her knowing smile. This wasn't the first time she'd brought him a stunning neophyte. *All right,* he nodded to her.

Mercedes could tell he appreciated her gift and had no doubt she'd soon be back in front of a camera.

He knew makeup artists who could help him make it happen.

"She doesn't know much about the business," Mercedes was telling him.

"Not a problem. I'll take her under my wing," he said, smiling.

Shaking hands, Molly took an instant liking to him in spite of her attempt to stay guarded. He seemed different from any of the guys at school. *Older—and more sophisticated.*

As she studied him, he was studying her. Her motions were so unaffected and perfect, a blend of elegance and naïveté. She was deliciously mysterious–especially her eyes. Mercedes was right. She was a natural. The photographer only had to tell her the look he wanted once, and she did it. Anson personally drove her on location and stayed for the entire shoot, not so much to check up on her work but to learn *her*, to discover the most effective way to get around the boss-employee thing.

His cell phone rang at four o'clock. He pulled it out of his pocket, "Anson here," he said, walking to a quieter spot.

"Mercedes Mauritz here," she cooed into the phone. "Well, love, how do you like her?" Her inveigled laugh reminded him of other women she'd found for him. She knew he couldn't respond and laughed again. "I knew you would, darling. Well then, what time will you be finished? I told Molly I'd give her a ride."

"I see," he said with a practiced smile.

Molly noticed his perfect teeth.

"Unfortunately, we've hit some lighting problems," he continued talking into the phone. "The client wanted outdoor shots, and–you know how long it takes to get it right." His frown was practiced, too. It conveyed exactly the

right amount of concern with only the slightest hint of irritation. "I think we're going to break so the crew can fix it, but
we're definitely running over."

"I know what you mean," Mercedes said, laughing like
the insider she was. "But, that presents a tiny problem— I
have to get back for a dinner party in my corner of suburbia—
a soirée of Jameson's I simply can't miss."

"Why don't I bring Molly home? I haven't been out of
the city in a long time." He turned to Molly, "Fine with
you?"

She nodded.

"Sounds like a plan."

"Marvelous," Mercedes enthused, giggling. "Oh, Anson,
you haven't lost your touch!" Suddenly eager to tell
Jameson his daughter was on her way to becoming a woman
of the world, she clicked the phone off, smirking as she
congratulated herself. Her mind raced its way through rush
hour.

* * *

Anson spoke first to his photographer, "We're going to
break for java while you get the lights fixed," then to the
models. "Take thirty, but don't be a minute late." He stepped
away from the others and spoke softly to Molly, "There's a
little coffee house down the street. Join me in five?"

She followed the other models to the trailer, where all
quickly shed uncomfortably-perfect outfits to ensure they'd
remain so for upcoming shots. She changed, then hurried to
meet Anson outside.

As they walked briskly toward the coffee shop, Anson
kept complimenting her work. "Molly, I've never seen
anyone as good as you are with the camera on the first day."

"I did have a few bookings last summer, you know."
Molly laughed. He'd teased her all day about her *vast*

modeling experience. No wonder she was so relaxed on camera.

They both ordered an iced mocha with a shot of caramel and found a small table in a quiet corner. Sipping slowly, Molly enjoyed listening to him. He seemed so open about everything, so mature, even admitting that Prozac pulled him through his dad's death.

"And your mom?" she asked.

"Remarried after their divorce. She lives in New York. No brothers or sisters."

He switched topics. "How about your family?"

"One sister, one brother. Parents divorced. But you knew that. I like Mercedes a lot." She paused briefly. "She wasn't why they divorced."

"I know." His smile was disarming. "She's like my big sister. If you have to have a stepmom, she'd be a nice one. Maybe you know she was almost mine, too."

Molly felt the bond between them growing. "She told me this morning. I'm sorry ... about your dad."

"We'll share her, OK?"

* * *

The drive to the suburb was even better than the day. They talked nonstop. Molly relaxed, discussing life with Anson as she never had before. She liked his extensive vocabulary—he used words no one else did, and she liked having to think about what he said.

He waited while she punched her dad's code, then walked with her into the lobby of her dad's building.

She joked about the disparity of modern art prints scattered among ostentatious antiques throughout the large foyer. "I call this the amalgamated passage of centuries," she quipped. He looked around, then laughed, the first one who seemed to get it.

"You're right. It's gauche," he said. "But some things in here have definite possibilities," he added, looking at her. "For once, I'm sorry we finished the job today," he continued. "But I know it won't be a problem to find bookings for you—please tell me you're coming back next week," he said, lifting her chin.

She broke into a smile. "If you think I can do it," she said, blushing under his gaze.

"You know what I think." He flashed her his perfect smile.

"Well, thanks … I guess I'd better go," she said, not knowing what else to say or do.

He nodded, his face a picture of understanding. "Yeah, the day started pretty early. See you soon," he said, squeezing her hand for a long moment.

Pushing the elevator button for her dad's floor, she could still feel her hand tingling.

She fell asleep thinking of him.

* * *

As Molly's modeling skills grew, so did the time she and Anson spent together off the job. He was always looking, waiting, watching to see how she'd respond. If her eyes said, "yes" he went one step further, casting his lure like a patient fisherman.

Molly was moved by his kindness. He never pushed her, but his tender kisses always left her wanting more.

The day he slipped his hand inside her blouse, he opened a door that he knew would soon open another. This was his favorite part, the tension of waiting. He caressed her gently again, still waiting, saying only, "How are you, babe?"

* * *

After her dad and Mercedes left for Spain, Molly invited Anson to see the apartment.

"Nice place," he said, holding her with his eyes. She quickly gave him the grand tour. She followed his gaze when they got to her bedroom. Wordlessly, they walked beside the bed. He slowly began to undress her. "I'll be gentle," he said.

She hesitated.

"Are you OK?" he asked with great concern in his voice.

"It's just that I, I'm … uh, I …," she stammered.

He reached into his pocket, smiling reassuringly. "Don't worry," he said. "I came prepared."

* * *

He slipped out early the next morning, leaving Molly reeling from unexpected loneliness. She called him on his cell phone. "When can you come again?" she asked softly.

He clicked to the other line to answer call waiting. His "quick second" turned into five minutes; she hung up and reached for her flute instead.

* * *

Later that night, he finally called back. "Hey, I got busy and couldn't get back to you," he began. Apologies out of the way, Anson dictated the terms of the relationship, telling Molly he couldn't see her every night—and they could never hang out at his place. "Roommate, you know, Mol. Just wouldn't work," he said, expecting her to understand.

"I see," she said blindly. Always accommodating, Molly still hungered for more time together. She was sure it would be enough just to be in his arms. She tried to believe she was happy; she wanted to think she was in love. She never felt quite whole again.

Even when he came to her dad's apartment every night for a week, she felt strangely empty.

"Dad and Mercedes are going to be back in two weeks," she said, laying her head on his chest.

He stood up, retying the knot on his robe.

"We can't get together here then," she added, assuming she'd spoken too softly.

"Relax, Mol, Mercedes wouldn't care," he said, pouring himself a drink.

"I would," she said, wondering.

"Oh, come on, you're not a kid anymore."

She didn't return his smile.

* * *

Mercedes was the first to speak the night she and Jameson got back from Spain. "You seem so grown up, Molly," she said knowingly. "I can't wait to hear all about your summer." She gave Molly a strange little smile. "How's it going with Anson?"

Molly was embarrassed that Mercedes seemed to know they were seeing each other. She quickly changed the subject, feigning interest in their vacation pictures. Mercedes hugging a matador. Mercedes in front of the Prado. Mercedes mixing with the locals. As soon as she could, she used her early morning shoot as an excuse to escape to burrow into her bed.

* * *

She awakened early to a spinning room and queasy stomach, forerunners, she dreaded, to inevitable chills and fever of the flu. Without opening her eyes, she groped for the phone on her bed stand, hitting the only number she'd programmed into speed dial. "Anson, I can't make it today," she said weakly. "I've got some kind of virus. Could you make a house call?" More than crackers and ginger ale, she wanted a pair of arms to hold her.

Mercedes stopped in the doorway, her eyebrows cocked. "Anson?" she mouthed conspiratorially.

"Yeah," Molly said, letting the receiver drop to the floor. Her expression answered more questions than Mercedes had asked.

"You two are together?" Mercedes enthusiastically asked, pretending not to know. "How long?"

"Almost two months." Molly couldn't talk any more. She ran to the bathroom. Waves of nausea kept her there for a week. Finally, Mercedes stepped in, "Are you pregnant, love?" she asked, seizing the chance to play the part of the wise, older sister.

"We've been really careful," said Molly, feeling too sick to be embarrassed.

"Stay there," Mercedes said firmly. "I'll be back." She was on familiar territory and considered herself an expert guide.

She brought Molly a pregnancy test kit. "Humor me," she said, handing it over and rattling off the instructions from memory.

Molly watched in disbelief as a delicate pink line darkened before her eyes. She went numb.

"Look, Molly, don't worry." Mercedes said, confident she understood just how Molly felt. "I know a great doctor who helped me out twice before I met your dad, and look at me! I'm doing just fine!"

Molly had never thought about abortion, but she'd never thought about pregnancy, either. While Mercedes was in the kitchen calling the clinic, she called Anson on her cell phone. "Anson?" She couldn't speak through her sobbing.

"What's the matter? Are you OK?" he asked, reaching for his sterling letter opener and a stack of unanswered mail.

"No. I'm not OK. Anson, I'm pregnant," she moaned.

"Molly, come on, babe, this is nothing we can't handle," he said soothingly. "I've been through this before."

His words reverberated in Molly's mind. She knew he was experienced—he'd made no secret of his long list of conquests. But, the thought of him impregnating other women sickened her. "I've got to go," she said, feeling utterly alone.

Minutes later, in walked Mercedes, planner in hand. "It's all set for Friday morning, so you only have two more days of this unpleasantness. Think you can last that long, Molly?"

Molly forced herself to reply, unable to quit replaying Anson's calloused words. "I'm not sure, Mercedes," she said. "I need some time to think about this, you know, to think through what I'm doing."

"What's to think about? You have a problem; here's the solution. The tissue can be safely, quickly and easily removed. Everything is going to be fine." She snapped her planner closed, then asked, "Does Anson know yet?"

"I just told him."

"What about your parents? Are you going to tell them?"

It all was happening too fast. She hadn't thought about saying anything to them. She looked as wretched as she felt.

Noticing, Mercedes said, "Would you rather not tell your parents? You're entitled to your privacy, you know. This can be our little secret."

"OK," Molly breathed, feeling a hint of relief when she looked at her stepmother, sitting cross-legged on her bed like a sympathetic sorority sister.

"Come here, love." Mercedes held her long thin arms open wide.

* * *

Finally, on Thursday evening, Anson called.

"Where have you been?" she asked, upset. He hadn't returned one of her calls.

"It's been a killer week. You knew that," he said defensively. "And babe, I hate to do it, but I can't get away tomorrow. I have a meeting I totally forgot with a client I can't afford to lose," he said breezily. "I knew you'd understand.

"Sure, Anson. I'm starting to."

* * *

Friday morning, Mercedes unknowingly rubbed salt in the wound. "That boy called me the minute after you gave him the news, totally distraught, to make sure I could be by your side today," she said. "Now *that's* love."

They didn't talk during the forty-minute drive to the clinic. Molly, lost in a world of frozen emotions, didn't notice where they were until the car slowed to a stop.

"Molly, we're here," Mercedes said matter-of-factly. "Traffic wasn't bad at all. Come on."

Numbly, Molly saw that they were parked in a lot adjacent to the clinic. As she opened her car door, she reflexively turned toward several people holding signs across the street.

Mercedes intervened at once. "Don't look over there."

"Why not?"

"They're a bunch of alarmists. Religious extremists."

Molly glanced at one of the signs before Mercedes steered her away. It said simply: "Life is a beautiful choice."

Before they walked a foot from the car, two women rushed to either side of Molly. Both wore bright yellow vests emblazoned with the word "ESCORT."

"We're here to help you get past these idiots," one of them said, smiling benignly at Molly.

The other escort chimed in, obviously following a script they'd used before. "Aren't you glad you chose to get on with *your* life?"

Molly stared at the sweatshirt of a teenager crossing the street. She looked away from the words, "choose life," printed between colorful drawings of babies.

The escorts talked nonstop, carrying Molly on a swift current of words. As they reached the clinic door, Mercedes jumped into the conversation. "Molly, I have to leave for a little while–brunch at the Hillcrest Club this morning– but I'll be back before you know it." She laughed the affected laugh Molly hated, then said, "Life goes on, you know."

Molly shivered, irrationally searching for a familiar face in which to take refuge, a warm hand to hold.

Pressing a bulging envelope into Molly's hand, Mercedes added, "You'll need this. See you later." Without another word, she turned toward the car.

The two escorts whisked Molly inside, depositing her in front of a receptionist who took the envelope of hundred-dollar bills Mercedes had stuffed into her hand, carefully counting them as Molly filled out a form requesting the names of next of kin and descriptions of health problems. As soon as she signed it, a nurse led her into another room, where the procedure was explained to Molly and the five other women of various ages who were already seated. One woman was loudly lamenting, "I want to keep my baby. I want to keep my baby. I want to go home."

The nurse was losing patience. "We need you to be quiet and calm down. Now. Your boyfriend is right. It's only tissue." A white-coated physician poked her head through the door, assessing the situation. She nodded to the nurse and disappeared. "Here," let the medication relax you," she commanded, inserting a needle into her arm.

The woman whimpered quietly, then fell mute.

Molly ignored the sounds around her. "This will be done before I know it," she repeated to herself over and over.

It was. Soon she was waking up in the recovery room, with Mercedes beside her, saying, "All done!" Mercedes seemed too bright, too cheerful, too loud. "You won't believe how well our little secret is working out. Your dad has a late meeting tonight, so you can be all tucked in bed when he gets home. He won't know a thing."

Molly heard Mercedes' voice. She saw her lips moving. But she could not comprehend her words.

"OK, let's check out and go home," Mercedes told her. "Want to get a burger on the way?"

Molly wouldn't let herself think as she watched the highway blur by. Some minutes or hours later—she could not tell—she found herself alone in the apartment, standing in the middle of her room. Like a sleepwalker, she methodically stripped off her clothes and put on her black sweats. Pinching the summer dress and underclothes she'd worn that day between thumb and forefinger, she held them at arm's length from her body. Expressionless, she walked down the hallway to the trash chute, dropping them in, letting the swishing sound they made as they vanished wash over her senses like an anesthetic. She went back to her room and saw her sandals lying against the wall where she had kicked them. Yanking them off the floor, she stumbled back to the chute, hurling them into the blackness, her mind traveling with them on their thumping volley against the metal walls. Downwards they went into blackness until there was silence, aflame.

Chapter Eighteen

➤❖

One week later, Anson called. "I have a job for you tomorrow. Interested?"

"I'm moving back with my mom tomorrow," Molly answered, her voice on edge.

"Oh, that's right."

Her heart surged. *He remembers,* she thought. *He cares.* "Yeah," she said, softening. "I have a lot to do before school starts."

"Next week, then. I could really use you for a spread on students in the city. We could do dinner afterwards. I know we need to talk."

Molly fought to keep her guard up. For a week, she'd waited to hear his voice, hating him more as each passing day proved his apathy. Locked in an internal debate, she struggled to tap into that anger, but connected only with her loneliness.

"Molly, what do you think?" he interjected. "Raphael's? That French restaurant you like?"

After a long pause, she conceded, hopeful she'd been wrong to doubt the only man who had ever loved her.

* * *

The job was exhausting. *Stand here, move there, let's try her hair another way for this shot.* Different people barked orders all day. *Do this; no, do that!* Molly felt like she was their toy, not a human being. She decided never to model again.

She barely spoke on the way to dinner. As usual, Anson filled the silence. "It hasn't been the same without you on the job the last few weeks," he said, reaching for his ringing cell phone.

"Great to hear your voice," he enthused, smiling into the air. "You've picked a fabulous time to sign with our agency." Molly was stunned by how quickly he shifted gears, soft and sensitive one moment, all business bravado the next. "This fall is going to be our busiest season yet."

He droned on, oblivious to the narcissism punctuating his every sentence. Molly heard him unfurl the same phrases he had used with her and wondered how she could have ever mistaken his manipulative flattery for love. He continued the conversation as they walked toward the restaurant and were seated at the table. "This won't do," he complained loudly, slipping the phone into his jacket with one hand, flagging down the maitre d' with the other.

By the time dinner was over, Molly couldn't remember why she had ever fallen for Anson in the first place.

"I'll cab home," she said as he paid the bill.

"Oh, let me drive you, for old time's sake," he insisted, reaching for her hand.

She dug into her purse to escape his touch.

"OK, then. I'll see you the next time we need a stunning blonde."

"Doubtful," Molly hissed under her breath, slamming down the onyx bracelet he gave her for landing her first cover.

He didn't move.

She wove through the candlelit maze of tables and disappeared into a taxi.

* * *

By September of her senior year, Molly knew she could no longer put off planning for college. Most of her friends had decided their top choice months before.

Her flute teacher urged her to apply for a music scholarship.

"Where?"

"You could try Pacific Harbor University, my alma mater," Mrs. Dennison responded with a rare display of enthusiasm.

"I think one of my friends is going there, but I don't know if it's what I had in mind," she said, not wanting to offend Mrs. Dennison (especially after all of the flute lessons she'd missed during the summer). "It's a religious school, isn't it?"

"There are people at Pacific from many backgrounds, Molly," her teacher explained. "I recommend it because it has one of the best music programs in the country." Noticing Molly's frown, she added, "Central State is another option. Their music program is better than average. In any case, you don't have much time to get your application in. That should have been done months ago."

Jeremy's alma mater was out of the question. "Tell me more about Pacific Harbor."

Molly left Mrs. Dennison's office with a catalog and a scholarship application.

Both came to her rescue that evening.

"Have you filled out your applications yet?" her mother asked, hardly hiding her anticipation of an empty nest.

"Mrs. Dennison is recommending me for a music scholarship at Pacific Harbor University—it's the school where she got her master's."

"A scholarship! I hadn't thought of that. Where is this school?"

"Southern California."

"You want to go out of state to school?"

"I like warm weather."

In less than a month, Molly received Pacific Harbor's request that she audition during Christmas break.

* * *

Molly began to question her choice the moment her plane touched down in California. As she walked into the San Diego terminal, lost in thought, a familiar voice jarred her back to reality.

"Hi, Molly! Bet you didn't expect to see me here!"

She looked up to see familiar freckles and an unmistakable smile. Kate.

"I don't believe it! What are you doing here?" Molly asked, incredulous. "Don't you live a couple of hours away?"

"You think I'd let you get this close and not come see you?" Kate asked, hugging her. "I called the school and told them I wanted to pick you up. Amazingly, they let me! Of course, it doesn't hurt that my uncle is on the faculty."

Molly smiled. She still considered Kate her best friend, even though they had seldom talked during the past year. She had thought about calling her before she came to California, but never followed through. At least they'd e-mailed once or twice in the past few months, which was more effort than she'd invested in any other friendship. Packing her schedule so tightly had almost shut Kate—and everyone else—out of her life.

Kate interrupted her thoughts. "Guess where you're staying this week?"

"Let me see—since you're here, and you've mentioned your uncle, I imagine I'm staying there."

"And?"

"You're coming, too? Oh, Kate, it's good to see you."

* * *

Sprawling above a rocky hillside overlooking the ocean, the Pacific Harbor campus was more beautiful than anything she'd imagined. Even though there wasn't a harbor nearby, it didn't matter; the view of the ocean was spectacular from this lofty perch. Molly chose the campus arboretum as her favorite lookout point. Benches were interspersed among the immaculately groomed flowerbeds for perfect observation of the scene below. Gazing down from the cliffs and listening to waves crash against the rocky shoreline, Molly could imagine spending all her spare hours immersed in the solitude.

By the day of her first audition, Molly felt none of the nonchalance with which she'd arrived. She knew Pacific Harbor was where she wanted to be. She also knew a scholarship was the only way she could buy the freedom to make her own choice.

The auditions were held on two different days. On the first morning, Molly played her favorite piece, Tomaso Albinoni's *Adagio in G Minor,* the pathos of her soul imbuing each note with intensity beyond her years. Oblivious to the poignancy of her interpretation, she nervously continued with Mozart's *G Major Flute Concerto*. That afternoon, a new panel of judges asked her to play numerous orchestra excerpts–from memory. Though she'd prepared all the required music, she hadn't realized how difficult it would be to perform it under pressure, and she was afraid she ruined her chances by forgetting an entire section of one of the pieces.

The next afternoon, when she and another scholarship-hopeful played Kuhlau's *Trio in G*, she suddenly felt grateful for her years of private flute lessons. Their piano accompanist was fantastic—and it sounded like the three of them had been working together for months instead of hours. It was exhilarating.

Before they left for home, the department dean announced, "We'll notify the two scholarship winners and the runner-up in early February."

Molly wanted to ask how good her chances of winning anything were—but she was afraid she'd look too desperate. She could barely choke out the words, "thank you for giving me the opportunity to visit your campus," as the dean of the music department shook her hand and thanked her profusely for coming.

Chapter Nineteen

➤❤️

Every day after school, Molly anxiously checked the mail. The letter from Pacific Harbor finally arrived in February, but she couldn't open it. She had to call Kate first. "It's here, Kate," she said.

Kate screamed. "What did it say?"

"I'm too scared to open it."

"Open it, open it!"

Molly began reading.

"Congratulations!" Kate yelled. "I knew you'd win!"

Molly's hands were shaking. It was the first thing she'd ever won.

"Still want to be roommates, Molly?"

"I'm planning on it."

"I've been checking on dorms. Uncle Dan and Aunt Zoë think Carmichael is best. It's the newest, and it has a pool, but there's usually a waiting list for it."

"Then there's probably no way we'll get in."

"We'll get in," Kate enthused. "I'll pray about it."

"You and everyone else who wants it," Molly said, lashing out. "Be a realist for once."

Kate fell silent on the other end of the line.

Even Molly was shocked by her quick-tempered sarcasm; Kate was the last person she wanted to hurt. "I'm sorry," she said, meaning it.

Kate rebounded quickly. "It's OK," she said, congratulating Molly again.

When they hung up, Molly's house was quiet—too quiet. She wanted to celebrate, but she knew her flute instructor was out of town. The kids from school were going to the Valentine's dance that night; calling them with her good news meant getting pressured to join them. Besides, her friends already questioned both her choice of schools and her decision to room with a grade-school friend. She finally decided to call her mother at work. "I got the scholarship, Mom," she said.

"Great, great. Now, that's an academic scholarship, right?"

"Music."

"Of course! Well, this is good news. Congratulations. By the way, could you throw a couple of wine glasses in the dishwasher and run it? I'm bringing a friend home for drinks."

Molly decided to finish her homework.

* * *

The newspaper staff of Eastwood High was crashing into their deadline. It had been a long week–and an even longer day. Nothing in their new format seemed to be working. At midnight on Friday, they were finally ready to go to press. "We've got to do something tonight to celebrate," said Jerrid, the senior editor.

"How about tomorrow?" His assistant, Sydney, spoke first. "I'm too tired to celebrate anything tonight." Molly was relieved when the others agreed. Her cozy down comforter was calling.

"Party poopers." Alex, the music columnist, was the only night owl in the group.

"I've got it," said Jerrid, ever the idea man. "We'll go into the city tomorrow morning. There's nothing going on tonight, anyway. None of us drinks. We'd all fall asleep if we rent a movie."

"I'll drive," Sydney offered. No one argued. The bumper sticker on her car read, "I'm not opinionated; I'm right."

* * *

On the way into the city, they kicked around their plans for the day. As usual, Jerrid insisted on checking details. Finally, with minimal bloodshed, they reached consensus. It would be Rush Street Giordano's for stuffed pizza first, then Omni Max at the Museum of Science and Industry and back in the Loop by evening.

"Isn't this plan a bit circuitous?" Jerrid asked, hunched over a map, his thick black eyebrows knitted together. "There's got to be a direct route." Outnumbered three to one, he finally admitted that having lunch at Giordano's was worth the detour.

With an hour to kill before the show started at Omni Max, they split up to explore the museum. "Hey, let's go to the Bio Annex," Sydney urged. "I haven't been there since I was little."

Molly had been to the museum on field trips, but the only display she remembered was Colleen Moore's Fairy Castle, with its hundreds of perfectly reproduced miniature treasures. "Let's go to the doll house next," she said. They took the elevator upstairs together, but Sydney rushed ahead. "This way," she called, veering right.

Molly followed her, ignoring the HIV/AIDS exhibit as she hurried past it. She saw Sydney ahead of her, standing on the edge of a long glass display case, and went to the opposite end of the room. Not sure what she was looking at, she stepped closer to see the row of glass containers. Each held a preserved specimen of a human, the lifeless forms representing every stage of fetal development. Molly's mind reeled. She stood facing a five-month old fetus, obsessively searching for signs that it was a fake. Not a real baby who somehow did not survive birth. Not a child suspended in time, trapped in a glass jar, naked before tourists filing by, year after year. Her eyes examined every detail. The dimpled chin. The plump toes. The downy mist of hair. The exact stage of development that her baby—she cringed when she thought of the word—would have been were it still growing inside her.

"Isn't this amazing?" Sydney asked, seeing only the form before her. "I forgot how cool these specimens were."

A mother crouched on the floor beside them, one arm pointing to the glass case, the other protectively shielding a pigtailed toddler from the passing crowds. "God designed each of you, too," she said, speaking loudly enough for her two other children to hear.

"Please keep your politics to yourself," a thirty-something woman with a sketchpad told her, glaring.

Molly turned away, hiding her tears as she hurried around the partition that obscured the exhibit from the rest of the room. She stood there, putting a barrier between now and then, forcibly pushing her emotions back in control.

Sydney caught up with her. "I didn't know where you were."

"I decided to check out another exhibit. Ready to go to the doll house?" Molly asked, walking.

* * *

She let school activities, studying, and practicing her flute–all with equal intensity–consume her life with more of a vengeance than ever. To further cram her schedule, she joined the Eastwood Thespian Troupe, quickly assuming the frenetic job of stage manager. She especially liked the first line of their motto: "Act well your part." It was her credo.

* * *

Christmas vacation brought Molly home to her dad and Mercedes for the first time since summer.

After Anson booked her for a few jobs that subsidized her fall wardrobe, Mercedes took time off for a blepharoplasty. "I hate to have you see me like this," she said the moment Molly arrived. "I know my eyes look terrible, and I wouldn't have had this surgery if your brother and sister were coming. But, I knew *you'd* understand. In our line of work, this procedure wasn't an option."

Mercedes droned on, "I had to get rid of those hideous circles, but I had no idea the process would be so dreadful. At least everything went well. I've been so nervous, because one of my dearest friends had too much fat removed on her lower lids, and she has a disgusting hollow place under her eyes. And they can't do a thing–not one thing– about it."

Molly dared not voice her thoughts.

For the next hour, Mercedes explained every detail of the procedure. "I decided to have it done with a scalpel instead of laser because it's a neater, cleaner cut," she said. "And I absolutely insisted on a lidocaine IV sedation—you can't imagine how much research I did to find the best plastic surgeon–someone with an oxygen chamber, you know. It's worth every penny. Look, you can hardly see the incision."

Nauseated, Molly looked for the invisible scar, wondering why her own procedure was barely acknowledged. She didn't dare let her mind go there, so she thought back to the long-ago Christmas when she was with Kate and her family.

She couldn't remember what they did, or what they discussed. *At least it wasn't somebody's bag job,* Molly thought. She excused herself and went to her room. Picking up the phone, she dialed Kate.

"Hello, Kate?" Kate and her mom's voices had begun sounding alike.

"Molly!" Kate's unbridled enthusiasm gave her away. "Where are you? Tell me you're in California!"

Molly smiled. "No, I'm at my dad's."

"Oh. I wish you were here. We just had a birthday party for Jesus. Did we do that when you were here for Christmas?"

"Uh, yeah, I think so." Molly hesitated, bracing for more Jesus talk.

Kate sensed her mood. "Are you OK?"

Without thinking, Molly plunged into a topic she'd wanted to discuss ever since she had agreed to be Kate's roommate. "Uh, Kate, there's something I've been wondering."

Kate, teasing, asked, "What? Are you afraid I'm going to be messier than you?"

"No," Molly paused. Both of them liked to have their rooms in order and could put up with occasional clutter. That wouldn't be a problem. "No, well, it's just that I'm not sure we'll be a good fit because ... ." She didn't know how to say the rest without hurting Kate.

Kate finished for her. "You're worried that I'm going to talk about God all the time."

Relieved, Molly exhaled.

"We've known each other a long time, Mol. Haven't I respected your opinions?"

"Yes, but, it ... well, it seems like you bring God into everything."

"I can't stop doing that, Molly. Ever since I surrendered my life to Christ when I was seven ... ."

Molly interrupted, "Why do you refer to that all the time? You were a little kid."

"It was the most important commitment of my life. It changed everything, Mol. But I've explained this before."

"About a million times."

"So I'm not supposed to tell my best friend about the best thing that ever happened to me?"

"Why do you always act like you're better than I am?" Molly retorted.

"There's no way I think that!" Choking out words between her tears, Kate said, "I accept you the way you are. Why don't you see that?"

"I'm sorry, Kate," Molly said, softening. "You're the best friend I've ever had. But the Jesus talk freaks me out. It's like you think he's standing right here or something."

"He is here, Molly. He's everywhere," Kate responded quietly. She paused. "I respect your beliefs. Will you respect mine?"

Realizing she demanded more from Kate than she was giving in return, Molly was forced to stare her hypocrisy in the face. "Kate, I'm sorry," she said. "I'm in a bad mood. Can we just forget this?"

* * *

Studying Molly's practice sheet, Mrs. Dennison frowned. "You need more practice, Molly—I want to see at least one to one-and-a-half hours a day. You're improving nicely, but the competition at college is going to be stiff."

"OK. I can get by on less sleep," Molly said, knowing her flute instructor was serious.

Mrs. Dennison paused briefly, then continued. "I got a call yesterday from the Alpine Institute. Are you familiar with it?"

"The summer music school near Lake Geneva?"

191

"That's the place— in my favorite part of Wisconsin. It's lovely in that area," she said, clearing her throat. Molly knew an important pronouncement was imminent. "I'm on the board and have been asked to recommend a student from the Chicago area to be an apprentice academician this summer. With your permission, Molly, I'd like to recommend you."

Molly hesitated, for a brief moment considering the possibility of taking the summer slowly. "What exactly is involved?"

"Besides keeping up with your own music studies and performing in ensemble and solo settings, you'd give private instruction to several students every day— a new group of students arrives every two weeks—in addition, you would be counselor to a different cabin of students during each Institute session." Sensing Molly's reticence, she quickly added, "The compensation is excellent. It is really quite a remarkable opportunity, and I'd like to see you have something like this on your resumé. What do you think, Molly?"

"I appreciate you considering me, Mrs. Dennison. Can I give it some thought?"

* * *

Several days later, her mother unintentionally helped her change her mind.

"Molly, your father and I talked last night," she said.

Talked or yelled? Molly wondered. She said, "Oh?"

"He and I agreed ... ."

Molly didn't hear the rest of her mother's point because she was still lost in thought, questioning, *you two actually agreed on something?*

"Molly, are you paying attention?"

"Uh, what did you say?"

"If I didn't know your SAT scores, I'd think you were an

imbecile. Pay attention. Your father and I think you should get a summer job and save your own spending money for college in the fall. We have several ideas."

"I already have a summer job, Mom."

"What are you talking about?"

"I'm going to be a student instructor at the Alpine Institute in Lake Geneva."

"That place is prestigious! How did this come up?"

"Mrs. Dennison recommended me for the position. She's on the board."

"Finally my investment in private flute lessons is paying off." Her irritating voice continued, "And when does this job begin?"

"I, uh, I'll find out Monday at my lesson," Molly said, hoping she would.

Chapter Twenty

Molly forced a goodbye wave to her mother as she boarded the train for Lake Geneva. Grimacing, she remembered the argument that began their day.

"Put your things in the other car, Molly," her mother had said.

"You want me to take your car?" Molly asked, incredulous.

"What are you talking about?"

"Well, I thought I'd drive the old BMW like usual," Molly explained.

That's when her mother started laughing. "You actually thought I'd let you take one of my cars to camp! Now *that's* funny."

"I've been driving it for two years."

"Out of the generosity of my heart," her mother retorted. "But I'm selling it this summer. You're going to college in the fall so you won't need it, anyway."

"But I assumed I'd take it to school ...."

"You assumed wrong." Seeing Molly's frown, she added, "Deal with it and move on quickly, because you have a train to catch. I'll drive you to the station—I'm sure there will be someone at your camp who can meet you at that end."

Molly used all her free time at camp to practice flute, which helped her get ready for college—and maintain a carefully spaced distance from the other counselors. Devin was the only one who tried to break through her impenetrable defenses. "Hey, Molly, we're going into town for ice cream. Come with us," he said, smiling. "The practice rooms are locked, so you don't have an excuse this time."

It was easily the hottest day of summer. *Why not?* Molly thought, joining the group of laughing counselors. She didn't notice that Devin carefully maneuvered into the seat next to hers, but she did start to bristle under his attention by the time they returned to camp.

"Want to go for a swim?" he asked, ambling next to her as she turned toward her cabin.

"No," she said without hesitation.

"How about trying out one of the new canoes?"

"I'm tired," she said, picking up her pace.

"You don't look tired."

"OK, so I'm not tired."

"Why are you so scared of me?" he asked, his smile irresistible, even to Molly.

"I'm not."

"Not tired and not scared," retorted Devin, elated. "I now know two things about you. We're finally getting to know each other."

A hint of a smile played on Molly's lips.

"She smiles, too! I knew you had teeth," he said, playfully hugging her shoulders.

Her smile disappeared at his touch. "Good night," she said, her armor springing back in place. For rest of the summer, she avoided Devin, setting her sights on starting college in the fall.

Chapter Twenty-one

S tepping off her plane, Molly unconsciously touched the form in her pocket, her mind replaying its contents. "Your dorm assignment: Carmichael Hall. The school shuttle will meet you at the airport." Looking ahead, she saw someone holding a sign announcing, "Pacific Harbor." The rest of the day was a blur.

That night, unpacking the last of the boxes she had shipped and the luggage that traveled with her, she sighed. She was used to having her own room, but this one felt too quiet. There were a few others on her floor, who, like her, had reported early for symphonic band section tryouts, but she had not met them yet. Kate wasn't due for one week.

A light tap on the door interrupted her. "Anyone home?"

Molly recognized the chirping voice of the overly caffeinated girl she saw—and heard— in band that afternoon.

The knocking continued. "I have chocolate chip cookies."

Molly reluctantly unlocked her door, and the lanky brunette bounded in. "Everyone's coming to my room to binge. No more practicing tonight!"

Molly couldn't think of an excuse fast enough, so she followed her down the hall. Molly was shocked at the difference between their rooms. The sterile mini-blinds had disappeared behind soft curtains. A braided rug camouflaged the gray-flecked linoleum. Framed candid snapshots dotted the desk and dresser: a tangle of kids in a leaf pile, a mom and dad on a snowy chairlift, two brothers lifting the brunette girl between them like a barbell.

Molly winced and looked away, suddenly aware that the noise level in the room had increased and a party was in full swing. The chaos scrambled Molly's thoughts, and she quickly slipped away, glad that no one seemed to notice.

Back in her room, she reached for a silver-framed portrait—three children perfectly posed around beaming parents—and quickly stuffed it into a dresser drawer.

The week evaporated in a constant stream of activities. Before she knew it, Molly was pacing the room, watching the clock, waiting for Kate to arrive.

The door burst open. "Molly!" Kate squealed, hugging her. "This is going to be so much fun!"

"Your hair—it's brown!"

"The box said 'espresso,'" she laughed. "The new me—but it only lasts for twenty more washes. It turned out kind of auburn, don't you think?"

Mrs. Johnson set down a suitcase to embrace Molly. "We've all been looking forward to seeing you, dear." A pile of boxes began to tip over, and she reached for them, taking charge. "OK, kids, let's set everything over here so we don't mess up Molly's side." Looking at Kate, she added, "Is this your dresser?"

Kate continued to talk with Molly, ignoring her mother—until she saw her unpacking. "This is my stuff, Mom," she said, an edge in her voice. "Let me take care of it later. I'm in college, not kindergarten."

"Hey, sis, you don't have to cut the apron strings with a chain saw. We'll be gone soon enough," Peter said, attempting to humor both mother and daughter.

"Hi, Peter," Molly said, turning toward him, surprised. "I didn't see you."

"I'm the family sherpa," he laughed, waving at the pile next to him.

Kate interrupted. "What do you think, Mol? We brought curtains for our room! Do you like them?"

"I do," she said, thinking of their room's imminent transformation. "I really do."

* * *

The first few weeks of school, Molly and Kate tried to eat at least one meal together each day. With their different class schedules, it took special effort to spend any time with each other, especially since they shared only one class, Psalms.

* * *

Pacific Harbor required that everyone take at least one Bible class each semester. Molly considered it a waste of time; she'd told her flute teacher as much during her last lesson before leaving for college.

"I imagine you're getting excited about getting to California—and my alma mater," Mrs. Dennison beamed, happy to have a student following her footsteps.

"Not really," Molly responded, the words slipping out before her usual reserve could stop them.

Her teacher's eyebrows arched. "And why not?"

Molly decided she might as well speak truth. "I read through the school's requirements last night. They expect us to take a Bible class every semester."

"Every school has some classes you'll value and some that you won't," replied Mrs. Dennison, her tone stern, but diplomatic. "Your job as a student is to learn to think critically."

"But I don't know anything about the Bible," said Molly, divulging her main concern. "It's like studying a foreign language."

Mrs. Dennison did something she rarely did—she laughed, her eyes twinkling. "Oh, Molly there will be many others there who have never looked at a Bible. I was one of those," she added. "Like you, I went to the school because of its reputation in the music field."

"Oh," Molly said, her anger defused.

* * *

She registered for the class in Psalms for one reason: she still remembered hearing one of them at her grandmother's funeral the summer before.

* * *

She didn't like remembering the night she went with her mother and her sister to see the body of the grandmother they barely knew. Her mother stood erect, her hands clenched in her suit pockets, her face devoid of emotion.

Dorothy Finster had lived in the same tiny town about an hour away from Babs, her only child, for all eighty-two years of her life. For sixty of those, Dorothy had resided in the same one-story, two-bedroom house. Molly had only been there three times.

They could have stayed there that night; Babs opted for a motel instead. Nothing about the accommodations—the carpet, the furniture, the room size—met with her approval.

"How repulsive," she said, pointing angrily at the wall. "Cheap laminate."

"Why is there a visitation the night before funerals?" Jennifer asked.

"Beats me," her mother said, shrugging. "Keep it short and sweet and be done with it! That's what I say."

"Maybe it helps people say 'goodbye,'" said Jenn, thoughtful.

"I did that twenty-five years ago," she fumed.

"Why?" asked Molly, looking up from her book.

"Don't even go there," her mother blazed. "You'll probably hear all about it tomorrow." She ended the conversation by picking up the remote. "Your brother was the smart one, too busy to come."

At the funeral, a small boy in a three-piece suit handed out programs—crisply folded sheets of white paper printed with the words "The Lord is my Shepherd." The minister talked about how Dottie Finster had helped tutor poor migrant children whose families worked area farms every summer. He told stories of the tree-trimming party she held each year and of the countless meals she carted to shut-ins. As he began to talk about Psalm 23, Molly glanced at the drawing on the program, losing herself in the simple sketch of rugged hands cradling a newborn lamb.

* * *

"We'll start with something familiar," her professor explained, giving their first assignment for the course on Psalms: write a letter to God based on Psalm 23.

"How weird," Molly said to Kate later. "I stopped writing to Santa when I was five."

Afraid Kate would offer to help her, she tackled the assignment at the campus library. After finding a secluded spot where she could plug in her laptop, she stared at the blankest of blank screens, wondering if she were going to launch her college career with an incomplete.

Through a window overlooking the courtyard below, she saw two birds in a small reflective pond and thought back to her professor's lecture.

"The Bible repeatedly uses nature to depict God the Creator as well as God the Lover of our souls," the kindly man had explained. "Here we see God portrayed as a Shepherd who leads us and actually cares where we go."

Molly opened her notebook and reread the psalm, unexpectedly recalling another portion of the lecture.

"Perhaps some of you have no idea what a loving father looks like. With over fifty percent of American marriages ending in divorce, many of you haven't even had a father at home with you; others of you have had fathers who are there but who aren't involved. You might wonder how one can begin to understand this metaphor for God's love."

"He leads me beside still waters," she read, startled that she was beginning to grasp her professor's explanations.

"Sheep are terrified of rushing streams, of noisy waters. They would stand and die of thirst before stooping to drink from water like that," he explained. "The Shepherd leads them beside still waters so they won't be fearful of the very thing that will keep them alive."

She began to write.

* * *

As soon as she got back to their room, Kate asked, "Did you do you Bible assignment.yet?"

"Yeah, I just finished it," Molly said.

"Want to read mine?"

"I'd better go practice," Molly said, not wanting to disclose her thoughts.

"OK." Kate seemed hurt. "Well, are you still going to dinner at my aunt and uncle's tonight?"

"Sure," Molly replied, irritated that she'd forgotten to write the date down. "I'll be back in an hour."

* * *

"It's good to see you again, Dr. and Mrs. Johnson," Molly said.

"Call me Zoë," Kate's aunt said, her chandelier earrings dancing as she extended her hand to Molly.

Daniel popped out of the kitchen to welcome the girls.

"Sometimes people think Aunt Zoë is my mom, because we look so much alike. Isn't that funny? Because we're not even blood relatives," Kate laughed. "Dad and Uncle Dan are brothers. But you know that."

It was true that they looked alike—but their similarities ended with red hair and freckles. Kate, constantly in motion, was rarely quiet. Her aunt liked to sit and listen to others, her chin cupped in her hands—typically pondering a person's comment long after conversation had turned elsewhere.

Zoë went to the kitchen to check on dinner, talking as she walked. "Kate, why don't you help Dan set the table? Molly, we'll get the food. You can kick off your shoes if you want to."

Molly followed her, noticing her peasant blouse and swishing skirt, intrigued as much by her Bohemian spirit as her eclectic fashion sense. Engrossed in the study of Zoë, Molly relaxed.

Zoë repeated her question. "Molly, how is your adjustment to college life going?"

It was obvious that Zoë didn't waste time on small talk. Molly didn't know how to answer. Her mind raced, quickly weighing pros and cons. If she told Zoë the truth, she'd think she was weird, but she couldn't think of a quick lie. Instead, she tried to frame an innocuous answer. "It's different from what I expected."

Zoë paused, thinking, remembering. "College was different from what I expected, too."

"How?" Molly asked her, both intrigued and relieved not to have to unveil herself.

"Oh, that is such a broad question," Zoë replied. "In a million ways, I guess—I wasn't ready to make my own decisions. And I made some poor ones. I didn't expect my assumptions about life to be challenged every day—and I didn't think I was as naïve as I was." She sighed, then looked at Molly, reflective. "How is it different for you?"

Forgetting herself, Molly answered directly, "I was hoping for something relevant to my life—not all this Bible mumbo-jumbo."

"I see," Zoë said, nodding.

Molly wanted to know what Zoë saw, but Kate and Dr. Johnson interrupted them.

* * *

Kate loved morning. "Hey, Molly, it's Thursday!"

Molly pulled a pillow over her head.

"Want to go to chapel today? You might like it."

"No one asked your opinion."

It had been an ongoing debate, a symptom of the irritation growing inside Molly.

"I'm an adult, Kate, and I don't appreciate being pressured every week to go to chapel."

"There's supposed to be a really good speaker—and great music."

"Kate, watch it." She didn't know why she so adamantly opposed going to the weekly chapel services. *I want to hear*

*the group that's performing today, but I can't tell her that. If
I go today, she'll expect me there every week.*

* * *

The campus shut down during chapel. The stillness of
the dorm was more disturbing than Kate's incessant chatter.
Restless, Molly rummaged through her bookshelves, notic-
ing the set of books Analese had given her for graduation.
Inside the cover, she read Analese's flowing script:
"Congratulations, Molly! You are one of my favorite people.
May your life take you on great adventures even more
wonderful than those you'll find in *Chronicles of Narnia*.
Love, Analese."

I forgot I already had these books. Reaching for the
phone, Molly spoke aloud, "I'll call her and tell her we're
studying *Narnia* in English Lit."

An automated voice intoned, "This number is no longer
in service. Calls are being taken by … ."

Sure she must have misdialed, Molly hung up and tried
again. Same message. She quickly jotted down the number
and punched it in.

This time the phone was answered by a voice that cheerily announced, "Hello, Harper Enterprises."

"Uh, I'm sorry, I must have the wrong number."

"Who were you calling?"

"Analese Harper."

"Analese is in Russia at the present time. May I help
you?"

"This is Molly Montgomery. I'm a friend."

"Oh, Molly! Great to talk with you! I'm Erica, Analese's
business manager. Analese has spoken of you often."

Molly was thoroughly confused. *Why does Analese have
a business manager?* she wondered, speechless.

"Molly, are you still there?"

"Uh, yes."

"I imagine you want to know what's going on. Analese said I could explain."

"I thought she cleaned houses."

A friendly chuckle preceded Erica's response. "She did that more as a hobby. We're both actually licensed stockbrokers, but making money isn't all that appealing to her. What she really likes is contact with people from all walks of life—I guess you could say she's a little bit eccentric—she doesn't need the money, because she inherited that from her family. That's how she got her start. Anyway, she's in St. Petersburg, Russia, helping some old friends of hers, the Lewellens. They're doing mission work in an orphanage. She'll be with them for at least six months."

Molly tried to think of something to say. "I, uh, I didn't know."

"Would you like her e-mail address?"

"So, uh, I can contact her there?"

"She'd love it."

"Well, thanks. Wow, this is a surprise. A stockbroker!"

"Harvard."

Molly hung up the phone, stunned. Reaching for her flute, she thought, *I'll e-mail her some other time. Right now, I need to play some Bach—at least his precision doesn't change like everybody else does.*

* * *

Lately, Kate had seemed too pious—always praying, reading her Bible, saying things like, "God showed me this; God helped me with that." *She even had the audacity to say God helped her with her physics exam.* Molly had to laugh at that one. "Kate, how is it that you're so special that God gets directly involved in your tests?"

"I don't have a corner on God, Molly. He wants to help

you, too—not just with school but with every part of your life."

"Kate, doesn't your Bible say 'God helps those who help themselves'?"

Kate's response still irked her. "Molly, that's not in the Bible. What it teaches is that God helps the helpless, not the proud who say they can do everything themselves."

"You have to make your own way in this world, Kate. What are you thinking? Are you thinking? I suppose God will even do your homework for you," she said, laughing.

Kate wasn't laughing. "Molly, you know I study three or four hours every day." *I'm also on the Dean's list*, she thought, but said only, "I'm not neglecting what I need to do. All I'm saying is that I simply ask God to guide me–and He does."

"You're saying you think you're smart enough to hear God," Molly sneered. "I can't sit around and listen to this garbage," she said, letting the door slam behind her as she stormed from their room. Even though she forgot to take her study notes, she stayed at the library until she was sure Kate would be asleep.

* * *

Walking across campus the next morning, she was still fuming—this time, at life in general. Cramming for an imminent English Lit. quiz, she wondered, *What's the point of learning things I'm never going to use? Why do they make me jump through the hoops of these general courses when all I want to learn is music?* She couldn't concentrate because she couldn't forget Kate's words, "Molly, I'm really sorry about last night," or her tears.

"What do you mean?" Molly feigned ignorance, wanting to brush off their previous discussion.

"You know—the argument."

"Oh, think nothing of it," she said, detached. "Look, I have to get to class."

* * *

The quiz was predictably simple, and Molly felt smug about it until she saw the final essay question: "Describe at least three similarities between Aslan and God's Son, Jesus Christ, and explain their significance."

She tensed. *He's taking this too far. I can't believe he's trying to complicate a children's story with a ridiculous religious theme.* After angrily scrawling an answer, she threw her paper on Professor Jenkins' desk.

* * *

Walking into philosophy class, she thought, *At least here I'm not assaulted with religion.* Dr. Newell stood at the front of the lecture hall, his back to the students as he wrote four words on the white board, "To know the good."

She sat near the back, her mind drifting to the Bach Partida she was memorizing, her hands unconsciously executing intricate fingering techniques on her notebook.

Two minutes into his lecture, the professor jarred her to consciousness by introducing the subject she loathed. "Religion isn't some kind of higher culture," Dr. Newell said. "It's not for elitists who think they're better than everyone else." He paused, his face charged with anticipation as he gazed around the lecture hall. "Can any of you offer another term other than *religion* we might use in this context?"

A hand shot up across the aisle. "Relationship?"

"A relationship but with what, or with whom? Do you know this as an object or as a subject?" Dr. Newell asked, prodding.

The student tried again. "A *relationship* with God is different from religion—uh, I see *religion* as people trying to work their way to God—doing what they think is right. But, Christianity is a relationship between the person and the living God, and it's made possible because of what Jesus did on the cross."

Molly tuned him out. *More Kate-isms. Why aren't we studying Plato's Republic? What does this discussion of religion have to do with what I'm supposed to be learning?*

Tapping the white board with his pointer, the professor got her attention. "What did Socrates mean when he said, 'To know the good is the highest knowledge that can be obtained by man'? Was he referring to a quality innate in human beings or was it something else?"

Waiting to understand the question, no one responded.

Dr. Newell continued, "Let me clarify. Is 'knowing good' simply understanding a command, like 'You ought to be good'? Are we to take this as a request, a recommendation or an order?"

A hand near the front went up, tentatively. "I can understand what an order means but still not do it."

"Well, then, did you really understand it?"

Another student entered the discussion. "I think that would depend on who gives it. If the command comes from someone who isn't good, there may not be any way to understand it. But, even if a command comes from somebody who is good, you can still ignore it."

"Hmm," Dr. Newell intoned, leaving everyone wondering what he thought. "So is Socrates saying that the meaning of knowing them is to *do* them, to actually *be* them? To know music, for example, is to subject yourself to that craft. Unless you subject yourself to it, unless you can actually play a note, unless you have disciplined yourself to master an instrument, then you don't really know music. Similarly, with respect to certain aspects of knowledge, you can't know it unless you *are* it. This is especially true of concepts like justice, goodness, wisdom, love—indeed, all moral concepts." He paused and looked around the lecture hall for what seemed a very long time. "Can anyone explain in one sentence what all of this means?"

The eager hand shot up again. "I think knowing *good* requires *being* good, which can't happen unless we're subject to God, since He alone is good."

* * *

Later, practicing her flute, Molly wondered, *Do I know anything at all? My life is all about doing, not being.* She shook her head, trying to forget the thoughts that invaded even her practice time. Her cell phone rang. It was her father.

"Mercedes and I are about twenty minutes away," he said. "Surprised?"

"Definitely." They hadn't called for months, and California was the last place she expected them to be.

"I'm here on business for a few days— we flew in yesterday. Thought we'd pick you up for dinner. Is thirty minutes OK?"

"I guess."

"Great. Give me directions."

* * *

Molly wondered, *Why this sudden interest? I don't even know if I want to see them.* She quickly changed into the still-new linen slacks and cobalt blue silk blouse Mercedes gave her for graduation. After deftly pulling her hair into one of the styles she'd learned as a model, Molly opened the case of custom-blended makeup Mercedes had given her to take to college. It was the first time she'd used it.

Molly didn't look anything like the girl who usually pulled her hair back into a casual ponytail and wore jeans and oversized T-shirts to class. Waiting downstairs in the dorm lobby, she noticed people staring, trying to figure out who she was. As soon as she saw her father and Mercedes pull up in their rental car, she hurried outside.

"You look fabulous, Molly," Mercedes said. "Why are you wasting your time studying when one phone call could get you back into the real world—modeling?"

Molly didn't reply.

Her father said only, "Great to see you."

Despite an elegant meal at an ocean front restaurant with a spectacular view, the conversation was flat and uninteresting. Molly wanted to get back to her world. *It's amazing how long two hours can seem,* she thought as they sped back toward Pacific Harbor.

Mercedes turned around, smiling. "Love, I know you'll want to know this—it's really important to get your teeth cleaned every two months. I know, I know—most people say to clean them every six months—but not with your face. You don't want those coffee stains distracting everyone from your important features, now do you?"

Molly tuned her out.

"Be good," her father said, waving as he and Mercedes left.

* * *

Molly walked into the dorm, thinking, *That word again! I wish I knew how to be good. But, is 'good' something I can be, is it even something I can objectively know?*

Kate was in the room when she arrived and, for once, Molly was glad to see her. She welcomed any diversion from her mental gymnastics.

"How did the time with your dad and stepmom go? I was—thinking of you," Kate said, gingerly.

Molly knew Kate substituted the word 'thinking' for 'praying' to avoid offending her, but it suddenly felt good to know Kate prayed for her. Pretending not to know, she said, "Oh, it was OK. Nothing too exciting."

"Peter called while you were out. He said to say 'hi'."

Molly's expression changed when she heard Peter's name. "How is he?" she asked, her face lighting up. "Is he coming home for Christmas?"

"Actually, he called to say our family is going to go to Colorado instead. One of his professors owns a condo in Breckenridge, and he's going to Florida during Christmas break. Since Peter has been working part-time for him, he told Peter we could use the condo—for free!"

"You'll have so much fun!"

"I know. I can't wait. The only hitch is for Peter to find a ride there. He doesn't have a car."

"You could always *pray* for him," Molly teased.

"Great idea!" Kate laughed, momentarily thrown off balance. "Why didn't I think of that?" Hey, why don't you come with us! It would be so much fun!" She hesitated. "Or do you already have plans with your family?"

"Actually, Dad just informed me that they're going to Hawaii. I don't know about Mom. I guess I could ask." Unexpectedly, she felt embarrassed, unsure of whether or not she'd been officially invited; after all she'd done to push Kate away, it was difficult to believe that her friend still cared. "But you don't need anyone intruding on your vacation."

"Intruding? You?" Kate said, reaching for the phone. "I'm only doing this so you won't worry." The conversation was punctuated with laughter, smiles and nods toward Molly. "Mom says you can only come if you promise never to ask a question like that again. She's thrilled! Here, call yours!"

Kate looked too eager to disappoint, but Molly hesitated, afraid her mother would veto the plan. She punched in the seldom-used numbers. "Mom?" she said, listening. Her expression calcified. "I know, but I study so much I don't have much time to write anything but papers," she said, all of the life drained out of her voice. "OK, I'll try to e-mail more." The corners of her mouth began to turn upwards.

Kate watched, puzzled, as the wide smile—one she rarely saw, it seemed—spread over Molly's face. "What? Tell me what she said—is it good news? What?" she asked, barely waiting for her to hang up.

"It seems that Mother has to leave town for Christmas. She hopes I don't mind 'fending for myself.'"

The only sounds louder than their screams as they jumped and hugged, were the noises of doors slamming. "We're trying to work!" yelled a disgruntled hallmate.

"We get to go skiing together for Christmas!" yelled Kate in response, eager to share her good news with the world.

Planning the trip took precedence over everything except studying. For the next week, Molly's life revolved around two objects: Her suitcase (packing seemed like a productive way to procrastinate) and her Palm Pilot, proof of her latest attempt to get organized. Late one night, it beeped.

"Just slowing down a little would help you a lot more than another gadget, Molly," Kate teased good-naturedly.

"I don't know what I forgot," Molly sighed, picking it up to check. She groaned. "It's Mercedes' birthday tomorrow. Oh, no. I've got to send her something."

"Flowers," Kate said confidently. "Flowers are good."

Molly was already online, ordering.

* * *

The next afternoon, Molly was alone in their room when the phone rang. Absent-mindedly, she picked it up. "Hello?"

Mercedes gushed with near-manic intensity. "The flowers are gorgeous, absolutely gorgeous, Molly! The bouquet has a simply darling combination of roses and iris as well as some chic miniature flowers—they look like lilies of some kind—well, the entire effect is pure elegance. I'm hosting a little soirée this evening and already have your flowers in the place of honor, right on the dining table," she gushed.

"Wonderful," said Molly, grimacing at the thought of her Visa bill.

Mercedes could turn a conversation on a dime. "I'm sure you've already taken care of this, love."

She hated it when Mercedes called her "love."

"Have you made an appointment yet?"

Molly evaded the question. "I'm glad you liked the flowers," she said.

Mercedes was not about to be put off. "Just in case you need a name, I've already contacted my dentist. He is a gem, absolutely a gem; he gave me the name of an excellent dentist—friend of his from dental school—who works just ten minutes from you." Her tone tensed. "Did you hear me?"

"Uh, I've been busy."

"Look, love, I know you're busy. That's why I made a back-up appointment for you. I just need to confirm it with your schedule."

* * *

In vain, Molly attempted to ignore the dental hygienist's steady stream of inane commentary. Even the soft music piped in through overhead speakers couldn't relax her.

"OK, Ms. Montgomery, we're going to take care of those coffee stains," she said, leaning over her. After a half hour of holding her mouth open, Molly felt frustrated when the hygienist said, "There are some tenacious stains here. I'm going to see if Dr. Zimmer can take a look."

He entered the room and lowered the back of Molly's chair until her shoulder rested against his leg. She pulled away. "I need you to sit still," he said gruffly. "If you'll just open your mouth a little wider, Nika here will help with the suction while I get you all fixed up." The perky brunette moved to the opposite side of the chair, making the space even more confined than it already was.

The ongoing sound of suction didn't bother her at first, but the longer it continued, the more Molly felt unexpected emotion welling up inside her. Despite her best attempts to regain control, her eyes filled with tears.

The dentist pulled back. "Am I hurting you?" he asked, looking at his watch and wondering how backed up the waiting room had become.

Molly didn't hear or see him; she had returned to another appointment, in another place with the same sound. A woman in a nearby room was crying out, "No, no, I want to go home. I want my baby." Was it her own voice she heard?

The dentist got busy. "Open your mouth again—wider now."

She promised never to set foot there again.

* * *

Peter met his family and Molly at the gate when they flew into Denver International Airport. "We can skip the rental," he said, smiling. "My professor loaned us his van. His flight just took off, so it worked out great."

Molly nudged Kate. "Answered prayer?"

Kate smiled and said, "I've heard that God does more than we can ask or imagine."

* * *

Even when they weren't skiing, Molly felt refreshed by being with the Johnsons. They weren't perfect—she'd seen them often enough to know that. But she had also seen them apologize and forgive each other. It was hard to believe it was real–and it was even more difficult to simply relax and accept their love. Molly's wildly fluctuating emotions kept her awake each night, long after everyone else was asleep.

It was well after midnight of their third night in the condo, and Molly was still wide-awake. When the quiet hum of the travel alarm began sounding like an angry bumblebee, she could lie still no longer. She could hear Kate's breathing from across the room—an even more maddening sound than the alarm. She slipped her fleece robe over her sweats, and then tiptoed around in the dark until she found her sheepskin slippers. After stumbling into the kitchen to make hot chocolate, she went to the living room, drawn to the sound of logs crackling in the fireplace. In the soft amber light, she didn't see Peter.

"Molly?"

She clamped her hand on her mouth in time to stifle a scream.

"I'm sorry—I didn't mean to scare you," he said kindly. "I couldn't sleep, so I came down here."

Still trying to calm herself, Molly didn't say anything.

"Are you OK?"

Finally she found words, "I'm OK, just a little startled. I, uh, I couldn't sleep, either." She backed up, not knowing what else to do, suddenly glad she was wearing sweats under her robe.

Peter, too, was dressed in sweats. "Nice slippers," he teased.

Molly slipped comfortably into the dynamic they'd shared for years. "It's dark in here. How can you tell?" She could relate to Peter like no one else.

He turned on a lamp, grinning. "Yep, still funny."

She laughed.

"Want to talk?" He took a couch across the room, motioning her to a chair. "That's my favorite. Try it—it's really comfortable."

She let herself sink into the soft cushions.

He spoke first, "You're having trouble sleeping?"

"Every night. All I do is toss and turn."

"I'm sorry," he said, his concern genuine. "Are you doing OK?"

Molly stunned herself when she said, "Not really."

"Can I help?"

"I— I don't know. There are a lot of things rumbling around in my head right now."

"Like?" Peter waited patiently while Molly processed her response.

With surprising candor, she began to tell him about her parents, her stepmother, and her struggle to understand God.

Peter listened and said little.

"Another thing that bothers me is the people at school," she continued.

"What do you mean?"

"Well, Harbor calls itself a church school or a Christian school–something like that. But some of the so-called Christians act just like the kids I grew up with. Some of them are a lot wilder. They sleep around, get drunk on weekends, do drugs."

"Oh, Molly, I definitely know what you're saying. Growing up, I went to a Christian high school and I got confused, too, when I saw kids saying one thing and doing something else."

"Double lives," nodded Molly.

"Well, they probably knew a lot about God but didn't know God. Make sense?"

"I'm lost."

"Let's see—it's as though they got enough of the message to immunize them to the real thing. They didn't let their head knowledge get into their hearts, their wills, their actions."

"We're back to Socrates, aren't we? 'To know the good, I have to actually be good.' I can't figure that one out—how to 'be good!'"

"I hear you. The guys on my floor at school keep pressuring me to party with them—and they party hard. I try to explain—but they don't get it. Even if I weren't a Christian, everything I see at work would make me want to stay away from that lifestyle."

"You have a job?"

"Work-study, at a boys' home. It's a rehab facility for kids who have gotten into all kinds of trouble, like drug or alcohol abuse. Some of their parents are in prison—and some of them will end up there if they don't shape up."

"I don't think I could handle a job like that."

"It's not easy. These kids' lives have been scarred in ways that are almost beyond belief." His voice choked. "I want to help them, but a lot of them have been betrayed so many times that they won't trust anyone."

She listened, feeling as if she were seeing him for the first time.

"Every day—no, every moment—I have to remember that only God can keep me on track. I could never live a good life without God's strength, without His wisdom."

The cynic in Molly burst forth. "With all the problems in the world, there must be a lot of people who don't understand anything about living the 'good' life," she said.

His forehead wrinkled in concentration. "Yeah," he exhaled. "God gets blamed for a lot of the evil people choose to do." He returned to where he'd left his thoughts, "Romans says a lot about this." He smiled, teasing her again— "Romans, you know, a book in the Bible?"

Molly pretended to cover her ears, but she couldn't suppress a smile.

"Anyway," he said seriously, "in Romans, Paul talks about his own failure and how God changed him from the inside out. I'm starting to see that living like a Christian has nothing to do with my strength or goodness at all. It's all about God in me."

There we go, back to 'good' again, Molly mused.

Peter interrupted her mental gymnastics. "What's next in your life, Molly?"

"Oh, I want to finish school, then hopefully get a job teaching flute somewhere near a good symphony where I can perform. You?"

"It looks like I can graduate in three years if I keep taking summer classes. Then, graduate school."

"What's your major, anyway?" Molly asked, for the first time noticing his eyes, reflecting both intensity and compassion in the flickering light.

"Human Development and Family Studies. I'm still deciding whether I want to go into youth work or do some kind of family counseling."

The fire burned down to embers and then went out all together. It was four o'clock before they finished their conversation, and Molly felt like they'd barely begun.

The Johnsons had planned to go to church the next morning. At 9:00, Kate tried to tease Molly awake, "You getting up today?"

No response.

"Couldn't sleep?"

"I was talking," came the muffled reply from under the pillow.

"In your sleep?" Kate hadn't noticed that Molly had been gone for several hours.

"Peter."

Molly jolted awake. All she wanted was to think about was their conversation—*the most wonderful conversation I've ever had.* She hadn't planned to tell anyone else about it. "He, uh, just happened to be up. We had some hot chocolate, talked about school—stuff like that."

Kate was uncharacteristically quiet.

Molly jumped out of bed, surprised to find she was looking forward to church.

The service was deadly. On the way back to the condo, Grace asked, "Why didn't they talk about God at church today? I thought we came to learn more about God." The youngest of the Johnson children, Grace, expressed her opinions liberally.

"From the mouth of babes," her mother said under her breath. To Grace, she responded, "Sweetheart, I guess this isn't like our church at home. We're sorry. We didn't know. Not every church teaches the same thing."

"Some churches don't believe the Bible is true," added her father. "I think we've been at a church like that today. They don't know the Bible is God's love letter, written just for them."

Grace didn't respond. She picked up her doll and began singing softly, "Jesus loves me, this I know, for the Bible tells me so."

For her, it's all so simple, Molly thought.

Chapter Twenty-two

➤❤

O nly one lure could draw Molly into a chapel service at Pacific Harbor University: The Flute. In November of her junior year, her ensemble was scheduled to perform. She never tired of performing Bach with the seven others who comprised their flute choir. The blend of bass and alto flutes, C flutes and piccolo was ethereal.

She planned to slip out immediately after they performed, but Dr. Knapp seated the group at the front of the auditorium. Molly was trapped.

She'd never heard of the guest speaker, a man named Tom Halden from Los Angeles. He spoke of growing up with divorced parents—alone, without a friend in the world. "At school," he said, "I was the runt. No one wanted me on his team—I was always the last one chosen. In junior high, I became the slave of some of the tough students in my school. In L.A., if someone tells you to do something or else, you know what they mean. And I did what they said. They had a group of kids they hated, and they used me as the one who would deliver their punishment. Every day, I had to put eggs in these kids' lockers, or smear paint on their clothes, or throw rocks at their houses, things like that.

In high school, that group broke up—by then, most of them were doing drugs and had dropped out of school—and I was 'free at last, free at last, thank God Almighty, free at last.'" He paused, his gaze piercing, his smile intense. Students' laughter faded, and the room fell silent. "A strange thing happened in high school. Remember those kids I'd been so mean to, the ones I kept hurting in junior high? They started being nice to me. One of them, Nate Roberts, was so nice it was weird. I didn't know what to think of it.

Nate invited me to his family's cabin on Lake Arrowhead, and it was the best time I'd ever had. The lake was beautiful, and we spent the weekend boating, hiking, fishing—normal, fun stuff I'd never done. Finally, I felt brave enough to ask, 'Nate, do you remember knowing me in junior high?' I'd always been too scared to say anything before. 'Yes,' he said.

I asked him another question. 'Do you remember any of the things I used to do to you?' He looked at me and smiled, then said, 'Yes, I do.' And he didn't say any more about it!

I thought, 'Why doesn't he hate me?'

A few weeks later, when Nate and I went with his parents to the lake again, I worked up my courage to ask him another question, 'Have you ever done anything bad like I did?' He acted like he didn't understand what I meant, so I said, 'Well, you seem so good, like you've never done anything bad.'

He looked at me and said, 'I did something so bad that my best friend had to die for me.' But he didn't tell me what he meant.

I kept trying to understand how someone's best friend could die for him—and what horrible thing Nate must have done to make him do it. A couple of weeks later, I finally asked him to explain it all to me, and to help me understand what he did to deserve to die.

He said, 'Tom, I've been waiting a long time for you to

ask me that question. It was Jesus who died for me, and it was because of my sin that He died. My sin was like a deep chasm, keeping me far from God. There wasn't any way I could reach God—not by going to church, not by doing good to others, not even by trying different religions.' Then he told me we've all done things—either in our attitudes or actions—that have separated us from God. The only way God could forgive our sins was to send someone else to pay for them. It had to be Someone who had never sinned. That's why He sent Jesus, His own Son. God sent Him to earth for one reason and one reason only: To die in our place, to pay for our sins, so we can have life forever with Him."

When Tom explained how he had asked Christ to forgive him and make him a new person, he told the assembled students that they could come and talk with him if they, too, were interested in experiencing God's love and forgiveness. At least fifty people stayed. Molly wanted to join them. But she didn't.

* * *

Later that evening, she and Kate were both in their room. Kate worked feverishly on a paper; Molly bent over a book, unable to concentrate.

"Popcorn?" Kate called from across the room. "I need a break."

Molly didn't answer, so Kate repeated her question, laughing, ready to tease her roommate into sharing her favorite snack. When Molly still didn't respond, Kate walked to her desk. Molly was gazing into space, oblivious of everything, twisting her hair. Concerned, Kate leaned over her, "... you OK, Mol?"

Molly's words were hesitant as she struggled to voice her thoughts, "Today at chapel, I really wanted to understand the speaker. I felt almost like God was right there talking to me, like there was something I was supposed to do—or respond to somehow. Kate, you know me, you know I've never said anything like this before. This is strange."

Kate spoke slowly, her voice serious, her words measured. "Molly, if God's speaking to you, it's wise to listen and act on what He shows you. But, don't do anything under pressure or because of some emotional high. This will impact your entire life."

Kate opened a page in her Bible and showed it to Molly. "In John, it says, '… to all who received Him, to those who believed in His name, He gave the right to become children of God–children born not of natural descent, nor of human decision or a husband's will, but born of God.'" She looked at Molly, her eyes kind. "You can become God's child at any time, by simply asking Him to forgive your sins and come into your life—and He will come in—and stay, forever."

Molly listened, pondering each of Kate's words. She bristled at one—"sins"—so violently that she almost missed hearing Kate's explanation.

"Sin isn't just what we 'do'— it's our attitudes, too. Our independence, doing things 'our' way." She laughed. "Like me, you know how stubborn I am!"

Molly's jaw tightened.

Kate waited

Finally, Molly asked, "How can you be so sure? I mean, isn't this what you grew up with? Don't you ever wonder if other religions are equally valid?

"Other religious leaders are still dead. Jesus is alive, He …"

Molly interrupted, "I think that should do it—I'd better get some sleep." But she lay awake, her anxious heart contradicting her words. *It seems so easy for Kate, but I'm just not sure I can believe it.*

* * *

The next day after classes, Molly rushed into a practice room. She put her flute together, savoring the precision of each piece and the exactitude of how they fit together, relishing the solitude of the small chamber. But even there she found no refuge from her thoughts. Trying to silence her mind, she played from her heart, a story so sad that she could hardly bear to hear it. The notes kept coming, each one a part of her, plaintive, begging her to listen. She set the flute down, admitting, *I have to consider more than I've seen.* She hesitated, first looking around the room, then counting ceiling tiles. *Ten, fifteen, twenty.* She stopped counting, and then studied the floor, engrossed in crumbs from someone's doughnut, then in an empty soda can, toppled on its side.

Kate's words reverberated in Molly's mind, "All you need to do is receive Him—and the gift of eternal life He is freely offering you." It sounded impossibly simple. She picked up her flute again, studying its design, marveling that a simple wind instrument could yield such complex music. *But an orchestra can't create music unless each member follows the conductor.* Suddenly she knew the source of her confusion. *I've ignored God all my life.*

Like the cacophony of a symphony tuning, her mind played conflicting notes. Emotion and intellect wove together, discordant and unrelenting. Then slowly—very slowly—they merged into a harmony that stilled and focused her heart. Setting her flute aside, Molly dropped to her knees, her heart forcing a gesture that her mind didn't fully understand. She knelt on the dusty floor, in awe, finally comprehending that the love encircling her was from God Himself. For the first time, she could hear the Father singing. To her. "He sent Jesus for me—He loves me!" She listened, trembling for joy as her heart wakened to the wooing. As His Spirit blanketed her with peace, she ran into God's open arms. The daughter was finally home.

Chapter Twenty-three

⋟⋞

The phone rang early Tuesday morning. Kate grabbed it so it wouldn't awaken her roommate. She succeeded; Molly slept peacefully as Kate talked softly with her brother.

When he began teasing her about living in California while he suffered in "the frozen hinterland," her volume increased. "You could always move back here, you know!"

"Oh, yeah, just drop out of school and lose all my credits. No, send me some seaweed or something so I can remember what it's like not to feel frozen all the time," he bantered.

Listening to him brag about his upcoming ski trip, she began to laugh. "Make up your mind—first you say you're freezing, then you want to torture me into coming there, too."

"Don't you wish you could?" he asked, knowing how much she liked to ski.

"Definitely—however, I don't think my professors would understand," she said, pausing while he changed the subject. "Sorry, Peter. She's still asleep."

"No, I'm not. I'll talk," Molly said, bumping her head on the top bunk in her hurry to reach the phone. "Hi, Peter."

"Hey, Molly—how's it going?"

"OK. I'll tell you more in a couple of minutes—after I wake up. What were you telling Kate that was so funny?"

"I've been trying to convince her to come to Colorado—the skiing is fantastic right now—perfect powder with a three-foot base. No patches of grass anywhere—nothing but ideal conditions. You should see it. You could go with me on a black run again—my current favorite is only *slightly* more difficult than the last one we tried," he laughed, reminding her about the previous Christmas—and skiing with his family. When he finally convinced her to "quit going down those baby blue runs and try just one really easy black slope," she vowed it would never happen again.

"You already know my answer to that, Peter. For some reason, I didn't enjoy wondering if I were about to careen over the mountainside into oblivion. I am quite content to stay on the rational person's blue—or green—slopes from now on." Her eyes danced as she joked, "Hey, don't you miss the beach, the waves, the warmth?"

"OK, OK. Blue it is." He started to tease her again and stopped when he sensed she had something more serious to tell him. "Sorry, Mol, I didn't mean to joke around—well, yeah, I did."

She laughed.

He continued, "No, really, what were you going to say? You said you wanted to tell me something."

"I ... I asked Christ to come into my heart last week," Molly said, shocked that with her words came atypical tears.

Kate could hear her brother's cheer from across the room.

Molly was surprised to hear him say, "Mol, this is the best news I've heard in years! I—I mean, our family ... has been praying ... for a long time!"

Molly was unable to respond.

Kate grabbed the phone from her. "Don't worry, Peter. She has that little flickering smile on her face that means she's really, really happy. I guess I'm going to have to talk for both of us now."

He groaned. "Not that. Anything but that. You already talk enough for two—or three people. Give the phone back to Molly."

Kate couldn't hear what Peter said to Molly, but she noticed her smile change from a flicker to a beam. After what seemed like a long time, she tapped her arm and whispered, "We're going to be late for class, Mol. Come on."

Reluctant, Molly hung up, dressing in record time, pulling her hair into a ponytail and grabbing everything she needed for the day. Mornings more often than not were a blur, so she'd begun setting everything out the night before. Today, she was glad she had.

"I miss my family so much—especially Peter," Kate said, rushing with her out the door. "I wish I were still a little kid living at home like it used to be—but then I'd miss you." She dabbed her moist eyes, then remembered to ask, "How's your family doing, Molly? You haven't mentioned them lately."

"The same," she replied, feeling an old sadness.

"Oh." Kate saw the light fade from Molly's eyes. She was fairly certain Molly hadn't talked with her family more than once or twice all semester. "Have you told them about becoming a Christian?"

"Not yet. I'm not sure ... how to tell them ... or what they'll say," she said, brushing a tear from her cheek.

Kate hugged her. "I'm praying. God cares about them, and He knows how you feel, too. He'll show you how and when."

"Thanks, Kate," Molly said, meaning it. "I still have a lot to learn. Thanks for reminding me that He ... cares." As Kate turned toward her class, Molly waved, lost in thought, her mind drifting back to the conversation with Peter. She was amazed at the changes in her life. *It's going to be a good day,* she assured herself.

It was. Everywhere she went, people were warm, friendly, caring. She smiled more than she had in her life—and noticed almost everyone smiling back. For the first time, she understood what her professors meant when they talked about a relationship with God or when they mentioned His love. She felt like she needed to pinch herself. *He loves me,* she exulted.

* * *

Everything is different now. She was glad she had told Kate about her prayer in the practice room, and even more happy that she'd been able to tell Peter.

With Kate, though, she said more. She had to tell her, too, how sorry she was for all the times she'd been rude, for all the times she wouldn't listen.

Kate didn't hold grudges. "How could I be upset when you've just made the most important decision of your life? You're different ... like a caterpillar—once it crawled in the dust, later it's a butterfly soaring in the heavens.'"

"Are you saying I'm a worm?" Molly teased her.

"Nope, but you sure are a new creation!" She spun around the room, singing, "You're a brand-new Christian!"

"I feel like a lot of things have to change ... like there's a lot of old stuff in me still."

"Give yourself time to grow."

"What do you mean, grow? Molly wondered. "I'm already grown up."

"There are different kinds of growing—I'm talking about spiritual growth," Kate smiled. "Just like babies change and mature—so should healthy Christians."

"I don't get it."

"One area where I *hope* I'm growing is that I'm starting to trust God instead of worrying about everything and everyone all the time." Her face crinkled with the effort of trying to describe the inner battle she faced. "I'm learning what God means when He said He's the vine, we're the branches. The times I fall flat on my face are when I try to do life—and overcome my weaknesses—in my own pathetic strength instead of remembering 'I can do all things through Christ who strengthens me.'"

"Is this as hard as it sounds?"

"Harder. The Christian life isn't just difficult; it's impossible. That's why it has to be lived in God's strength, not ours."

* * *

Second semester evaporated in a seemingly endless study session for Molly—leaving rumpled bed sheets as the only sign that Kate still had a roommate. Her friend could barely contain her loneliness. Although she thrived in an ever-widening circle of friends, she always felt a certain sense of relief around Molly, the one person who didn't look to her to play social director. Grounded as it was in a long history together, their friendship brought calm and comfort to her life. She needed Molly—something she knew her friend had never understood.

Wednesday mornings—when they both had discussion groups across campus—gave them a rare mid-week opportunity to connect. Kate cherished that time, a chance to have her friend all to herself. Molly loathed early mornings and started each Wednesday by blasting the teaching assistant who scheduled such "absolutely ridiculous 7:30 AM meetings." Yet even she looked forward to those mornings—although she never admitted it—and the ritual they had created: Giant to-go coffees and glazed doughnuts from the dining hall, topped off by thirty minutes to catch up.

"No cream," she muttered, lifting the lid to her Styrofoam cup as they set off in the early-morning fog. "They forgot the cream."

Kate licked sugar from the corners of her mouth, having devoured her doughnut in record time. "Finishing yours?" she asked.

Molly pulled the paper sack possessively closer. Before she could deliver the sarcastic answer that Kate—a vulture when it came to sweets—had come to expect, her friend interrupted.

"Oh, I almost forgot to tell you!" she said, abruptly stopping in her tracks and looking at Molly with wide eyes.

"Who died?" Molly deadpanned.

Kate ignored her. "Uncle Dan and Aunt Zoë want to have us over for dinner Friday. Can you?"

Dr. Johnson, the head of the psychology department at Pacific Harbor University, was one of the most easy-going people Molly had ever met. His wife, too, was effortless company, although the tall, elegant woman, a former art-director for Architecture Today, was a woman of few words and, to Molly, much mystery.

"I'm crazed this week," she said, mentally scanning her schedule. "As long as they don't mind if I'm comatose."

"They were thinking six-ish. Does that work for you?"

"Probably. I may be late."

"Doing what?" Kate asked with mock exasperation. Molly always hedged when it came to social commitments.

"Memorizing 'K' numbers," she shot back, knowing Kate hadn't the slightest idea what she meant.

"Are you making this up so you don't have to go with me?"

Molly saw Kate's dazed look and explained, "They're classification numbers—to identify Mozart's compositions.

And I want to come—I promise to *try* to be on time."

Laughing, the two friends gave each other a quick hug and headed to separate classes.

* * *

From study group to the music library, Molly's morning was packed. Still focused on getting ready for her music exam, she was not in the mood for small talk as she dashed across campus for an appointment to work on her next major hurdle—an anthropology project.

"Hey, Molly." It was someone she didn't want to see— Trevor, a guy from class who always turned up without warning—and when she had the least amount of patience for him. He smiled at her like an eager puppy, his dark brown hair in a just-rolled-out-of-bed mess, his flannel shirt untucked. As usual, he asked her out. "How about dinner tonight?"

Molly cringed. With a forced smile, she told him, "Sorry, Trevor, I have plans."

He looked disappointed. "How about tomorrow?" His eyes lit up in anticipation.

"I'm pretty overloaded right now," she said.

"That's what you said last week, Molly. I'm beginning to think you're avoiding me."

"Really?" she said cynically, turning abruptly into Warner Hall, breathing a sigh of relief when he continued in another direction.

Her friend Sally met her at their professor's door, as planned. The two were partners on a research project and were meeting to divvy up responsibilities before the weekend. They quickly walked to the coffee bar in the student activity building. Sally ordered an orange-mint-chocolate iced mocha double espresso; Molly, her usual cappuccino.

"Why don't you step out a little?" chided Sally.

"Because I like this," Molly smiled, sitting down on an overstuffed sofa. "How can you stand iced coffee when it's freezing out?" After three years, Molly was fully acclimated to California. The damp spring weather chilled her to the bone.

Sally beamed from the plaid chair next to her. "I'm warm on the inside."

"What's going on?"

"Corin asked me to marry him last night!" Sally exclaimed, pulling a sparkling hand out of the pocket of her jacket, where she had kept it hidden.

"I'm happy for you," Molly said, forcing herself to smile—and shocked by the emotions roiling inside of her, seemingly out of nowhere.

Sally didn't notice and gushed on, giving the blow-by-blow of the proposal.

"Hold that thought," Molly said, standing up and feeling suddenly dizzy. "I'll be right back."

She braced herself against the stall door in the bathroom, trying to manufacture some feelings of happiness for her friend. Her eyes landed on graffiti scrawled on the wall. Inexplicably, she broke down.

Sally knocked on the door. "You OK in there?"

"I … I must have the flu or something."

"Can I help?"

Molly stepped out. "I'd better go to my room and lie down."

"Do you need me to go with you?"

"I'll be fine."

* * *

Molly didn't notice sunlight breaking through the cloudy sky. Oblivious to her surroundings, she sprinted toward her dorm, her emotions pelting her first with one accusation, then another, clamping her mind in a vice of darkness. *I'm so rude*, she thought. *Why couldn't I enjoy Sally's news? What's wrong with me?* Without realizing it, she scolded herself aloud. "Get it together, woman," she demanded.

"Get what together?" interrupted a voice at her side. It was Trevor.

She looked away and took off running, not caring where she was going as long as she found an escape.

Trevor's concerned voice disappeared into the air behind her. "What's wrong? Can I help?"

Compelled by a crippling urge to hide, she stumbled to her room—not even sure how she got there—locked the door, and collapsed on her bed, winded. In an instant she was back on her feet, obsessively checking the lock again and again and again as a thin thread of connection spun out from her mind. Suddenly she understood the panic that had driven her to her room and the nausea that was expanding in her stomach. In countless ways, Trevor mirrored Jeremy. His tousled hair, his persistent pursuit, and his uncanny ability to catch her off guard were an eerie prelude to the hideous word on the bathroom wall, that repulsive slang that was Jeremy's favorite pet name for her.

Molly lost all awareness of time and space as nightmarish images tumbled from the storage vault of her mind, surging out of control, coming at her like boulders hurtling through a river at flood stage. Churning out of all restraints, each thought bombarded her with more crushing weight than the one before it. Powerless to stop their onslaught, she curled into a ball on the floor.

The phone rang, again and again, at last jarring her to action. She stood, then staggered across the room.

"Hello, Uncle Dan here," she heard Dr. Johnson's warm voice calling from another world.

Molly couldn't speak.

"This is Daniel Johnson," he said, thinking he'd misdialed. "I'm trying to reach my niece, Kate Johnson."

"This is Molly," she said, her voice choking.

"Oh, I'm sorry. I didn't recognize you. Aren't you feeling well?" he asked, concerned.

"Yes, er, no— not really," she said, beginning to sob.

"Can I help?"

Afraid to return to the terrifying place she'd been, she forced herself to talk, clinging to the phone like a drowning victim gripping a lifeline. "Dr. Johnson, something is happening to me. I keep remembering horrible things."

"I'm listening."

"My brother," she moaned. "He came to my room. He did things—he made me do things. I forgot them until now. I feel like I'm going crazy," she whispered, shocked by the admission of her deepest fear.

Each of his words was framed in kindness. "Molly, I'm very, very sorry. Would you like me to help you sort through what you're experiencing? A good deal of my training has been in counseling people during times like this."

"Can you?" she asked, still rocking back and forth on the floor.

"It sounds like you're having what's known as a flashback, where thoughts you've pushed down for years force their way out. You can't stop them, right?"

"Yeah, I can't slow them down, either." Twisting her hair, she described how the thoughts surfaced. "There's this guy on campus. He's in one of my classes, and he keeps asking me out, and I give him lame excuses. He's not the problem, it's just that—I don't know how to say this, but— today I realized that he reminds me of my brother, Jeremy."

"How old is your brother?"

"Twenty-nine—nearly eight years older than me." Stopping often, she described the abuse she remembered. They continued talking for over an hour, until Molly's voice cracked with the strain of the remembering.

"Do you want to take a break and rest now?"

She murmured a reply, hoping he understood.

"Let's set an appointment to continue sorting through this. I'm here for you. And remember that God is with you all the time; He is your Healer."

The dial tone hummed as she cradled the phone in her hand.

* * *

Kate had an international students' dinner that night. As part of the planning committee, she stayed, as usual, until everyone had left. Molly pretended to be asleep when she heard her roommate's late night return. The next morning, her eyes were still red; her voice was hollow. She knew she couldn't hide the truth from Kate, nor did she want to; although she did not feel ready to relive her nightmare, she was even more reluctant to experience it alone. One concerned look from Kate was all it took for the story to tumble out.

Kate wept. "I didn't know; oh, I'm so sorry."

They continued talking for hours, until Molly noticed the clock. "We've both missed our first two classes. I'm sorry."

"Don't be. I wouldn't have gotten anything out of it, anyway. I'd be too worried about you."

"I hate laying all this on you."

The phone rang, interrupting them. It was Zoë, calling to see if they were still coming for dinner Friday.

"Does she know?" Molly whispered.

"No way," Kate mouthed the words. "My uncle wouldn't tell her unless you told him to." "OK. I'll go. I'm just not ready to talk about it yet."

* * *

Molly looked pale and gaunt Friday, but she went with Kate to her aunt and uncle's home, unwilling to break their dinner commitment.

Neither she nor Kate felt much like eating.

When everyone refused dessert, Molly said, "I shouldn't have come. I'm sorry. I feel like I've ruined dinner for everyone."

Zoë hugged her, "Honey, we care about you, that's all. Is there anything we can do?"

Looking at Molly, her husband cut in. "I'm not sure Molly is ready to talk."

"I'm not," she whispered, "but you can tell her for me. I told Kate. I just don't want anyone else to know but you three."

"Shall I tell her now?" he asked.

"We could watch a DVD while you tell her," Kate volunteered, knowing Molly didn't want to hear it again.

"Molly?" he asked.

"Sure," she nodded, following Kate to the den, fearful of what Zoë would think of her.

Dan and Zoë cleared the table together, as they often did, then moved to the kitchen to load the dishwasher and talk.

It wasn't long before they called the girls. "Want dessert now?" Zoë asked. "We could eat it in the den." Neither Molly nor Kate had been paying attention to the movie. They bolted to the kitchen, hungry more for encouragement than food. The Bavarian apple torte looked wonderful; each of them carried a plate of that and a steaming cup of coffee. As her Uncle Dan sat in his favorite leather chair, Kate took a seat next to him, on the rocking chair where she played as a child. Molly hesitated, then eased into the yellow chintz sofa beside Zoë. They began eating dessert in silence, each one wondering what to say, each one waiting for the time to be right.

Molly broke the silence. "I appreciate you all—more than I can say." She stifled a sob, and then forced herself to continue. "I've never talked about anything ... like this ... before, but I know—from what you said yesterday, Dr. Johnson—that I can't hide from it any longer." She looked around the room, her eyes stopping first on Kate, then Zoë and Dan.

Kate began to cry. "Oh, Mol, I'm so sorry—I wish I could have helped you, I wish I could have stopped all this from happening ... ."

Her uncle explained, "You're here for Molly now, Kate—and in some ways, the pain is even worse than it was then. As repressed memories continue to surface, they'll be frightening. The flashbacks can continue to occur unexpectedly, triggered by a current event or by something inexplicable, and Molly will need you to keep caring."

The evening became a blur of trying to understand.

"God allowed you to sublimate childhood events so you wouldn't have to face painful memories before you were ready."

Molly grimaced. She pushed the fringe of their Oriental rug with her foot, first one way, then another.

Zoë looked at Molly for permission, then reached an arm around her. "God was there, Molly. He cares. He didn't want this to happen."

The silence in the room was deafening.

"Molly?" Dan asked, his voice compassionate. "It hurts—I know it hurts. But remembering can become a good thing, because it can help you move away from what was to hope and healing. We're here to help you, and—more importantly—God is with you constantly. He will help you get beyond this."

* * *

In the following months, the discussion continued, sometimes between Dr. Johnson and Molly in his office, sometimes with Kate in their dorm room late at night, and other times, with Zoë.

There were days when Molly wished she could repress her memories all over again. "I don't want to feel anymore," she told Dr. Johnson. "I don't want to tell you anything else that happened, either; I just want to move on."

"What would happen if you had a boil and just put a band-aid over it to hide it?"

"It would still be there, under the band-aid."

"And it could also spread. I had a staph infection on my arm when I was in jr. high, and I had to go to the doctor and have a needle inserted to drain it. Then, I had to have a shot of penicillin and oral antibiotics. The next time I went to the doctor, he pressed on my arm—until the pain was so bad that I cried—and that didn't faze him. He told me the infection could spread throughout my body if he didn't get rid of it."

"So you're saying my past is going to impact my future if I don't deal with it."

"Exactly. You're going to make your present and future decisions based on the misconceptions of your past unless they're exposed to the truth."

"There's no easy way out," she sighed.

"God gives you this promise, among many others: 'I can do all things through Christ who strengthens me.'"

* * *

It was easy to forget that promise. Sometimes Molly found herself going back to old habits, numbing her pain with a flurry of activities and relentless studying accompanied by sleepless nights.

When a professor asked her to stay after class, she couldn't imagine why.

"Molly, is something going on ... ?" he asked.

"Wasn't my paper all right?" she interrupted, nervous.

"No, it's not that. Your work is fine. But you're falling asleep in class. Are you well?"

Mumbling an answer, Molly hurried out. She felt violated by his sympathy.

When Zoë called her that afternoon, she tried to refuse her invitation to coffee.

"Please come, Molly. I miss you," Zoë said, her words candid, her tone almost pleading.

Sipping coffee with her the next day, Molly was shocked to discover herself describing her strange reaction to her professor's sincere compassion. "I feel like I can't trust anyone—especially myself. My responses are so unpredictable. What is happening to me?"

For two hours, Zoë listened, saying little. Finally, she responded. "There's one solution," she said, gently brushing back a wisp of hair on Molly's forehead. "I think you already know it."

"Set your mind on things above, not on things on earth?" Ever since her experience in the practice room, Molly had immersed herself in reading the Bible, amazed to see how the words sprang to life before her—and seemed to take root in her heart.

"Exactly," encouraged Zoë. "Anything you let yourself dwell on will eventually lead your emotions, your choices, your actions."

Molly groaned. "This is hard work."

"Give it time. You're going to be fine."

Molly's eyes filled with tears. "I'm not so sure."

"Are you still meeting with Dan?"

Nodding, Molly relaxed, realizing that she wasn't an object of discussion in their home.

"You're my friend, Molly," Zoë continued. "Dan and I both care about what happens to you."

"But I feel like I'm a burden. I'm always bothering you with some new problem."

"The Bible says we're to 'bear one another's burdens'—and you don't bother us, Molly," she added quickly, seeing Molly pull back. "We want you to come see us—anytime."

"You two seem like the perfect couple," Molly said, the edge in her voice revealing her discouragement. "I go to Dr. Johnson's office and get homework, and then I come here to see a home that works."

"Don't be under any false illusions. Our home 'works,' as you put it, because of the love of God, not because we're perfect people. We trust in God, and He leads us; He gives us the strength we need for each day's challenges. It's as simple as that. He's leading you, too."

"So the only way to go through it is to go through it," Molly sighed.

"Something like that," Zoë said, hugging her again.

* * *

Exhausted by the hard work of excavating her past, Molly almost cancelled her next session with Dr. Johnson. Her resilience had always pulled her through tough times, but somehow now her old coping mechanism was failing. She felt broken and dependent, two deeply uncomfortable sensations that panicked her at times, leaving her feeling utterly naked, her soul on display to the world.

"I feel like I drag everybody down," she said reluctantly, sitting on the familiar couch the next week, wearily dreading yet another hour of introspection.

Dr. Johnson smiled gently and listened.

She looked away, hugging her knees and gazing at a lemon tree outside the window. "I feel so stupid," she said.

"Cognitive distortion," he interjected, reminding her.

They had spent many hours together talking through

the condemning thoughts that replayed like a critical tape in Molly's head, denouncing her every turn. At first, Molly had to work hard to spot them; the self-defeating voice in her mind had been with her as long as she could remember and she trusted it as truth. Questioning her automatic thinking meant doubting her take on reality—which was exactly what Dr. Johnson repeatedly told her she needed to do. Not only had he taught her how to identify wrong thought patterns; he had taught her to chart them and consciously replace them with truth. "I still feel stupid," said Molly.

Hearing her denigrate herself, he pointed to the campus newspaper story: "Girl from Windy City Suburb Hits Harbor Like a Storm." It detailed Molly's GPA, her achievements in music, her stellar performance at the university. "Long ago, we established that your concern regarding 'stupidity' is simply not true," he said, his tone matter-of-fact, once more training her to refute the lies in her thinking. "What *is* your worth based on?"

"God's opinion of me, not my own, not other people's; not what I do, but who I am." She knew the words; they hadn't yet reached her heart.

"Why do you think you're struggling with this all over again?"

Molly didn't know where to start. She concentrated, remembering, still at a loss to describe why Dr. Knapp's directive upset her so.

* * *

"We need to set the date for your senior recital," Dr. Knapp had told her months ago, launching Molly into a frenzy of learning new techniques, memorizing music, and making all the necessary preparations to ensure success. She began to carry her flute with her wherever she went, ducking into empty rooms to practice whenever she could snatch a spare minute. Although she hadn't noticed, her body was beginning to rebel.

Warming up before her last lesson, she had winced, shifting position to ease the pain searing her arms, neck, shoulders and legs.

"How long has that been going on?" her teacher asked.

Molly hadn't heard Dr. Knapp arrive. "Oh, I'm fine," she said, believing it.

Her professor wasn't deterred. "You won't be able to play at all if you continue pushing your body beyond its limits, Molly. You're still practicing three to four hours a day?"

Molly nodded; at least she could admit that much.

Dr. Knapp continued, "Are you doing the stretches I gave you?"

Molly shook her head, "No."

"Lift up your flute for me," Dr. Knapp ordered—kindness in her eyes, firmness in her voice. "There," she said, touching first Molly's shoulders, then her neck. "Feel that?"

Molly felt surprised, aware of the throbbing for the first time.

Dr. Knapp dug through her purse. "Take this," she said, holding up a business card. "I want you to make an appointment this week with my massage therapist; he knows the specific needs of musicians. You need treatments at least twice a month—more often if possible—until after your recital."

* * *

She reached into her backpack and handed Dr. Johnson the card. "This is why I feel stupid," she said. "My flute teacher wants me to get massages—and I'm terrified. I can't tell her why."

Dan read the name on the card and brightened. "This could be a good thing," he said. "I've sent clients to him before. If you'll give me permission, I'll give him a call first."

"And explain that I'm insane and might strangle him if he comes near me?" Molly said, laughing miserably.

"This is a safe way to learn the difference between good and bad touches, Molly," said Dr. Johnson. "Trust me on this one?"

A slight nod indicated her assent as she lost herself in the fringe of the sofa pillow, pulling it first one way, then the other. "I feel like I go backwards more than I go forward," she said at last.

"That won't last forever, Molly. God promises to finish the healing He started."

Molly threw the pillow down, jamming it into a corner. "But why does it take so long?"

"Your wounds have been years in the making," he answered. "They won't disappear overnight. Make your first massage appointment and read Psalm 69. Then pray it back to God."

* * *

Her nightmares unaccountably returned, with unnerving intensity. The first terrifying dream invaded Molly's sleep when Kate was out, studying late at the campus library.

It was almost one o'clock when she awakened, screaming, at the click of the door closing behind her roommate.

"It's Kate, Mol. You're OK. Everything's OK."

Molly sat up in bed, wrenched alert. "I saw your shadow, and I thought you were Jeremy." Curling into a fetal position, she cried, "I'm so scared. It feels like it's all happening again. Oh, Kate, what can I do? I'm afraid to go back to sleep."

Kate pulled a chair next to her bed and sat beside her, praying, then reading aloud until Molly's breathing relaxed into peaceful sleep.

* * *

The next morning, Kate went to her uncle's office on campus with questions of her own. Pacing back and forth, waving her arms, she described the sleepless night. "Uncle Dan, I didn't know what to do last night, but I prayed. I read to Molly from Isaiah— 'When you pass through the waters, I will be with you; and when you pass through the rivers, they will not sweep over you ... For I am the LORD your God, the Holy One of Israel, you Savior.' After that, I read Psalms until she finally fell asleep." She sat down, fidgeting still. "Was that the right thing to do?" she asked, her eyes mirroring her distress.

"Kate, don't worry!" He walked to her chair. Melting into her uncle's arms, she began to cry. "We have a phone right by our bed, Kate," he said, handing her a tissue. "You can call anytime. But, don't worry, you did the right thing last night. Molly will be fine in time. But keep me posted on what you notice. During times like this, people sometimes get so distraught that they need medication or other special care."

"Can't you just give her something now, to help her?"

"I could."

"But ... ?"

"Drugs aren't necessarily the best solution. It's essential to deal with the root of the problem so it doesn't keep resurfacing. The pain can actually be her ally."

"Oh." Kate stared out the window. "If only Molly had a family to help her."

"She does—us." He looked at her, waiting for her to look back. "One more thing, Kate. I'm really proud of you," he smiled. "You remembered to do what some professional counselors forget."

"What's that?"

"You pointed Molly to God. The best thing we can do for Molly is consistently teach her how to trust God."

Her uncle usually saved his most important point for last, so she sat there, paying attention, not wanting to miss it.

"Years ago, when I finished my PhD and was finally a 'psychologist'— I thought I knew everything." He glanced at his diploma, on the wall behind him. "Now, I'm amazed at how little I really know. I look to God for guidance every day, with every person who walks through that door."

"So," she said, pretending to have an epiphany, "are you telling me man isn't a product of blind evolutionary forces after all?"

"You're definitely a Johnson, aren't you? Just when I think I'm imparting some deep truth and you're hanging on every word, you sound just like my brother." He laughed, then quickly grew serious. "I wouldn't be here unless I believed in a Creator Who cares. Otherwise, I, too, would despair at all the heartache I see."

Her face solemn, she said, "Actually, I was hanging on every word. But I don't want you to get a big head," she teased again.

* * *

Molly was practicing Varèse's *Density 21.5* when Kate walked into their room. Unaware of her roommate's entrance, she continued, playing first at the low edge of the flute's register, moving rapidly higher and higher until she approached the upper end of the flute's range, hitting the same piercing note over and over.

Covering her ears, Kate screamed in mock agony. "Deliver me!"

Molly wasn't amused. "For your information, this piece represents my current life—a never-ending series of highs and lows. Excruciating, isn't it?"

"Let's hear my life in music," Kate laughed.

Without hesitation, Molly played several sprightly bars from a laundry commercial.

Kate interrupted, genuinely startled. "Really?"

"You have no problems," said Molly. "You have it together, perfect family, plenty of friends."

"I have problems."

"Name one."

"That's easy: I'm having an identity crisis! Last week, I took this test online to identify my temperament traits and help me find the perfect job." She groaned. "Now I don't know how I can even begin to write a six-word objective for my resumé to get ready for the job fair next month. I can't begin to tell the job market what I want when I'm totally confused myself!"

"Slow down. What do you mean?"

" I've always thought I was an extrovert, but the test said I'm not—it said I'm really an introvert who is passionate about life and that I only *seem* outgoing! Then I took a personality analysis in this magazine, and it said I give mixed messages! I'm a total freak!"

"Don't let your uncle hear you say that," Molly interjected.

"You're not taking me seriously."

"Trust me, Kate. You don't need therapy for this one. Frozen yogurt's your answer." Molly had already put on her shoes and was holding the door open. "My treat."

* * *

Classes were a never-ending chain of studying, homework, and tests. Molly was surprised when she actually began to look forward to the work in Bible class, even though she still struggled with her lack of knowledge. "I don't know anything about missionaries, Kate," she said, puzzling over their latest assignment. "I don't even know what a 'missionary' is!"

"A person who is sent somewhere to tell people about God's love," she called across their room, wholly immersed in writing her own paper. "Can you imagine starting an orphanage like George Mueller did, never telling people you didn't have money to buy food?"

Molly didn't respond.

"And he sat all the kids down to breakfast and thanked God for the food—except they didn't have any," Kate continued. "Then, a guy shows up at the door and says his milk cart overturned, 'You want some milk? I can't sell it now that the cart spilled the rest of it.' The same morning, a baker brought them bread. They had what they needed, without asking anyone but God! I need to trust God like that," she mused.

Still staring at the assignment, Molly demanded, "How am I going to find a missionary to write about?"

"Look outside our dorm; it's named after one," said Kate, staring at her computer screen.

Molly grabbed her shoes and ran out the door, happy for an excuse to procrastinate.

She had passed the life-sized statue every time she walked in and out of their building but had never taken time to look at it. The engraved placard next to the sculpture said, "Miss Amy Carmichael, 1867-1951, pioneer missionary to India. She saved children from a fate worse than death." Underneath the heading was one of her poems. Molly stood there a long time, trying to understand it.

No wound, no scar?
Yet, as the Master shall the servant be,
And pierced the feet that follow Me;
But thine are whole: can he have followed far,
Who has no wound nor scar?

Returning to their room, she heard her roommate down the hall, "talking a break," as Kate described time off from studying. Molly, glad to have time to think, reached for the Bible Kate had given her for her birthday and turned to the passage Dr. Johnson asked her to consider.

Save me, O God, for the waters have come up to my neck. I sink in the miry depths, where there is no foothold. I have come into the deep waters; the floods engulf me. Rescue me from the mire, do not let me sink; ... deliver me from those who hate me, from the deep waters. Do not let the floodwaters engulf me or the depths swallow me up or the pit close its mouth over me. Answer me, O LORD, out of the goodness of your love; in your great mercy turn to me.

Overwhelmed, she knelt by her bed. "God, thank You for pulling me out of the flood and keeping me safe." Beginning to see her own rescue and what it cost, she hurried to the library, wanting to learn more about the woman whose understanding of wounds and scars compelled her to help hurting children.

In a rare reversal that night, it was she who talked while her roommate tried to sleep. "Kate, did you know Amy Carmichael went into Hindu temples and rescued little girls who were sold to be temple prostitutes? And when Amy was young, her mother told her God answered prayer, so she asked Him to give her blue eyes—like the rest of her family—and then was utterly disappointed to wake up and look in the mirror to see that they were still brown! Her mother taught her to wait, to discover God's purposes. In India, God used her brown eyes," she said. "She couldn't have gone where she did if they had been blue. God cares about every detail. If her brown eyes had a purpose, then everything about my life must, too. The bad can be used for good, somehow."

* * *

Molly's journey continued, filled with the predictable peaks and valleys. Her first massage appointment was a definite low. No words could describe the sheer terror it brought to her heart.

"Hi, my name is Bob Becker," the therapist told her. "Dan Johnson called me; I'll be extremely careful to respect your concerns."

Molly couldn't meet his eyes.

"I'm leaving the room now," he said. "Please take off whatever clothing is comfortable for you. Open the door a crack when you're ready." He set a sheet on the massage table. "You can cover up with this."

The door shut and Molly was alone. Ten minutes passed. Finally, she cracked open the door. Then she quickly hopped onto the table, fully clothed except for the shoes she had placed next to her purse.

"Shall we get started?" said the therapist, reentering the room. "Are you comfortable lying down, or would you like me to work on your neck and shoulders while you sit?" He spoke so gently that she had the courage, at last, to lie down. Every muscle tensed as his body leaned over her. She couldn't think; she didn't dare feel. But she stayed, only because both Dr. Johnson and Dr. Knapp had insisted.

* * *

Nightmares returned full force that night. It was near dawn before Kate successfully comforted Molly back to sleep. For several more hours, Kate herself lay awake, sifting through her own childhood memories of Molly, in search of clues that she had missed. She stayed in bed, pretending to sleep, until Molly left for classes the next morning. Then she let herself cry, her emotions running the gamut from fury to utter sorrow. Not knowing what else to do, she called her uncle's office, her voice agitated as she groped for words. "Uncle Dan, Molly remembered more last night—horrible things. Do you know about her birthday, the time her parents blamed her instead of her brother? They accused her of lying—not him! And they didn't try to help her!"

"That's fairly typical, unfortunately," he said, sighing. "Parents often pretend nothing is happening and blame the victim instead of the perpetrator."

"Why?" Kate yelled into the phone. "Didn't she suffer enough?"

Her uncle paused, struggling within himself. He hated having to explain the inexplicable. "Their response could be an escape mechanism—or it could be that one or both of her parents were once molestation victims or perpetrators themselves. We simply don't know."

Kate interrupted, "I'm furious at them." Whispering, she added, "And I'm mad at God for letting this happen."

"Be careful not to accuse God for people's mistakes, Kate. God cares far more about Molly than either of us could. He wept when Molly's brother hurt her and when her parents failed to protect her. Do you really think He is to blame?"

"It wouldn't be in His character, would it?" Kate said, calming down enough to think clearly. "He's all-loving, merciful, kind ... ."

"Exactly. Now, think back to Adam and Eve. They had everything–a perfect environment, all of their needs met, and what did they do?"

"They rebelled against God and chose to do the only thing they weren't supposed to do."

"Right. Do you think God wanted Adam and Eve to reject Him and all that He'd given them?"

"No. I get it—it was their idea, not God's." She sobbed, thinking of Molly's family. "But where was God when Molly suffered?"

"He was with her, wanting to show her His love."

Kate wept, her face in her hands.

Dr. Johnson's eyes filled with tears, too, thinking of Molly—and of all the men and women who came to him with similar stories. It wasn't the first time he lamented the enormity of incest's wounds—more insidious than a massive toxic waste dump, leeching hidden poison into every walk of life. Cradling the phone, he prayed aloud with Kate, "Oh, Lord, we grieve for Molly—and for each person suffering from incestual abuse. Please use us to bring hope and healing. Comfort and encourage Kate as she helps her friend ... ."

"God, please forgive me for not helping her," Kate interjected with a sob.

As soon as her uncle finished praying, he asked, "You feel like you haven't helped?"

"I feel like it's partially my fault that she was abused."

"Why, Kate?" he probed, gently.

"I've known her since kindergarten–her brother must have been hurting her when I first met her. And I didn't do anything! I should have helped her! All the times we were together, I should have known. I should have helped her—I should have known," she repeated, nervously entwining her feet in her desk chair.

"It would have been impossible for you, a child her age, to see what was happening. Child molesters are very careful not to get caught. Kate, it wasn't your fault."

"But something else is," Kate sighed. "I promised her I wouldn't tell anyone what happened. Even though I didn't really tell, one of the girls on our dorm floor figured it out. I feel like I've betrayed Molly."

"What happened?" he asked, waving his secretary away, giving her the look that said he'd be late for his next appointment.

"A girl on our floor asked me why Molly has been sad lately. I said she was working through some things, and Heather asked me if it were incest. Somehow the look on my face gave it all away, even though I didn't really admit it. Heather told me about her cousin who went to a counselor who said she needed to go back and remember her childhood—she helped her discover that all her problems were because she was an incest victim. Then she broke off communication with her entire family for years, until somehow she realized it was a lie, and she knew she wasn't an incest victim after all. In the meantime, it nearly destroyed their entire family."

"You're wondering about Molly's memories?"

"Well, yes—but I think hers are real."

"It's a legitimate concern. But there's a significant difference between Molly and the woman you mentioned." He sighed, wishing there were an easy explanation. As he looked across his desk, he unconsciously remembered faces of those who had sat there with him; their contorted anguish was mirrored in his expression as he spoke. "Molly's memories surfaced on their own. No one led her to conclusions. And those memories have been confirmed in various ways. What's important now is she's on the road to healing. We can help her on that road by praying for her and for her family to realize God's love and forgiveness. You and I need to forgive Molly's family, too, Kate. Choosing not to forgive is like drinking poison and hoping your enemy will die," he said gently. "Remember that God's love transforms people from the inside out. He wants to lift Molly away from those horrible circumstances into His own goodness and joy."

"Oh, Uncle Dan, it's so easy to forget."

* * *

That weekend, Molly went with Kate to visit her family, who lived two hours away. It was a bittersweet visit. On the one hand, she felt happy to be with people she loved. But the contrast between what she saw there and any vision she held for her own future was stark and painful. The conflict in her soul awakened her early on Sunday morning and drew her out on the patio to pray. Through an open window, she heard muted sounds of the wakening family. It reminded her of another time she'd stayed with them, when Grace was only three. In the middle of that night, Grace had cried, "Daddy, Daddy, where are you?" He responded with, "I'm right here, my darling, right here. I won't leave you. You've had another bad dream, haven't you?" The memory filled Molly with hope. *That's how God cares for me. He hears me; He knows my needs. I have a Father who will never leave.*

Sitting with the Johnsons at church later that morning, she bowed her head. "Our Father who art in Heaven," they prayed together. Gazing around the sanctuary, for the first time she understood: they were united in a family that would last forever.

* * *

Another friendship—with Dr. Johnson's wife, Zoë—was also putting flesh and blood on her experience of God's love and faithfulness. They continually discovered that, despite their age differences, they had a lot in common.

Whether they were talking over coffee, playing a flute and piano duet, or walking along the beach, conversation flourished. Molly began to grasp the depth of God's acceptance.

It was on one glorious day at Laguna Beach that she glimpsed His forgiveness, too.

Tired from climbing, the two women sat on a rock overlooking the ocean. "I can't tell you how much I appreciate you taking time to be with me," Zoë said, musing aloud as they stared at the crashing waves.

Molly was incredulous. "Me? I'm the one you're babysitting through this nightmare!"

"Maybe our friendship began that way," Zoë responded, giving Molly a playful shove. "But, that's not how it is now. I treasure time with you."

Fighting tears, Molly couldn't speak.

"Are you OK?"

"You wouldn't like me if you knew what I'm really like."

"Molly, there's nothing beyond God's love, and He tells us to love each other with the same love He has given us." She reached to give a hug, but Molly pulled back.

"You don't understand," she choked out the words. "I've done something beyond God's love."

Embracing Molly with her eyes, Zoë asked, "When did you have your abortion?"

Molly was shocked into silence.

"With the kind of abuse you've suffered, other behavior often follows." She paused, her voice gentle, "Molly, God loves you."

"I killed my own baby! How can God forgive that?"

"Because Jesus died for all sin—'all' includes past, present and future sins."

"But this was worse ... ."

"Psalm 103 promises us, 'As far as the East is from the West, so far has He removed our sins from us.' What do you think? Did God forgive all of your sins, or only part of them?"

She whispered, "All?"

Zoë smiled. "Yes!"

Her tenuous smile flickered, then grew.

"It's important that you know for sure that Jesus accomplished what He said He did. Otherwise, you'll always be wondering whether or not He loves you and whether or not you can trust Him. His death proves that He does love you. And His resurrection proves that His payment for sin was eternally enough. That should free you, Molly, to live as God's beloved daughter."

"But what do I do when I feel guilty for the same thing over and over again?"

"Thank God again for His forgiveness—you no longer carry the weight of your sin—Jesus did that on the Cross. It's right to grieve—you did lose your innocence and your child—but it's wrong to carry guilt."

"I'm lost," Molly said.

"Since Jesus willingly died to pay for sin, you don't have to live in the pain of guilt any longer. That means you're free to move gradually from denial and anger to acceptance."

"Acceptance? How can I be expected to *accept* what has happened?"

"Not in the sense of liking it, Molly, but in the sense of embracing the loss."

"I have no problem accepting that," Molly sighed. Her face began to relax as understanding dawned. "You're saying that guilt leaves you in pain, but grieving leads to healing."

"And eventually, you'll experience relief from the pain."

"What about—?" Molly choked, unable to continue.

Zoë addressed Molly's unspoken fear: That she'd never have a good marriage. "God is the great restorer, dear. I've experienced Him that way. He promises strength for each day—just take it a day at a time. And He says that when we're weak, then we're strong." She tossed a rock into the water. "As long as we try to do things ourselves, we won't understand His power. The sweetest times are when we really can't 'bear' something and we grasp God's supernatural strength to overcome. You're going to be just fine, Molly," she smiled, gently clasping her arm.

They began to climb again, and Molly let the soft ocean breeze envelop her.

Chapter Twenty-four

➤❤❮

"**D**r. Johnson?" Molly noticed his raised eyebrows. "Uh, I mean 'Dan.' I don't want to be a nuisance. I feel like you and Zoë have both spent so much time helping me … and here I am again."

"Molly, you're dear to both of us—and you are definitely not a nuisance."

His mock frown set Molly at ease. She began to talk, hating to admit another struggle. "I'm feeling a lot of anger again—toward a lot of people. Sometimes I just want to call my family up and tell them how they ruined my life."

"Do you really think they ruined your life?"

"Of course they did," she answered, feeling uncooperative. "How else could I empty an entire box of tissue in under an hour?" For the next thirty minutes, Molly's pent-up hatred emerged, raw and unvarnished. Sometimes her tears came hard and fast. Just as quickly she could turn stone cold, as if bitterness were freezing her very soul. A war was on, and the opposing forces were hate—for each one who had inflicted her suffering—and mind-boggling love for them, the only flesh-and-blood family she had. Yes, they had ruined her life, together scarring every inch of her body and soul. Molly railed against the injustice, mentally flinging stones—hatred, isolation, and mistrust—at the people in her past. The battle left her limp. "I want this to go away," she whispered, leaning back against the couch and drawing her feet up under her. "Maybe I should just write them all a letter and be done with it."

"Has anything changed since the other times you've tried to talk with them?"

"Not really. I spoke with Jenn last week and she said Jeremy's still drinking; he's already talking about sending his second wife the route of his first one."

"They divorced?"

"Family tradition," Molly said, smiling wryly.

"That's sad," Dr. Johnson added, skillfully blocking her escape route and forcing Molly to wrestle with the deep disappointment she so badly wanted to ignore.

"My parents and my stepmother are too consumed with their own lives. They're not going to talk with me and they're definitely not going to listen. It would be the same old thing. I'm sure they'd find some way to blame me."

"I'm inclined to agree with you," he said. "Molly, I think any change is going to have to come from you."

"But what else can I do?" she asked, confused.

Dr. Johnson waited, sensing the moment. "Forgive them," he said, his voice barely audible.

Molly looked at him in stunned disbelief.

"I know I've asked you to do the impossible," he said, as if reading her mind.

"Well, yes," Molly retorted, questioning his judgment for the first time. "They stole my childhood." Her flashing eyes defied him to speak further—but he did.

"If you don't forgive them, Molly, they'll steal the rest of your life, too. They'll continue to control you until you forgive them, each one."

She mouthed, "How?"

"'To forgive' is to 'untie' or 'release' someone. When you make a conscious choice to pardon your family for hurting you, you decide not to hold their faults against them. It's not the same as saying they didn't do anything wrong—you know that they did. But, Jesus told us to 'forgive everyone who is indebted to us' just as He forgave us our sins."

"I'm not quite sure I'm ready to do that—or that I want to."

"Forgiveness isn't something we do because people deserve it. We do it because of Jesus. If He forgives us our sins when all we deserve is punishment, then we can't help but do the same for other people. And you don't have to wait until you feel like forgiving them, Molly. You can choose to act on what's right rather than what you feel."

"Isn't that hypocritical?" she demanded, jumping up from her chair. "I don't see why it's right to forgive them for something so unconscionable, so destructive."

"Did Jesus forgive you?"

"Yes," she said, dropping back into her seat.

"And He says we're to forgive others as He has forgiven us. If we don't forgive those who hurt us, we keep on living in the past—trapped in ropes of anger and bitterness. Eventually, those negative emotions seep into every area of our lives, including other relationships."

"That's already happened," she whispered. "I constantly run from close relationships—I'm afraid to be around men. I can't imagine ever being intimate with anyone," she said, weeping.

"Those feelings are like warning lights."

She looked away, staring at nothing, her hands folded below her chest.

The stillness screamed her pain.

At last, she spoke, deliberating over each word. "Intellectually, this makes sense," she began reluctantly, her hand cradling her face. "I just can't begin to take it into my heart."

"I'm not suggesting you deny your feelings, Molly. But you can act apart from them, stepping out in truth and letting your emotions follow." Dr. Johnson stopped, wondering if Molly heard him, if she understood how much he hurt with her—enough to push her beyond the past, when he knew it felt like he was only adding to the pain. He wanted her to let God transform her from the inside out—He wanted her to see she could live in joy regardless of how her family treated her. He watched her head drop further down into her hands, and saw her shoulders rise and fall with each labored breath. He did not hear her prayers.

Chapter Twenty-five

➤❖

Months after Molly began getting biweekly massages, she experienced her first breakthrough. This time, instead of tensing when Bob came into the room, she relaxed, anticipating the relief each session brought with it. He gently pressed her tight shoulders and upper arms, reminding her as he always did, "Be sure and tell me if I do anything that feels uncomfortable to you, and I'll stop it right away." She had been too numb to notice during her first few appointments and never said a word. But on this day, she surprised even herself., "Could you work on my lower back, too?" she asked, lifting her head from the table. "No, over there—it is really tight today." A contented smile washed over her face as she dangled her fingertips toward the floor.

* * *

The year evaporated. In next to no time, graduation was only two weeks away.

"This is going to be the best summer I've ever had," Kate enthused. "I am so excited about grad school."

"I'm glad one of us is," said Molly, ruing the day she applied to be a graduate assistant.

"Peter's coming for graduation," Kate said, smiling, waiting for a response.

"He is?" Molly forced herself to remain calm.

"He's skipping his so he can come to ours. Must be nice to make it through school in three years."

"He went to summer school before college and every summer during college, didn't he?"

"You don't have to defend him, Mol. I'm just kidding!" She smiled, loving to make her wait. "He called last night—he wanted to talk with you, but you were at the library."

Molly felt alternately elated and despairing—a complex emotional mix that only her best friend could read on her face.

"What is it?"

"Oh, nothing," Molly said, afraid to voice her recurring fear.

"You're thinking Peter couldn't possibly like you, I know it."

Molly began to cry. "How did you know?"

"Four years rooming together, maybe? Best friends since kindergarten?"

"If he knew everything I've done—he'd never speak to me again ... ."

"You forget, Molly—he does know. When I went home last Christmas, you asked me to tell Peter and my parents what you were going through. I told you how much they all love you and how sad they were about what happened to you—remember?"

"I don't know. Maybe." Her shoulders slumped. "What did Peter say ... about everything?"

"Mostly he just wanted to know that you were doing OK."

"Is that why he calls me now—because he feels sorry for me?"

"I thought you knew him better. He calls you because he likes you. Haven't you figured that out yet?" She lobbed a pillow across the room. Molly tossed it back, ignoring her comment.

"Peter could have anyone he wanted," she said, despondent. "He could pick someone who has lived like he has, instead of someone with all my baggage."

"Molly, did it ever occur to you that Peter cares for *you*, not someone else? Trust God with this. Ask Him to lead you *and* Peter."

* * *

The phone rang. Unable to identify the sophisticated voice, Kate shrugged, passing the phone to Molly.

Molly listened intently, finally recognizing her stepmother's timbre.

"Molly, is your father with you for graduation?" Mercedes asked.

"Uh, graduation isn't for two more weeks," Molly said, wondering.

"Oh, certainly, certainly. He must be visiting his ... his ... uh, parents, then."

Confused, Molly asked, "Isn't he in Illinois—with you?"

Laughing the phony laugh Molly hated, Mercedes said, "Oh, he has been so busy with work lately—silly me—I'm quite sure he'll be here any second now. I, uh, thought he might have come there to surprise you—for graduation, you know."

Both Molly and Mercedes knew her father had no intention of coming to her college graduation.

"Yes, I'm sure he'll be here momentarily. Goodbye, then," Mercedes hung up abruptly.

Molly stood unmoving, the phone still in her hand.

"Who was that?" Kate broke the silence.

"Mercedes. That was undoubtedly the weirdest call I've ever received. She actually thought Dad was here now, for graduation."

"I wonder where he is?"

"So do I."

The phone rang again, and Molly cautiously answered it. "Hello?"

"Molly?"

"Hi, Nana," she said, surprised.

"Are you excited about graduation, dear?"

"I'm too tired to be excited," Molly said.

"We wish we could come. Are your parents coming?"

"No," she replied, hesitating, wondering if she should mention the puzzling call from Mercedes. "Dad said he couldn't come—but, Mercedes called a few minutes ago and asked if he were here—or there with you."

"In Florida? He told us he'd be going into Chicago for meetings all this week."

"Interesting. It seems strange that Mercedes doesn't know."

* * *

Mercedes hadn't moved from Jameson's desk since her call to Molly an hour before. She usually stayed away from the den, since Jameson was so obsessive about his privacy. *I wonder why he never lets me see his papers?* she questioned as her thoughts propelled her to action. Trying to open the top two desk drawers, she yelled, "These didn't have locks before!" In reality, she knew why he resorted to locks–it was after he told her to quit helping herself to his charge cards. *He actually accused me of forging his signature*, Mercedes remembered, still irritated at being caught. When she finally found an unlocked drawer, she was surprised to find his Palm Pilot there. *That's odd—he never goes anywhere without this.* Scanning through meticulous schedules, she went to the address section—noticing the first entry under 'S'— Beth Shepard. Scowling, she picked up the phone and tried calling the number.

Mercedes knew how to turn on the charm when necessary, and she used it to purr sweetly into the phone, "Hello, is this Beth Shepard?"

"Yes," Beth hesitated.

"This is Mercedes Mauritz," she said, pausing for effect. "I'm married to Jameson Montgomery—I believe you know him."

There was a long pause. "I once knew him," she said at last.

"I thought perhaps he might be there visiting you and your daughter?"

"Well, no—we haven't seen him for quite some time. He—uh, only met my daughter one time, last year. That's the only time we've seen him since before she was born."

"Oh." Frustrated, Mercedes slammed down the phone without another word. "Another dead end," she told the empty room.

* * *

A few days later, Molly watched Kate answer the phone with her customary enthusiasm. Almost immediately, her smile was replaced by a look Molly couldn't identify. Kate hugged her as she gently placed the phone in her hand.

Her mother's voice was strained. "Molly, I'm sorry to have to call with bad news right before your graduation."

She remembers I'm graduating, Molly thought, wondering why she couldn't come. "Molly, I don't know how to say this— your father," she sobbed, "he, he ... ."

"What's wrong, Mom?"

There was a long pause, and all Molly could hear was her mother's labored breathing. "Something happened to your father— the police found him last night. His parents asked me to call you—they're too upset to talk."

Unable to absorb the words, Molly stammered, "What happened?"

"Your father killed himself."

"What? I don't understand ... ."

After a long pause, her mother spoke—rapidly, as though she had to spit out everything to get it over with as quickly as possible. "They found him in a storage unit he rented. Apparently he drove his car into it and died. Carbon monoxide poisoning."

Molly listened, paralyzed.

"Did you hear me? You need to be here for the funeral day after tomorrow. Call me with your flight number."

Numbly, woodenly, she said, "OK, I'll let you know."

* * *

Sitting on a teal leather sofa in her elegant living room, Mercedes looked like a mannequin. Finally, she moved to pick up a piece of paper from the alligator coffee table in front of her. Her hand caressed the table, just as it had the day she bought it last month. As soon as the interior decorator saw her touch it, he exuded, "Ms. Mauritz, with your impeccable taste, you know this is a steal at $11,000, and that price reflects a significant markdown." Knowing her weakness for costly things, he smiled ingratiatingly. "We made it custom for another client who unexpectedly had to move to a new place with an entirely different décor. But it has your name all over it." Fondling the table, he reminded her, "You can't put a price tag on one-of-a-kind quality."

His appeal to her pride had precisely the effect he anticipated. Seconds later, she glibly handed him Jameson's charge card, rationalizing, "I really do deserve a nice little treat like this. I haven't done anything to our apartment since I put in new carpeting and window treatments last spring."

That day seemed like a long time ago. Scowling at the paper in her hand, Mercedes read aloud, "Mercedes: Attached to this you will find a life insurance policy, purchased precisely two years ago. In other words, it's valid, which is the question foremost on your mind. I only ask that you use it to pay your current debts instead of creating new ones. Since you've made it quite clear that you're disappointed with a bank president's income, I'm sure you'll be much happier with your ample proceeds from my estate than you are when you occasionally happen to be with me. My attorney will give further instructions as to the allocation of all other assets. Brace yourself—my four children will each receive a share. Signed, Jameson W. Montgomery."

Her lips curling into a sneer, Mercedes screamed, "This is ridiculous. I can't believe he expects me to divvy up everything with those spoiled brats. Even the illegitimate one!"

Smoothing her silk slacks obsessively, she tried to think of something else. "I know what will help," she said as she reached for the now-familiar Palm Pilot. "I'll call Beth." The phone was answered on the third ring. Quickly, she pursed her lips into a simulated expression of compassion and said, "Oh, Beth, dear, I was wondering if anyone let you know ... ." Irritated, she waited while Beth replied. Then, she said, "Oh, yes, I should have known that his parents would call. Well, I wanted to be certain you'd be at the memorial service early tomorrow. That's right—2:00, Colonial Oaks Funeral Home—but do remember to come early. I'm sure his other children will want to meet their sister. Be sure to bring her, won't you?"

Chapter Twenty-six

M olly awakened, looking as disoriented as she felt.
Her face was crinkled from lying on top of the book
she was holding when she fell asleep. Her hair stuck out in
several directions; she was still wearing the jeans and T-
shirt in which she'd flown the day before. Tears filled her
eyes when she remembered why she was in her mother's
house.

Wanting to be ready for this difficult day, she made
herself get up. In ten minutes, she was showered and
dressed, and no one else in the house was moving. *Good—
I still have time,* she thought. Opening her Bible, she knelt
by her old bed, knowing she couldn't face the day—or her
family—without God's strength. She followed the sticky
notes Kate had secretly inserted throughout her Bible
before she left. "God knows just how you feel," she'd written on the first one. "My soul melts from heaviness;
strengthen me according to Your word." "I'm praying for
you," Kate wrote on another: "God is my refuge and
strength, a very present help in trouble." For an hour, Molly
read, lifting her heart to God. " ... those who hope in the
Lord will renew their strength. They will soar on wings like

eagles." When the sounds of other family members reached her, she was ready for the day. Still praying, she walked downstairs.

Obviously agitated, Babs shrieked into the phone. "This is a fine time to find out. No, I'm not telling them—you tell them." Frowning, she handed the phone to Molly. "It's your Grandmother Montgomery."

"Hi, Nana. I hope your flight was OK." Molly's time on her knees kept her calm, unworried.

Her grandmother apologized, "I'm so sorry—I didn't want you to find out at the funeral today. We should have told you before."

"Told me what?"

"Your father had another child—with Beth. That's why he ended their relationship. He didn't want the child then, but later, he changed his mind. He told us about a year ago. He felt like we needed to know we had another grandchild. Her name is Renae, and she's eight now. She'll be nine in July."

Molly was quiet, absorbing the shock. "Will she be there today?"

"Both of them—Beth and Renae—are coming. Mercedes insisted."

"Oh," she said. Molly had given up trying to understand Mercedes a long time ago. "Can we meet them?" she asked.

"I'm sure you will. Mercedes said she told them to come early—even wants them to sit with the family. I think she wants everyone to feel worse than we already do. She didn't count on us knowing about Renae, though—she thought she was the only one who knew. But, your dad took us with him to meet her. She reminds me of you, Molly." Weeping, she asked, "Will you tell your brother and sister about Renae for me? It's still hard … to talk."

"I'll tell them. And, I'm praying for you and Grandpa today. I love you, Nana."

She broke down. "Your father was our only child—and now he's gone—he's gone."

Almost as soon as Molly hung up the phone, Jennifer and Jeremy walked into the room.

"Tell them the latest," her mother ordered.

When Molly finished explaining their grandmother's call, Jeremy laughed with anger, not humor. "Our father was a busy man, wasn't he?" he asked, nudging his mother. Molly felt sick.

Jenn stared out the window. "I wonder if we can meet our new sister before the funeral?" She sighed. "We haven't even met Beth yet."

"Oh, yeah," Jeremy laughed again, his face distorted, mocking. "I was the only one who had the privilege of meeting her—but now we all get to meet our precious little sister together." His scathing voice continued, "Now, that's quality time."

The doorbell rang, and Molly answered it, relieved to have an excuse to escape the room. It was flowers—a huge bouquet of lilies. The attached card said simply, "God cares. Love, the Johnsons." The scent of the flowers surrounded her, a tangible reminder of God's love and the prayers of friends. *I'm not alone. God will get me through this,* she thought, smiling.

Jeremy took the card from her hand and looked at it with contempt. "Who are the Johnsons?" he demanded, tossing it into the trash.

"My best friends," Molly said, fishing it from the wastebasket. "Their daughter, Kate, is my roommate."

"I suppose she's the one who put you up to writing that stupid letter to me last year."

"Jeremy, I wrote that— to let you know I forgive you for..." All sounds ceased; Molly had to force herself to speak over the silence. "... for everything that happened in the past."

"I imagine it was a letter like the one you wrote me," her mother said, her face flushed. "I'm only going to say this once, Molly. I don't want to hear any more of your Jesus talk."

The doorbell rang again, and Babs showed a colleague in, thanking him profusely for his bouquet, urging, "Come on into the living room. Sit down. I'll get you some coffee," She wasn't the same woman who had been in the kitchen minutes before.

Jeremy, Jennifer and Molly sat around the table, alone with each other for the first time in four years. Their silence was broken when Jennifer sobbed, "We never got to really know him. He left us without saying goodbye. He left us again."

"Hey, what's the big deal? For years he acted like we don't exist. Now he doesn't exist—that's it, plain and simple," Jeremy said, his tears contradicting his stoicism.

Molly took his hand in hers, astonished that she could touch him without bitterness. "God thinks every life is valuable," she said. "He knows how much we hurt, and He cares."

He snatched his hand away from her, grimacing. "Give it up, Molly! After I read your first letter about your life as a wacko religious fanatic, I've thrown all the other ones away without reading them. Save your time and mine. I don't need any sermons from you."

The back doorbell rang, and Jennifer opened the door. Sheldon Wendham came in carrying a pan of brownies; Lauren Wendham bore a casserole. "We're so sorry to hear about your dad," she said.

After showing her first visitor to the front door, Babs rushed to greet their neighbors. "Coffee, anyone?" she asked, suddenly remembering how much fun it was to play hostess.

* * *

Molly put on the dress she had planned to wear for her college graduation. She tried to remember shopping for it, and couldn't. For a moment, she was overwhelmed with forgotten sights, sounds and smells leering from every corner of the room. She silenced them, praying, "Thank You, God, for grace to survive this. Oh, Lord, I don't know how to talk with my family but You do. Please show me."

After a tense drive to the mortuary in her mother's car, Molly noticed the clock in front of the building, a visible reminder of mortality that only she seemed to notice.

There was no wake the previous night. They braced to see their father's body for the first time. Jennifer stepped back, sobbing. Molly looked and began weeping for all that never could be. Turning away, Jeremy riveted his eyes on his watch. "Two hours 'til the Big Goodbye," he said, feigning nonchalance.

Inadvertently, Molly turned to the door and saw a man and woman entering with a petite girl dressed in blue, her blonde hair pulled back into a French braid. One look at her eyes—which were so similar to her own—told Molly exactly who she was.

"I'm Molly Montgomery," she said, reaching out her hand.

"I'm Beth, and this is my husband Andrew Shepard," she said. Putting her arm protectively around her daughter's shoulders, she continued. "This is Renae."

Molly whispered, "My half sister?" Leaning down, she smiled, "Hi, Renae."

"Hi," came the soft reply. She knew that her birth father had other children, but she felt awkward meeting the one her grandmother had said was like her. "Daddy," she said, not knowing what to do but reach for her adoptive father's hand. The tall man with square shoulders walked outside with her, listening intently to her whispered concerns.

275

Beth breathed a sigh of relief. "You knew about Renae?"

"Not until this morning. Our grandmother called."

"I'm so sorry you had to find out like this. I—I don't want to hurt anyone again."

Molly gently interrupted, "You're not hurting me. I'm grateful we can finally meet. I've been praying for you ever since I became a Christian."

Incredulous, Beth asked, "You're a Christian?" A smile of recognition lit her eyes. "I am, too—but I wasn't when I knew your father. I'm so sorry for everything that happened to your family," she said, her eyes pleading for forgiveness. "I made a lot of choices I regret—and it wasn't until my daughter was born that I was willing to admit how rebellious I'd been about everything my parents tried to teach me. I named her Renae because it means 'reborn.' God used her to help me find new life," she paused, too overcome by emotion to continue.

Molly hugged Beth, her eyes filling with tears. "I hope we can get to know each other better someday," she said.

The man returned to Beth's side. Still holding Renae's hand, he put his other arm around his wife. "God brought Andrew back into my life just after I became a Christian," she said. We knew each other in college, but he was already a Christian then. He thought I was, too," she said sadly.

Andrew drew Beth closer. "God promises to use everything for good and He did," he said, smiling at Renae, who was putting her doll to bed on a nearby bench.

Molly recognized the rosebud coverlet as one Nana Montgomery had made. Saying goodbye to Beth and Andrew, she slowly walked over and knelt down beside the bench, pulling a caramel from her purse and slipping it into Renae's outstretched hand.

Mercedes walked into the room like a cover girl on a catwalk. Her face hidden behind the black veil of a wide-brimmed hat, she walked toward the coffin for a final view of her dearly departed. After the appropriate interval, she let a tear trickle down her cheek, slowly dabbing it with an embroidered handkerchief. That's when she saw Molly playing dollies on the floor with the child. With disgust—and visibly angered at having lost her one consolation, Mercedes accompanied Jameson's parents to a private waiting room. She was miffed when Beth and her little family declined her invitation to join them—and irritated even more when Molly sat next to her grandmother, too far away to hear the verbal jabs Mercedes had prepared for this tender moment.

* * *

Molly's family couldn't understand why she wasn't furious about Renae. When she gave them a reason—crediting God for giving her and Beth peace and forgiveness—they went on the attack, quickly labeling her a "self-righteous prig." But those words didn't make her cry. The tears flowed, unchecked, when the reality of her father's death hit full-force, decimating any hope for reconciliation. Hours passed, and she lay awake wondering why he gave up on life, ultimately placing the blame on her own slender shoulders. Somehow convinced that words alone could have saved him—that he didn't find peace with God because she failed to show him how—she finally fell asleep on a pillow damp with tears.

* * *

The phone rang early the next morning. "Molly!" her mother yelled.

Molly jolted awake, quickly grabbing her robe with a fearful glance at the door. Taking a deep breath—the split second she needed to get her bearings and remember that she was not a little girl and this was not her bedroom anymore—she walked out. "Hello, this is Molly," she groggily answered the hall phone.

"You weren't up yet?" Mercedes asked, oddly chipper for a grieving widow.

"I guess I'm still on Pacific Time."

"Look, why don't I come get you for brunch! I know a great little place with a marvelous chef. Ten-thirty sound about right?"

Molly hesitated, giving herself time to think, to pray. "OK," she answered, setting aside her qualms.

When Molly went downstairs at 10:25, Jenn was still in bed. She didn't go into the kitchen to sidestep an energy-sapping explanation of her plans. Watching for Mercedes from the front hallway, she overheard Jeremy talking with their mother.

"It went through two months ago and Peg got custody of Cody and Samantha. Two ex-wives and four kids—that's some payroll, right?" His voice bitter, he added, "Nice time for my firm to ask me to leave."

"But you can still work in finance … ."

He cut in, "Not anymore. I'm in a tight spot I can't explain." He used a loud staccato laugh to change the subject. "I have a great future ahead of me in California!"

"You're not moving, are you? That's a lot of stress to take on, sweetheart."

"Now's the perfect time, Mom," he said, his voice growing spirited. "Remember that agent who said she'd read my script? She said to call her when I'm in town. That's the way this business is. If you're not right there, people don't take you seriously."

"So you set up a meeting?"

"She wanted to keep it loose, but she's my first call once I land."

"And where, exactly, will that be?"

"Funny thing, I got an e-mail from Bill Sanderson the other day. I ran my plan by him and he offered his guest house until I get settled."

"I heard he designed a spectacular beach house after Ingrid died. Did he tell you about it?"

"Actually, I've seen it when I've been in L.A. on business, oh, once or twice a month for a couple of years. Amazing how long it took for Peg to catch on." His laugh was hard, his voice a crater.

"Jeremy, what are you saying?"

"You figure it out, Mom. And, while we're on the subject, don't tell Molly I'm moving. If I need a preacher, I'll go to church."

Molly silently closed the door and slipped outside to Mercedes' waiting car.

* * *

The restaurant was quiet, a perfect place to talk. Molly waited until their coffee came to ask the question uppermost in her mind. "Mercedes, I can't stop wondering why Dad did this. He didn't seem like the type."

"Oh, it's always the high achievers who kill themselves," Mercedes said, clicking her nails on her saucer. "That's what all work and no play does to a person."

"Did he seem depressed?" Molly asked, wiping a tear.

"He was ranting and raving about money, bills, you know, that sort of thing. He always was like that, though," Mercedes responded, signaling the waiter. "A tightwad— but you knew that."

Waiting as Mercedes ordered for both of them, Molly remembered that generosity had been her father's nicest quality. She grew quiet, considering Mercedes' comment. "Hmmm," she said, absently.

"What do you mean by that?" Mercedes demanded. She hated the new Molly even more than she'd always secretly loathed the old. Since her funeral plans had been foiled, she decided that only one strategy remained: To make Saint Molly stumble. Now she waited, coiled, anticipating the perfect moment to spring.

"I guess I don't remember him being like that," Molly said, looking unsure.

"Well, maybe he wasn't when you were young, but he is–or was–lately," said an injured Mercedes.

"I didn't mean to offend you, Mercedes. I'm only trying to understand what happened—I, I haven't seen him very often during the past few years." She reached into her purse for a tissue.

"You talked on the phone with him last month," she said, accusingly.

Molly remembered the sad conversation, her most recent failed attempt to extend forgiveness—and share her faith—with her family. She choked as she recalled her father's words. "This subject is closed until further notice, Molly. I'm warning you, don't bring it up again. I see absolutely no reason to bring up the past, and I will not listen to you rant and rave like a religious fanatic."

"Dad, I'm not a religious fanatic," she'd told him. "I'm not even religious. I'm talking about a relationship—with God."

He cut her off and, in less than thirty seconds, ended the call and left the last memory Molly would ever have of her father's voice.

Clasping her hands and sighing, Mercedes deftly changed subjects. "I imagine, after what you saw yesterday, you couldn't help being grateful."

Molly didn't have any idea where Mercedes was going.

"Could you picture yourself in Beth's shoes, hauling a kid around?"

Tears came to Molly's eyes.

Mercedes continued, determined not to let the opportunity get away. "Just think, one day of cramps versus eighteen years of headache!"

"I wish I had a child to hold, or at least given my baby up for adoption," Molly interjected, the words tumbling straight from her heart.

Like a lion going for the kill, Mercedes pounced. "Darling, if your god is so big, why didn't he stop you?"

Molly felt righteous anger rise from her heart as she returned Mercedes' stare, her eyes steady. When she finally spoke, her voice was strong. "I don't blame God for my wrong choices," she said. Her face, though resolute, radiated peace and confidence. "Since God has forgiven me, I can finally forgive myself."

"Well, god isn't going to forgive 'Daddy' now, is he?" Mercedes screeched, her face contorted with barely-contained fury. "If memory serves me right, I believe your father has committed what you wackos call the unpardonable sin."

Silently praying, Molly stayed calm, knowing the strength she felt was a gift from God. "That's an interesting topic, Mercedes," she said.

Mercedes flinched, frustrated that Molly had, once again, failed to take the bait.

"A professor of mine says that occurs in only one circumstance—when someone refuses to accept the gift of life God gave when His Son died on the cross to pay for our sins."

"Oh, I see," Mercedes spoke the words slowly, not seeing at all. "And isn't that precisely what your father did? Look, Molly," she said, speaking as though Molly was a very small, very stupid child. "He killed himself," she hissed. "You can't reject your so-called gift of life much more blatantly than that!" She waited triumphantly for Molly's reaction.

Molly's reply came in a whisper, but it was packed with power. "We can't judge what was in my father's heart when he died, Mercedes," she began. "Only God knows that."

Furious, Mercedes leapt from her chair. "Don't you dare try to cram your pompous pat answers down my throat! You and your religious rhetoric disgust me!"

Chapter Twenty-seven

Molly leaned her head against the plane's stiff headrest. Only dimly aware of the other passengers, she felt like she was somewhere else, far from anything she had ever known. She didn't have to force herself to stay calm; she was numb. Tears filled her eyes, and she fumbled in her purse for a tissue, finding instead the card Kate had tucked there when she left. "Come to Me all you who are weary and heavy laden," it said, "and I will give you rest." Kate's scrawl at the bottom brought a slight smile to her face. "It's a promise from Jesus Himself. He's with you, so you're going to be OK." Any comfort she gathered from those words was crowded out by pain. She remembered her last conversation with Jennifer.

"How are you doing with all this?" Molly had asked. "I can't believe this is happening."

"Believe it. Dad died to us when he left Mom," Jennifer retorted angrily.

Molly knew the comment was an invitation to mudsling their father's memory. In the past, denigrating their parents—and Jeremy—had been something that bonded the two sisters, who shared very little else in common.

This time, Molly didn't go there. "I can tell you're still really hurting from that," she said sadly, but without rancor. "I'm so sorry."

"Spare me," said Jennifer, her eyes blazing. "You don't need to feel sorry for me, and you can quit exuding your little message of peace, hope and joy."

"What do you mean?"

"You've changed, Molly. You used to be—well, more like everybody else. Now—I don't know—you're different. I feel like you've died, too."

"I'm still me, Jenn, but some of what you're saying is true. I am different. Totally. The Bible calls it being born again, which is another way of saying I have a new life. God has given me faith, hope, peace. Isn't that what you want, too?"

"I liked you better the first time you were born," said Jennifer. "I'll find peace my own way."

Molly was still mulling over the conversation when Kate found her at the gate. "Hello, friend," Kate told her, putting her arms around her neck.

Molly looked up—surprised to see Peter by her side. "Hi," she said, unable to keep from crying as the emotions of the week tumbled out.

"Molly, we love you and we're so sorry—about everything," Kate said.

"We've been praying," added Peter. In one motion, he reached for her carry-on bag and expertly guided her through the crowds toward the luggage carousel. Her heart quieted.

"So?" he asked.

"It was hard. Every person in my family thinks I'm an idiot. And ... ." She choked, remembering. "... and no one but me and my grandparents even cares that Dad's gone."

"We care," Kate said. "We cried for you, Molly—all of us. She stopped, searching for words.

"Don't believe your family's opinion about you," said Peter, protectively. "I don't."

"But I couldn't do anything right."

"Remember John chapter fifteen?" Kate asked.

She nodded.

"God is doing good things and is at work, no matter what has happened. He is in control."

No more words were needed. The trio drove home in soothing silence.

* * *

When they arrived at their dorm, it was obvious Zoë had been there while Kate was at the airport. The room was filled with fragrance from the bouquet on Molly's desk. Next to it sat a plate of chocolate chip cookies, with a card. "We hurt with you," it said. "If you want to spend the day at our house tomorrow, please just come. Love, Dan and Zoë."

The next afternoon, both of them rushed to greet Molly as soon as she stepped out of Kate's car, enveloping her in every expression of love imaginable, from the smell of her favorite meal—lasagna—baking in the oven, to hugs and the gift of listening, perhaps the one she most needed.

Zoë and Kate started setting the table just before Peter arrived. His aunt teased, "It's always the one who lives closest who arrives late!"

"The last thing I want to do is be late for one of your great meals, Aunt Zoë," said Peter, uncharacteristically serious.

"Actually, it's going to be awhile."

"Good," he said, relieved, motioning Molly to follow him outside. "I saw this yesterday," he said, pointing to a baby bird peering over its nest. "The same God who sees even the tiniest bird in His creation cares about you. He understands what you're going through ... ." Overcome by emotion, his voice cracked.

They stood there, listening to the bird chirp, watching its mother fly to its side with food. Both were quiet for several minutes before Molly whispered, "It isn't easy, is it?"

"Life?"

"I thought it would never be this hard again." She paused.

He waited.

"I wish I could sail through life like you do, Peter."

Peter resisted the urge to laugh. "I think everyone experiences some kind of suffering," he said. "But you're right, some people get a bigger serving than others. We all have one thing in common: God promises to sustain us through it and even make us stronger because of it—if we'll let Him."

"Why doesn't He make it go away?" she asked, only half kidding.

"You ask tough questions, Molly," he said, smiling, resisting the urge to hold her, knowing that his heart's desire was to make her smile forever. Losing himself in the sea of her eyes, he felt himself falling fast and hard. *Yes,* he admitted to himself, *I love her.* The time wasn't right to tell her how much.

Her eyes framed the question again.

"Before I left Colorado," he nodded in response to her question, "I was hiking alone in the mountains. I came to this cliff, and stood there awhile trying to figure out how to get down—maybe a few rocks I could use as a foothold or something. Then I saw a stairway someone had carved into the mountain, and I followed it down into an incredible rock garden that someone had made. It was gorgeous, but I would have missed it if I hadn't kept going forward, if I hadn't kept going when it was hard."

"If only life were so simple."

"Grab a couple of chairs and talk with us while we finish the French bread and salad," said Zoë when they came back inside. Amid the flurry of activity in the kitchen, Molly's heart quieted. She looked at her friends, one by one, and knew she was really home.

"Did Peter tell you his news?" Zoë asked, interrupting her thoughts.

"Not yet," he quickly jumped in. "I, uh, I was waiting ... ."

"Tell me," she begged.

"Are you sure? I didn't want to talk when ... "

"Please ... ." she smiled.

"He's moving here to go to graduate school!" Kate announced.

"But I thought you were going to Denver."

"Not anymore," he grinned. "I decided to apply here a few months ago, but I wanted to wait until everything was final to say anything. I start summer school next week—just like you and Kate."

"But why ... what happened?" Molly's cheeks burned. It felt like everyone was looking at her.

Kate propped her elbows on the counter, not wanting to miss a word.

"I think I forgot to put napkins on the dining table, Kate. Could you go in there and check?" Zoë said, motioning Peter and Molly toward the back door. Take your time; the food will keep," she whispered to him.

"I'm sorry," he began as soon as the door closed. "I meant this to be more private; I wanted to plan everything and, and ... ," he stammered, obviously uncomfortable. "I was going to wait until later, when you had time to rest...and, well, you know."

"I'm pretty much in the dark," she said, baffled.

His cheeks were flushed and his eyes shone with an intensity she'd never seen before. "Molly, I've liked you ever since the night of your un-birthday party—first as my sister's best friend, and now as mine."

She looked up at him, puzzled, trying to understand.

"I'm making a mess of this," he said, his words tangling into knots. "We've talked on the phone a lot, and every time we talk, I want more time with you. But, I've never dated and never plan to. Molly?" he said, looking at her for reassurance.

She nodded, ever so slightly.

"I want to begin a more serious relationship with you— one that might lead to marriage someday." He was out of breath. "I don't want to be 'just friends' or 'Kate's brother' anymore."

"I'm not sure what you mean."

"I mean I love you. I know this is horrible timing, but I want to be here for you, to help you through your sorrow. I guess what I'm asking is this: would you consider spending time with me—with others around, too—so that you can see if you love me as much as I love you?"

"I'm afraid I'm not going to be very good company for awhile."

"By whose definition?" He smiled—and his smile was contagious.

They walked inside, and Molly had the strange feeling everyone else knew more than she did. She was only partly right—Peter had asked his aunt and uncle for advice; Kate was still in the dark.

That night, Molly tried to tell Kate about her conversation with Peter, still thinking she knew. Kate jumped up, screaming, hugging her. "Oh, Molly, you're falling in love with my brother!"

"Not so fast, friend. I'm still not sure what to think about this."

"Trust in the LORD with all your heart; lean not on your own understanding," Kate began the verse they'd been learning before Molly left for Illinois.

Molly continued, "In all your ways acknowledge Him, and He will make your paths straight."

"I love happy endings," Kate sighed.

"This isn't an ending yet. Perhaps it's a beginning."

Chapter Twenty-eight

It was a summer of indescribable beginnings—first to hope, then to joy and finally, to love. Pure love. At a level she didn't know existed.

It was also the beginning of laughter. Over pizza one Friday night, a tradition was born that carried them through the summer: Saturdays at Newport Beach. On the inaugural trip, Peter emerged from the trunk of the car with two kites. "Excellent!" Kate enthused. "I can't remember the last time we did this!" He looked at Molly, who was already sitting on her beach towel, staring at the waves while their other friends jumped in with boogie boards.

"Try it, Molly," Peter said, handing her the reel.

"I'm an expert at crashing them. I'll watch."

Laughing, he ran ahead with the kite, leaving the reel in her hand; the Delta instantly lifted into the wind. She felt the line tugging, bobbing as the kite soared. "I'm going to lose it," she yelled.

"No way," he said, encouraging her. "Just let it go."

Molly ran along the beach, letting out more line by the second, marveling at the simple thrill. She backed into the cool, shallow water, letting it lap at her feet. She forgot herself and burst into uncontrollable laughter.

Peter appeared next to her, relishing their joint venture. "It's at least five hundred feet up there!" She handed him the reel and they took off running, both of them looking upwards at the red kite against the blue sky.

The air was cool that night, but not too cool. Peter and Molly stood with friends, gazing at the sailboats dotting the harbor. Seagulls swooped overhead, waiting for someone— anyone—to toss morsels their way. "Here, Molly," Peter said, reaching into his backpack. With three gulls surging toward her at once, Molly yelped, dropping the bread and back-stepping. "Take it," she called, making a face at Peter, who was rapidly encouraging the masses by spraying more breadcrumbs at her ankles.

A reggae band launched into its first number, and people around them took off to the beat. Two little girls ran past, arms outstretched, abandoned to the sound of the beachside concert. Peter looked at Molly, his eyes inviting, "Come on."

She shook her head, "I can't dance." He laughed, "Neither can I." He dropped to his knees, begging. "All right, I surrender," she smiled, following him into the noisy crowd. Like kids on a playground, they spun, the night sky whirling with them, the stars a blur, the music becoming their own. Inside, though, her thoughts spiraled in another direction.

Peter noticed. "What's wrong?" he asked, pulling her aside.

"Nothing," she replied, believing it.

"Something's bothering you, I can tell," he persisted, guiding her away from the crowd toward a rock. "Did I do something?"

"No," she said, sure of that much.

"What were you thinking out there?"

She recoiled from the pressure, reflexively standing and moving to a rock nearby.

She traced her thoughts backwards, wanting to understand. "I'm afraid," she said at last.

"Of?"

"Not you," she sighed. "I'm afraid ... to be happy, afraid I'll do something wrong to make ... this all go away."

After several minutes of silence, he spoke. "Believing the truth will set you free from all of your fears—old *and* new."

* * *

Fall came, bringing with it a move from the cozy dorm room to graduate student housing. Molly had always hated uprooting, but this time the transition barely registered. Peter was there, helping her.

The day of the move was hot and humid. Sweat dripping down his back, Peter dropped the final box on Kate and Molly's new threshold. "You have a lot of stuff, Kate," he said in mock dismay. "This feels a bit too much like déjàvue."

"The workout will do you good, little brother." Kate craned her neck to grin at Peter, who easily towered a foot above her. "Don't mess with a tired redhead, mister."

Peter patted her head, nonplussed. "Yesterday our professor explained the axiom: 'Change is inevitable; growth is optional.' Witness Exhibit A," he said, waving at their piles, his spirits diffusing their moving-day stress. He turned to Molly, bowing. "Experienced sherpa at your service."

* * *

As soon as they were settled, Molly checked e-mail, dreading the number of messages she'd need to answer. She groaned when she saw her mother's address. No subject, as usual. She clicked it open, knowing her mother never wrote unless she had a reason.

Jeremy's in your area, but I can't get through to him. He hasn't cashed my check this month. Before I stop payment, do me a favor and drop in on him, see what's up.
Tell him to call.
His address: 25 Shorewood Estates.

Molly called Peter. "Will you help me with something difficult?"

"Of course."

"I'm supposed to find my brother."

He drove her to the prestigious area, both of them intently searching for the correct address. It felt strange to be winding along the mansion-lined road. Anticipating the imminent encounter felt even stranger. She looked up as the car slowed in front of a contemporary custom home. As if in a dream, Molly followed Peter to the door. It sprang open, revealing none other than Bill Sanderson himself. "Well, this beats all," he said, white teeth gleaming from leathery skin stretching across his face like a mask. "Hey, Jer," he called. "You've got company."

Jeremy didn't hear him. "Are we picking up my Porsche today?" he asked, tucking in his silk T-shirt as he emerged from the bedroom. Stunned, he glared at his sister. "What are you doing here?"

She answered the question.

"My life here is none of Mom's business," he said.

"She wants to know why you haven't cashed her check."

"What is this, grade school?" He turned to Bill, but he was already walking on the beach yards away.

"I'm just doing what Mom asked," Molly said, smarting.

Jeremy turned from her, for the first time noticing Peter. "Who's your friend?"

Peter stiffly shook hands and introduced himself, fighting the urge to tackle the man who had so wounded Molly. His stomach tightened when Jeremy threw an arm around her.

"Now that you've found me, Sis, how can I contact you?"

Peter stepped between them, handing Jeremy a slip of paper. "You can call me," he said.

"Oh, I will."

Peter squirmed under his gaze.

* * *

Molly picked up her phone—and then set it down again. She wanted to call Jeremy, yet didn't know what to say. Partially to protect Molly, Peter counseled her to wait, letting Jeremy make the first move. When fall semester began, taking with it little time for anything but school and work, Jeremy's life faded from their minds. Until October.

Peter and Molly were ordering pizza with friends when his cell phone rang. "Sorry," he said, reaching into his pocket. "Hello," he said brightly, his eyes smiling. The smile quickly faded, then disappeared.

Molly looked at him quizzically.

"Where are you now?" When he responded, his voice was dull. "All right. Give me an hour."

She couldn't read his face. "Who was that?"

"Your brother."

As her past invaded her present, Molly reeled. "Why?"

They stepped away from the group, whispering. "I guess he had nowhere else to turn. Bill kicked him out; he found someone new. Your brother doesn't even have a car," Peter added, incredulous.

"He still had your number," she said thoughtfully, almost to herself. "What are you going to do?"

"Pray with me, OK?"

"Are you thinking what I think you're thinking?"

"Probably."

"This isn't like working part-time at a boys' home," she said, not wanting Peter to get wounded.

"I know I'm not a rehab expert. But, I think the principles we used in Colorado at the boys' home could help him."

"What if he doesn't want help?" she murmured.

"I can't shake the idea that I'm supposed to try. I actually talked with Uncle Dan about this after I first met your brother."

Her eyebrows arched.

"I didn't say anything about my idea because I didn't want to worry you; I didn't know if your brother would ever call. Dan and Zoë said they'd help, too—if there were any opening to intervene in Jeremy's life. But I need to ask your permission first; I don't want to hurt you."

Molly's emotions ran the gamut from terror to hope. She leaned on Peter's shoulder. "What if something happens to you?"

"My apartment's in the back of Dan and Zoë's house, remember? They'll be right there."

* * *

Peter drove alone to a halfway house that was a far cry from the luxurious home where he'd been before. When he saw Jeremy waiting on the front porch—his beard scruffy, his clothes a mess—he was glad he'd insisted Molly stay behind. Peter knew his story had to be as complex as Molly's—the only thought that kept him from driving away in revulsion.

In one hand, Jeremy clutched a slip of paper; in the other he gripped a bag that held all his belongings. "Thanks for the lift," he said with a slurred voice. "One strike and you're outta this place. Who needs it? They say the place downtown's better anyway because their volunteers are wimps. Nobody's going to breathe down *my* neck."

Peter put the duffel bag in his trunk, grimacing at the stench. "Jeremy, he said, "I have an extra room until second semester. You can stay with me."

Smirking, Jeremy leaned against the car. "So, you going to save me?"

Peter shook his head, clenching the car keys. "No. That's not my job."

CPSIA information can be obtained at www.ICGtesting.com
Printed in the USA
BVOW01s2225290816

460545BV00001B/7/P

9 781591 608912